Secret Sister 19 85
Minnie Co

bought by

Don Green.
Oct 26, 1996 Sale

DAILY PROMISES

DAILY PROMISES

by
Herbert Lockyer

publishers since 1798

Thomas Nelson Publishers
Nashville • Camden • New York

Published in Nashville, Tennessee, by Thomas Nelson, Inc. and distributed in Canada by Lawson Falle, Ltd., Cambridge, Ontario.

Printed in the United States of America.

Library of Congress Cataloging in Publication Data

Lockyer, Herbert.
Daily promises.

1. Devotional calendars. I. Title.
BV4811.L59 1984 242'.2 84-25428

ISBN 0-8407-5916-9

There has not failed one word
of all His good promise.

I Kings 8:56

DAILY PROMISES

January 1

The promises. ROMANS 9:4
The promises of God. GALATIANS 3:21

Deciding to dwell upon the significance of promises on this opening day of another year, I find the exhortation of D. L. Moody appropriate:

> Take the promises of God. Let a man feed for a month on the promises of God, and he will not talk about how poor he is. You hear people say, "Oh, my leanness! How lean I am!" It is not their leanness, it is their laziness. If you would only read from Genesis to Revelation and see all the promises made by God to Abraham, to Isaac, to Jacob, to the Jews and to the Gentiles, and to all His people everywhere—if you would spend a month feeding on the precious promises of God—you wouldn't be going about complaining how poor you are. You would lift up your head and proclaim the riches of His grace, because you couldn't help doing it.

As it is our purpose to feed upon God's promises for all twelve months of the year, we need to gain an understanding of the nature of a promise. A *promise* can be defined as "a statement, either oral or written, assuring that one will or will not do some something." It is a vow. The power of a promise depends on the one making it. God assures His people that all promised blessings or judgments will be fully realized. For example, the fifth commandment is called "the first commandment with promise" (Eph. 6:2) because God declared that they who honor their parents shall have their days lengthened on the earth. Thus, as you face another year, be confident. Trust the vast and varied promises of God associated with the needs of your earthly pilgrimage.

You know the power of almighty God who created you and redeemed your life. Trust His promises to guide you through each unknown day of the future.

January 2

He who promised is faithful. HEBREWS 10:23

The character of a person has a great deal to do with the fulfillment of any promise he or she makes. We may have friends who are free with their promises but who fail to keep their word. They are like those Jonathan Swift describes, whose "promises and pie-crusts are made to be broken." A proverb states: "To promise and give nothing is a comfort to a fool." John Wilmot, of the seventeenth century, wrote the following epitaph for King Charles II:

> Here lies our sovereign lord the King,
> Whose promise none relies on;
> He never did a foolish thing,
> Nor ever did a wise one.

How different was the reputation of Joseph Addison as given by Alexander Pope:

> Statesman, yet friend to truth! of soul sincere,
> In action faithful, and in honor clear;
> Who broke no promise, serv'd no private end,
> Who gain'd no title, and who lost no friend.

"God is not a man, that He should lie" (Num. 23:19). Paul reiterated the truth that "God is faithful" (1 Cor. 1:9). Such a virtue is the guarantee of promise-fulfillment. "For all the promises of God in Him are Yes, and in Him Amen, to the glory of God through us" (2 Cor. 1:20). Great is His faithfulness. No despair can cause us fear as we claim the promise of our never-failing, infallible God. The consciousness of all God is in Himself enables us to appropriate His promises. Not "one word of all His good promise" can possibly fail (1 Kin. 8:56). May grace be ours to rest in these glorious tributes to God's reliability! Frances Ridley Havergal, the saintly blind poetess, often extols the divine promises in her heart-moving poems. Let us say, along with her: "We would claim this mighty gift."

January 3

Exceedingly great and precious promises. 2 PETER 1:4

To understand God's precious promises, we need to look at them in detail. Peter followed that practice, which led him to pronounce the promises of God as "exceedingly great and precious." He discovered their boundless diversity and scope.

Human promises can meet few needs, but divine promises cover all our needs, as their abundance clearly proves. The apostle described them as being "exceedingly great," implying their extraordinary nature, going beyond or surpassing human promises. Peter also called them "precious," a word he used frequently in his epistles: "The genuineness of your faith, being much more precious than gold" (1 Pet. 1:7); "the precious blood of Christ" (1 Pet. 1:19); "chosen by God and precious" (1 Pet. 2:4); "a chief cornerstone, elect, precious" (1 Pet. 2:6); "To you who believe, He is precious" (1 Pet. 2:7); and "precious faith" (2 Pet. 1:1).

Sin and death may rob us of our nearest and dearest possessions, but nothing can rob us of the rich, abiding promises of God's Word. Truly our needs seem insignificant beside such wonderful promises. But why were these promises given? What is their ultimate purpose? Peter gives us the answer: "Through these you may be partakers of the divine nature, having escaped the corruption that is in the world through lust" (2 Pet. 1:4).

The believer needs to bear in mind that the promises themselves cannot purify our hearts. Only the Lord who gave them can purify. Scripture is the medium of sanctification. "Sanctify them by Your truth. Your word is truth" (John 17:17).

January 4

Through faith and patience inherit the promises. HEBREWS 6:12

As the heirs of God and joint-heirs with Christ, we have a rich inheritance. We are heirs of the promises of grace, of salvation, and of righteousness in all that has been promised us. The kindred words *inherit* and *inheritance,* occurring over two hundred times in Scripture, afford a profitable line of study. *To inherit* means "to come into possession of money or goods at the death of those who willed the same to us." With God, however, the meaning is somewhat different. All His promises do not wait for fulfillment at His death because He is "the living God," the One who is eternal. The question is: Are we claiming our inheritance as heirs? We often live as spiritual paupers, bankrupt as far as spiritual wealth is concerned.

We need both faith and patience when claiming our inheritance. Although the promises have been made by God Himself, they are unavailing unless we believe that He will never go back on His word and that we will receive what He has promised by faith. May we be strong in faith, never doubting what God has said. He is always ready to perform on our behalf! We certainly must have patience before some promises are fulfilled. George Mueller believed God would answer prayer for an unsaved friend, but he had to wait some forty years before God granted him the desire of his heart. If God seems slow to fulfill a promise you daily claim, be patient, friend. God never acts before or behind His time. He knows, because of His omniscience, the right moment to act. We read of Abraham, that it was only "after he had patiently endured" that he "obtained the promise" (Heb. 6:15). Delays are not denials, according to the prophet Habakkuk:

> For the vision is yet for an appointed time;
> But at the end it will speak, and it will not lie.
> Though it tarries, wait for it;
> Because it will surely come,
> It will not tarry (Hab. 2:3).

The Christian who waits on the Lord will see promises fulfilled.

January 5

Having these promises . . .
let us cleanse ourselves. 2 CORINTHIANS 7:1

In 2 Corinthians, Paul referred to many Old Testament promises. He concluded with the one in which God promises to be our Father and to recognize us as His "sons and daughters" (6:18). The apostle then made his appeal, "Therefore having these [a word most emphatic in the original] promises, beloved, let us cleanse ourselves from all filthiness of the flesh and spirit, perfecting holiness in the fear of God" (7:1). This passage reminds us of the immediate function of a promise and also of its ultimate goal.

The immediate purpose of acquired promises is the meeting of our various needs, physical and material. But their ultimate design is the separation of our lives from everything alien to the holy will of the divine promiser. Jesus could say of His disciples: "You are already clean because of the word which I have spoken to you. . . . sanctified by the truth" (John 15:3; 17:19). Promises, then, should make us pure. Such a process of purification through truth is continuous. The claiming of specific promises related to material needs should ultimately result in holiness of life.

Paul declared that we must "cleanse ourselves" from all that is antagonistic to the holy purpose of God. This action is not adverse, in any way, to John's declaration that "the blood of Jesus Christ His Son cleanses us from all sin" (1 John 1:7). When ours is the definite will, desire, and endeavor to be clean, we allow the precious blood of Jesus to be the channel of necessary cleansing.

James Elroy Flecker, twentieth-century poet, tells us "songs beguile your pilgrimage." Says the psalmist: "Your statutes have been my songs/In the house of my pilgrimage" (Ps. 119:54). The promises of God can only lead to praise and adoration as they result in the sanctification of our heart and life.

January 6

He did not waver at the promise of God through unbelief. ROMANS 4:20

Abraham is the classic biblical example of the inheritance of a promise by faith. This father and founder of the Jewish race had no uncertainty through unbelief regarding the fulfillment of a specific divine promise. He faced all obstacles, believing that God had promised faithfully. Abraham exhibited an acting faith, proving, thereby, that the trial of faith is "much more precious than gold that perishes" (1 Pet. 1:7). William Booth's slogan for his Salvation Army soldiers was: "Keep up your repeated acts of faith."

Abraham knew what it was to laugh at an impossibility and believe it could be done. It was indeed overwhelming to tell a man about one hundred years old that his wife, not much younger than he, would give birth to a son. Yet such was the faith of Abraham, who against hope believed in hope. The physically impossible did not trouble him. God had promised him a son, and that was the end of the matter as far as he was concerned.

Many of the promises of God often stagger our minds. They appear to be too good to be true, but God never mocks the human heart. He always says what He means. Our difficulty is the failure to meet great promises with great faith.

Shakespeare said of one of his kings: "His promises were, as he then was, mighty!/But his performance, as is now, nothing." With the King eternal, however, it is totally different. He immediately performs a promise, once its condition is fulfilled on our part. Job could say to the Lord: "I know that You can do everything" (Job 42:2).

Paul affirmed that "what He had promised He was also able to perform" (Rom. 4:21). God's Word is His bond. Behind what He offers to do, there is not only His faithfulness but also His omnipotence to execute His promise.

January 7

Has His promise failed forevermore? PSALM 77:8

The psalmist was overwhelmed with sorrow. With a soul that refused to be comforted, he felt that God had forgotten to fulfill His gracious promise. Have you felt these emotions? Sometimes our doubt causes us to question the ability of God to carry out a promise we have sought to claim. The psalmist, however, quickly answered his own question. He confessed: "You are the God who does wonders" (Ps. 77:14). To think that God could fall short of the fulfillment of any promise He has given is an impeachment of His perfection. He would not be God if He had the possibility of any kind of failure in His being. David could declare: "As for God, His way is perfect;/The word of the LORD is proven" (Ps. 18:30). Addressing His disciples, Jesus commanded: "Therefore you shall be perfect, just as your Father in heaven is perfect" (Matt. 5:48). All God has promised, He can bring to pass.

According to our laws, a breach of promise, which represents the violation of one's plighted word to another, is a justifiable and punishable offense. Because of His absolute perfection, God cannot be guilty of such a breach—a fact encouraging to us as heirs of the divine promises. In his New Testament translation, Dr. Weymouth says that the promise of Hebrews 13:5, "I will never leave thee," can be rendered, "I will in no wise fail thee."

David Livingstone's favorite promise was: "Lo, I am with you always" (Matt. 28:20). The renowned missionary would say of this verse, "That's the word of a perfect Gentleman, and that's the end of it." Is it not comforting to know that amid all human failures and broken promises, we have an unfailing God?

In his well-known hymn, *Onward, Christian Soldiers*, Sabine Baring-Gould wrote these confident words:

> Gates of hell can never
> 'Gainst that church prevail;
> We have Christ's own promise,
> And that cannot fail.

January 8

The promise made of no effect. ROMANS 4:14

In this verse Paul was referring to the specific promise that Abraham would be the heir of the world (see Rom. 4:13–25). The apostle's contention was that adherence to the law nullifies God's work of grace. The promise to bless all, through the righteousness of faith, is made of no effect by the works of the law. What we must remember, even though we are under grace, is that the promises are conditional and that failure on our part to comply with their conditions cancels them. The tragedy is that so many wonderful promises are rendered void by misapplication, or by sin, unbelief, and disobedience. The promises are always effective when cashed in by faith, proving thereby their reality.

It is a tribute to Abraham's dauntless faith that the adverse experiences he endured in no way nullified the fulfillment of the promised multiplied seed. The Lord tested him by delay. Satan tried him by temptations. People around him tried him by jealousy, distrust, and opposition. Hagar tried him by scorning her mistress. Sarah, his wife, tried him by her peevishness. But Abraham remained steadfast and immovable. He never questioned God's veracity, doubted His faithfulness, or limited His power. He bowed to divine sovereignty, yielded to infinite wisdom, and remained silent under delays. Having received the promise, he was satisfied. He discovered that patient waiters are never disappointed.

How imperative it is for us to imitate Abraham's example! You and I need to share his assurance that God's promises cannot fail. Every promise is plain, positive, and permanent.

I leave to Thy disposing hand,
Events I cannot mold;
With steadfast faith serene I stand,
And see Thy plan unfold.

January 9

"You have promised this goodness to Your servant."

2 SAMUEL 7:28

At the outset of today's meditation, I feel it important to indicate the difference between facts and promises. A *fact* implies actuality, a definite existence distinct altogether from the realm of fancy. The indisputable fact of Scripture is: *God is love!* A *promise* is a pledge of one to another to do something distinctly specified. Jesus said: "I will give you rest" (Matt. 11:28). Such a promise is conditional on our coming to Him and learning of Him.

David, in his praise to God for the building of a temple, spoke of a promise of goodness. Woven into all the promises of God is His unfailing goodness. How great is His goodness! Because He is the God of goodness, all promises for the "children of promise" (Gal. 4:28) are better promises. Such promises bear the imprint of His character and have, at their heart, the present and eternal good of those to whom they are given.

A promise of life can come from wrong sources. Ezekiel called such promises made by false prophets "lies" (Ezek. 13:22). But because of who and what God is, He cannot utter a word contrary to His nature and attributes. How good is the God we adore! We are thrice blessed seeing we have such a loving, faithful God who is ever eager, ready, and willing to enrich our lives with abiding benefits. No wonder Peter called divine promises "precious" (2 Pet. 1:4).

C. H. Spurgeon, the renowned London preacher, once declared he had personally tried and proved the promises. He believed all the promises of God. He said: "I have seen that they are true, for they have been fulfilled in me."

What satisfaction is yours if you can write beside every promise that has enriched your life—*tried and proved*! One of the most blessed of the promises is related to our eternal presence in heaven: "Those who are called may receive the promises of eternal inheritance" (Heb. 9:15).

January 10

He will be our guide/Even to death. PSALM 48:14

As pilgrims traveling through "the whole world . . . under the sway of the wicked one" (1 John 5:19), we have dire need of this reliable guide. What a privilege and joy it is to have God as our sufficient and safe guide who will lead us continually!

Is it not soul inspiring to realize that God has promised to be with us always? As day follows day and year follows year, His watchful eye is ever upon us. We may not know the way, but we know the Guide. Thus we trust Him, although we cannot trace Him. Our Lord referred to "blind guides, who strain out a gnat and swallow a camel!" (Matt. 23:24). He is no sightless guide. His eyes, as a flame of fire, are always open. David reminds us that God has promised to guide us with His eyes (see Ps. 32:8); with perfect vision and knowledge, He never takes a wrong turn.

Promises associated with divine guidance are as numerous as they are precious. In presenting the pleasing profile of the Lord as our unfailing and constant guide, I hope to inspire you as you step out upon the untrodden pathway of the future. As He guides you skillfully with His hands, He will never lead you astray.

What happens when we reach the end of our pilgrimage? Will the faithful Guide leave us? The psalmist would have us believe that the Lord is our guide not only unto death but also "through the valley of the shadow of death" into the beautiful and broad country of heaven (Ps. 23:4).

Guide me, O thou great Jehovah,
Pilgrim through this barren land;
I am weak, but thou art mighty;
Hold me with thy powerful hand;
Bread of Heaven,
Feed me till I want no more.

January 11

You-Are-the-God-Who-Sees. GENESIS 16:13

Most commentators do not recognize that these six words constitute one of the names of almighty God. Hagar called the name of the Lord who spoke to her: "You-Are-the-God-Who-Sees." She also said: "Have I also here seen Him who sees me?" (Gen. 16:13). Then she called the well where this revelation took place Beer Lahai Roi, which means the "well of the one who lives and sees me."

When John Milton reached his twenty-third birthday, he wrote: "All is, if I have grace to use it so,/As ever in my great Task-Master's eye." Surely this confidence is a most profitable way to live as a pilgrim in a barren land. As we journey through the year, may it be with the assurance that the eyes of the Lord are ever upon the righteous. Note 1 Peter 3:12, where the apostle speaks of His eyes, ears, and face. His eye is not only upon sparrows but also upon saints. But the question is: Does what He sees, gladden or grieve His loving heart? We may successfully hide certain actions from the knowledge and gaze of others, but we can never hide anything from God, whose eyes "are in every place/Keeping watch on the evil and the good" (Prov. 15:3).

The realization of God's omniscience produces comfort for the saint and conviction in the sinner. The latter endeavors to hide from His all-seeing eye, while the believer rejoices that such a compassionate eye is ever upon him. Truly there is no nobler way to live than as "the apple of His eye" (Deut. 32:10). We may feel a sense of inferiority and count ourselves as mere worms of the dust; yet we are never out of God's sight, whose care of His children is personal and intimate.

May the eyes of the Lord see nothing in your life and mine alien to His holy mind and purpose. The days before us will be the most blessed we have experienced if we are daily conscious and confident of the life we live to bring constant joy to the eyes of the Lord that never close in slumber.

January 12

"He kept him as the apple of His eye." DEUTERONOMY 32:10

The repeated figure of speech, "the apple of the eye," in the Old Testament conveys a comforting image. The *apple* is the pupil of the eye, which has a keen sensibility. It is easily injured but is very valuable to its owner. Such a delicate organ is continually preserved by the eyelids and continually cleansed by the tear ducts. Therefore, this expressive metaphor denotes God's willingness both to protect and to purge His children.

The chain of biblical references containing the phrase forms a profitable meditation. The expression was used by God of Jacob and later of the nation of Israel: "He instructed him,/He kept him as the apple of His eye" (Deut. 32:10). God cherished His people as jealously as a man seeks to protect his eyeball. Israel was, and is, precious to God who spoke of her as "Israel My glory" (Is. 46:13).

David spoke of himself as being the apple of God's eye: "Keep me as the apple of Your eye;/Hide me under the shadow of Your wings" (Ps. 17:8). The pupil of the eye is a symbol of that which is tenderest and dearest to a person. Wings also are a frequently used figure of protection. David felt that he was easily hurt by his foes, yet so valuable to God that he dared pray that God would preserve him.

Solomon gave us the same illustration in advice to his son: "Keep my commands and live,/And my law as the apple of your eye" (Prov. 7:2). The pupil, the center of the eye, is one's most precious possession, and the Word of God is here presented as a valuable gift to be guarded and preserved most carefully.

The phrase also appears in the book of Zechariah, "He who touches you touches the apple of His eye" (Zech. 2:8). God notifies the world that Israel is unusually dear and precious to Him. He will protect her from all her foes.

Rejoice that God will keep you as the apple of His eye.

January 13

"He shall pray to God, and
He will delight in him."

JOB 33:26

What a privilege it is to carry everything to God in prayer! Thomas Brooks would have us remember that "the best and sweetest flowers of Paradise God gives to His people when they are upon their knees. Prayer is the gate of Heaven." Effectual prayer, however, is that inspired by the Holy Spirit for the ears of God alone, who never fails to hear and answer prayer when it is the natural breath of a redeemed soul. Prayer is the voice of faith.

When our approach to God is characterized by reverence, adoration, and faith, He is delighted to grant us favorable answers. God never withholds any good thing from those who are prayerfully dependent upon Him. At times, however, some answers appear to be most unfavorable to our finite understanding. We pray to God to be kept in health, but sickness comes. Has God forgotten to be gracious? Of course not. Because of His infinite wisdom, He knows what is best for His own. Therefore, if He permits sickness, He knows that is the most favorable experience for us. Often a bed of pain makes a far more powerful pulpit than a healthy body.

How striking is God's indictment of Israel: "I will hide My eyes from you;/Even though you make many prayers,/I will not hear" (Is. 1:15). Because Israel was a sinful nation, with hands full of blood, their prayers were shams. There are prayers God will not answer. Jeremiah has this striking description of God in respect to prayer: "You have covered Yourself with a cloud,/That prayer should not pass through" (Lam. 3:44). What a waste of breath and time it is when we talk into the deaf air and not into hearing ears! In the passage from Isaiah, the prophet condemns Judah for her departure from God. Laden with iniquity, she sought to keep up religious appearances, sacrifices, and oblations. But such mock worship only earned God's saying: "I am weary of bearing them" (Is. 1:14).

May we be found among the number who believe, as John Bunyan states it, "Prayer is a shield to the soul, a sacrifice to God, and a scourge for Satan."

January 14

*The nations . . . shall beat their swords into plowshares, . . .
Neither shall they learn war anymore.* ISAIAH 2:4

We can link this bright promise of a warless earth with that of the psalmist: "He makes wars cease to the end of the earth" (Ps. 46:9). Such a glorious prospect of a warless world seems far removed from the war-stricken and blood-soaked earth on which we live. The threat of a nuclear war, with its universal destruction of persons and property, makes worldwide peace seem like a dream. Yet here is the promise that nations are to transform the death-dealing engines of war into instruments of profit.

In World War II, there was a constant drive for metals, and people brought to the center of cities piles of farm and kitchen utensils and deposited them in public squares. Then taken to factories they would be transformed into weapons of fearful destruction. War always robs us of the necessities of life and destroys all that is peaceful and pastoral. How often we pause and cry: "Oh, God, why do nations make wars?"

But the promise of heaven is that earth's travail will cease with the appearance of the Prince of Peace. He alone has the prerogative to "make wars cease to the end of the earth:/He breaks the bow and . . . burns the chariot in the fire" (Ps. 46:9). Presently, international crises are heavy with prophetic significance, as Jesus declared.

Jesus predicted "distress of nations, with perplexity" (Luke 21:25). The word *perplexity* means "no way out." Rulers of our war-torn world see no way out of the problems resulting in the destruction of so much human life. Our Lord used a word in Luke 21:28 you should underline in your Bible—it is the word *begin.* We have come to the age when we are witnessing the beginning of those signs Jesus said would herald His coming. As we see these things come to pass: "Look up and lift up your heads, because your redemption draws near" (Luke 21:28). Our redemption is His appearance as the Prince of the kings of earth. As we wait, may our attitude be that of supreme confidence in the realization of divine sovereignty: "Be still, and know that I am God;/I will be exalted among the nations" (Ps. 46:10).

January 15

Woe to those who call evil good,
and good evil. ISAIAH 5:20

In this promise of judgment is a warning to all who make light of sin. Rudyard Kipling, in *The Islanders,* has the Pauline phrase: "Given to strong delusion, wholly believing a lie." Paul declared that in the last days: "God will send them strong delusion, that they should believe the lie" (2 Thess. 2:11).

Modernists have invented softening terms to hide the hideousness of sin. They claim sin is a mistake, an error, an accident, an element in our spiritual education. Festering sores are covered with satins. Guilt is veiled, and iniquity is garnished. Man is no longer thought of as a miserable, hell-deserving sinner.

God alone is the power enabling us to see ourselves as we are in His sight. Camouflage is necessary for soldiers to deceive their foes in battle, but for soldiers of the Cross any camouflage is sinful. Satan delights in picturing the Christian life as something drab, unwelcome, and undesirable. Sin entered the world when Satan persuaded Adam and Eve that God was a liar. Today, there is widespread denial of what God has declared. The way of holiness is pictured as rough, thorny, perilous, and therefore undesirable. Adherence to divine laws seems too narrow a life to live.

Christ died because *all* persons had sinned and come short of the glory of God; none were righteous on their own merit, no not one.

Just as I am, poor, wretched, blind;
Sight, riches, healing of the mind,
Yea, all I need, in thee to find,
O Lamb of God, I come! I come!

January 16

"He will not fail nor be discouraged." ISAIAH 42:4

Chief among the common ailments affecting the human mind is discouragement—a bane of both saint and sinner. When in distress, David would chide his heart with the question: "Why are you cast down, O my soul?/And why are you disquieted within me?/Hope in God" (Ps. 42:5). God's people can grow discouraged. The godless age of today with its wars, murders, suicides, robberies, broken trusts, and natural calamities breeds discouragement.

The Bible has some interesting things to say about discouragement. The Israelites were "very discouraged on the way" from Mount Hor to the Red Sea (Num. 21:4). Moses rebuked those who "discouraged the heart of the children of Israel" (Num. 32:9). "Go up and possess it . . . do not fear or be discouraged" (Deut. 1:21). Paul urged fathers not to provoke their children in any way "lest they become discouraged" (Col. 3:21).

As for the more pleasant ministry of encouragement, when Joshua set out to enter Canaan, the people were urged to "encourage him" (Deut. 1:38). Isaiah referred to a society of encouragers in which its members "encouraged" one another—a society in which all of us should have membership (see Is. 41:6–7).

From Isaiah we have the promise and prophecy that when Christ appeared on earth He would be a stranger to discouragement. This was, indeed, characteristic of His life. As the captain of our salvation, He never grew discouraged. The taunts of men could not frighten Him. In spite of Satan, demons, and foes, the word *depression* was never found in His vocabulary. Believing in His ultimate victory, He courageously endured the cross.

Can it be that as you read these lines that, for some reason, yours is the feeling of discouragement? Bid it farewell. Consider the children's chorus:

> Don't be downhearted, cheer up, cheer up,
> For Jesus is on the throne.
> And He will supply every need from on high,
> Cheer up! Cheer up! Cheer up!

January 17

"The blood of this just Person." MATTHEW 27:24

After our Lord was betrayed by Judas, He endured blasphemy in the presence of Caiaphas and mockery in Herod's presence. He was bound and led by the chief priests and elders to Pilate, whose conscience told him that the august prisoner was innocent. Jesus was then scourged, crowned with thorns, and condemned to a criminal's death. Pilate delivered Him up to be crucified, and thus Jesus died, the Just for the unjust.

There in Pilate's judgment hall, the heavenly Governor stood shackled before a Roman governor who failed to govern righteously. All judgment had been committed by the Father into the hands of His Son, and although He will yet judge the world, He submitted to the unjust sentence of an earthly judge.

As a man, Christ stood at the judgment seat of one of His own creatures. The marvel of marvels is that the Perfect Man, who is "the express image" of the Father (Heb. 1:3), suffered Himself to be branded as a criminal and to die between two thieves. When Jesus stood before Pilate, He was conscious of His complete innocence, a claim the one thief testified to when he said: "This Man has done nothing wrong" (Luke 23:41). In spite of the cynical miscarriage of justice by the religious leaders, climaxed by Pilate's pronouncement, Jesus was silent. Accepting the verdict by His submission, He delivered up Himself, rather than being delivered up by others. He had said He had power to lay down His life, which He did. His life was not taken but given. Presently, He is the Savior. But the time is coming when He is going to act as the judge of all the earth at the great white throne when just judgment will be pronounced upon all whose names are not inscribed in the Lamb's Book of Life.

What Thou, my Lord, hast suffered
   Was all for sinners' gain;
Mine, mine was the transgression,
   But Thine the deadly pain.
Lo, here I fall, my Savior,
   'Tis I deserve Thy place;
Look on me with Thy favor,
   Vouchsafe to me Thy grace.

January 18

There stood by the cross of Jesus
His mother. JOHN 19:25

Some ran away and others were prostrate with grief as Jesus died a brutal death. But the three Marys—Mary, his mother; Mary, the wife of Clopas; and Mary Magdalene—were found standing by the cross. Jesus, through His pain-filled eyes, saw His mother near the cross. What a sight it was for her to see her firstborn, dying in agony and shame! That was the moment when the prophecy of Simeon was fulfilled: "A sword will pierce through your own soul also" (Luke 2:35). Yet as she looked up lovingly and loyally at her son's mangled body, her face did not reveal despair. It was as if she were saying by her posture: "I am with you, son, even to the bitter end."

As our Lord's mother, Mary was associated with Him in suffering, since He was the only babe the world has ever known who did not have a human father. The shadow of the cross began to darken Mary's life in the early days of motherhood when, in her heart, she knew that "the holy thing" born of her was to be the Savior of the world. Later, as she stood by the cross, her spirit more than ever rejoiced in Him who was to be her Savior as well as the Savior of a lost world.

There had been the hour when Mary had to learn that earthly relationships must not interfere with heavenly obligations. In the temple came her son's mild rebuke: "Did you not know that I must be about My Father's business?" (Luke 2:49). Mary knew, only too well, that the business would be fulfilled in the sacrifice and death of her son. From that hour she prepared herself to drink of her son's bitter cup. The hour of His death came, and she followed Him to Calvary. There she stood by the cross until Jesus yielded up His spirit to God the Father. No wonder all generations call her blessed!

Around us we have many enemies of the Cross. May grace ever be ours to stand by it in wonder, praise, and gratitude!

January 19

He came to His own,
and His own did not receive Him. JOHN 1:11

When Christ came into the world, the promise was that all who received Him and believed on His name should become the sons of God. But a mixed reception greeted Him. Some welcomed Him, but others seemed to say: "Go where you are wanted, for you are not wanted here." Thus some people despised and rejected Him. If only they had esteemed Him worthy of reception, they would have been the heirs of the promise to be received by Jesus at His coming for His own.

Perhaps no experience is comparable to that of being unwanted, undesired, or rejected by one's own friends and relatives. Alas, many unwanted persons are around us. The heart of John must have been moved when he wrote of the One who came from glory, where chief honor was His, to earth with its door closed against Him. It is sad enough to read that "the world did not know Him" (John 1:10), but how sorrowful it must have been for Jesus to know that "His own" failed to receive Him as heaven's representative. He came to His own world, which He Himself had created, to His own people, but they saw no beauty in Him that they should desire Him. Disregarding the promised king, the Jewish hierarchy would not have Him reign over them, and they crucified their king.

The sad fact is that the intervening centuries have brought little change of attitude, for Jesus is still the unwanted One by the majority in our godless world. As for those of us who name His name, are we not guilty of affording Him only a partial reception? We have Him as our Savior but fail to recognize Him as the sovereign of our life. We rejoice that our guilty past is under the blood, but our present is marked by defeat because we fail to proclaim Him as Lord. May grace be ours to crown Him Lord of all we are and have!

January 20

"You also go into the vineyard, and whatever is right I will give you." MATTHEW 20:4

Among the metaphors used in Scripture, that of the vineyard has frequent mention. Old Testament references are associated with Israel whom God deemed to be His vineyard—and a disappointing one at that! Our Lord, in His parables, employed the figure of the vineyard. On one occasion, He told the parable of the two sons (see Matt. 21:28–33). The parable of the householder in Matthew 20:1–16 is the one claiming our attention today.

As the divine husbandman, God has planted us in His vineyard, or field of labor, and He expects us to be fruitful and thus receive the right reward at His judgment seat. God's lament over Israel was that "many rulers have destroyed My vineyard" (Jer. 12:10). Are we among the laborers cultivating to the full "the vineyard of the LORD of hosts" (Is. 5:7)? Many of the Lord's servants have a larger part of the vineyard to care for than others, and consequently, theirs is a larger responsibility. But whether our sphere of service is conspicuous or obscure makes little difference. What the Lord of the harvest expects is the very best from us wherever, in His providence, we have been placed.

The truth each of us must realize is that when God graciously saved us and made us His own, He endowed us with gifts or talents to be used in His service and likewise promised rewards if such talents were fully and rightly employed. Our quantity of talents may vary, but their quality must honor the Lord of the harvest. Whether we have a single gift or many, what we do have must be laid on the altar for God and used to the limit for His glory.

A boy had little to give Jesus—only five small loaves and two fishes. But all he had he fully surrendered, and Jesus multiplied the gift. The most enduring activity in the part of the vineyard we represent is that of the winning of the lost. May grace be ours ever to watch for, pray for, and win over lost souls!

January 21

From whom the whole family in heaven and earth is named. EPHESIANS 3:15

Will we recognize each other in heaven? What kind of a home would it be if its members are strangers to each other? Each of us will possess in the afterlife a recognizable personality superior to the one we had on earth. We may not recognize each other in the same way we do now, but there is no doubt that we will know each other. "Then I shall know just as I also am known" (1 Cor. 13:12). Heaven will give us a more holy and blessed intimacy than our human frailties presently allow.

This desire to know each other in heaven has been with us throughout the ages. Heaven could not be heaven if it did not offer reunion with the dead in Christ. All love is of God, and such love cannot be buried in a grave. The beautiful but broken relationships of earth will be resumed in the Father's home. As members of the same family, we will dwell together there in perfect harmony.

The Bible offers much evidence that the occupants of heaven recognize each other. The two angels found at Jesus' tomb proclaiming His resurrection certainly recognized each other. Jesus talked of sitting down with Abraham, Isaac, and Jacob in heaven (see Matt. 8:11). Moses and Elijah came from their dwelling place with God to have a conversation with Jesus about His death. Peter, James, and John were with Him on the mountain when the two appeared. Peter, of course, had never seen those saints in the flesh, but he recognized them immediately.

Jesus retained His identity in His resurrected body and appeared to Mary in the garden. The two disciples on the road to Emmaus recognized Him when He broke bread with them.

If you have a loved one in heaven whom you long to see, do not despair, for you will be together again. The voice you miss so much, you will hear again. Your loved one is only lost for a little while.

We are given this assurance by Cardinal Newman in "Lead, Kindly Light": "And with the morn those angel faces smile,/Which I have loved long since, and lost awhile."

January 22

His visage was marred more than any man. ISAIAH 52:14

The prophet Isaiah combined the brutal rejection of Jesus and the promise of His reign as King of kings. A study Bible reminds us that the literal rendering of the maltreatment Jesus received from the soldiers of Pilate is terrible in the extreme. It reads: "So marred from the form of man was His aspect that His appearance was not that of a son of man." The implication is that He was cruelly battered, almost beyond human recognition. We will never know what it meant for Him, as the holy, innocent one, to bear away our sin.

Legend has it that among the daughters of Jerusalem who were moved with compassion as they looked upon Christ's crimson-stained countenance was one named Veronica. Pushing her way through the crowd, she wiped His face with a handkerchief. Accepting her kind action with gratitude, the Suffering One performed a miracle. On her linen cloth was the image of His marred face. The pitiable creature Veronica helped had every shred of beauty, majesty, and dignity torn from Him. To those who watched Him as He stumbled pitifully along, looking like many a criminal who had walked the *Via Dolorosa*, He was without form or comeliness.

That face bruised, gashed from the soldiers' blows, and heavily lined for all the agonies He had undergone aroused no pity in some who hounded Him to His cross. Veronica saw beauty in the blood. The godly woman may have wiped the blood from His face, but she could not save Him from further bloodshed. On the cross, He shed His heart's blood to wipe away sin with all its disfigurements and restore God's image in us. The promise is that as astonishment was caused by His humiliation, still greater astonishment at His exaltation would appear (see Is. 52:14–15). John declared that the saints "shall see His face" no longer marred but diademed with majesty and glory (Rev. 22:4).

January 23

"Behold, the Lion of the tribe of Judah." REVELATION 5:5

Of all the metaphors used to describe Jesus, none is so expressive as that of the lion. Because of the fearful state of the wicked, God promised to "be to them like a lion. . . . I will devour them like a lion" (Hos. 13:7–8).

Naturalists observe that an enraged lion has a majestical, fierce look. Persons nearby run for their lives when the animal rises up for its prey. When the Lord "will roar from Zion" (Joel 3:16), what fear and terror will overcome the wicked!

As used of Christ, the metaphor of a lion is full of spiritual import. First of all, the lion is called "the king of beasts." Majesty adorns its very face. The Lion of Judah is King of kings on the earth.

The lion is also noted for its strength. Said Samson in a riddle: "Out of the strong came something sweet" (Judg. 14:14). None can match the Lord who is mighty to save and strong to deliver.

The lion is courageous, fearing no foes. The ancients applauded it as symbolizing dominion. Christ as the lion exhibited superlative courage and emerged from His conflict with another like a roaring lion, more than a conqueror. Proverbs 28:1 expresses the idea that believers are equally courageous: ". . . the righteous are bold as a lion." Indeed, we should be bold and courageous, just as Christ, the Lion of Judah, was strong in the face of His adversaries.

Pliny recorded about the king of beasts: "The lion alone, of all wild beasts, is gentle to those that humble themselves unto him, and will not touch any such upon submission, but spareth what creature soever will prostrate before him."

January 24

"Is not life more than food and the body more than clothing?" MATTHEW 6:25

Bound up with anxiety over material and physical needs is the promise that our heavenly Father knows what they are and will supply. The health and holiness of the body are of greater importance than its covering. Since we are children of God, our bodies have been fashioned into the temple of the Holy Spirit. Christians have to be more concerned over the body's functioning as a medium of blessing than as a mere model, displaying the latest fashion creations. The spiritual is more important than the material. To attach greater priority to clothes than we do to necessary, nutritious food, whereby the body can be kept healthy and made to render the utmost service in the cause of Christ, is surely unworthy of any Christian.

If God is able to feed the birds and to feed our bodies, has He not power to provide the raiment these bodies require? Surely, if He clothes the birds with lovely feathers, He will not be indifferent regarding what His children must have to wear. "Your heavenly Father knows that you need all these things" (Matt. 6:32). Good clothes are expensive these days, and saints who are materially poor need have no worry as to necessary raiment. He who clothes the fields with grass will surely care for their food and clothing. "I will clothe you with rich robes" (Zech. 3:4).

A hesitant new believer might ask how long this divine help is offered. "Through this weary pilgrimage," as Philip Doddridge describes it, the God of Bethel will make ample provision for us. He has promised to be our unfailing companion until traveling days are over. Until then, as we are to discover, He has given us manifold promises to assure our hearts that He will be our all-sufficiency as day follows day. The variety and value of these divine promises are our unfailing source of succor, solace, strength, and spiritual impulse during the varying circumstances of life.

January 25

"Then you will lay your gold in the dust." JOB 22:24

Although Eliphaz appears in the book of Job as a religious dogmatist who uttered many true things, much of his philosophy was his own. In Job 22, Eliphaz's third discourse sets forth the old theory that Job must have sinned; therefore, God allowed him to suffer. Poverty-stricken as Job was, let him but return to the Almighty and material prosperity would return was the contention of Eliphaz. Such advice, however, revealed the mercenary mind of Job's friend.

Experience proves that some of the purest of men and women are the poorest. Many of God's saints are not able to lay up gold as dust. The Lord sees to it that their every need is met. Further, the use of money in Christ's service means laying up treasure in heaven.

Later on Job answered his critics: "If I have made gold my hope, or said to fine gold, 'You are my confidence' . . . this also would be an iniquity worthy of judgment" (Job 31:24, 28). But gold had never been Job's hope or confidence. Gold had never been his god.

If the world's silver and gold are the Lord's, and they are because He created all metals, then He has the prior claim upon them. There would never be any lack of support for God's work at home and abroad if only all His children looked upon their substance as His money.

Regrettably, too many around us think more of their silver than they do of their Savior. If it is true that money talks, then with a loud, commanding voice it demands worship, and gold-greedy souls listen to that call and bow in obedience to that which makes them as hard as the metal for which they live. People will go to terrible extremes for riches. If a man possesses a million dollars, we call him a very rich man. But if his heart is destitute of Him whose price is above rubies, then like the rich Laodiceans, he is poor and miserable.

Heaven's millionaires are those who, apart from what they have, know and love Jesus, to whom the wealth in every mine belongs.

January 26

To be admired among all those who believe. 2 THESSALONIANS 1:10

In the opening chapter of 2 Thessalonians Paul emphasized the righteous judgment of God. He promised that when the Lord appears in the day of His power to take vengeance upon the wicked, He will be also "glorified in His saints, and...admired among all those who believe." The last phrase is the one commanding our attention. It prompts us to ask our hearts the question: Is Jesus being admired by others because of our reflection of all He is in Himself? The consuming passion of Paul was that in every way: "Christ will be magnified in my body, whether by life or by death" (Phil. 1:20). *Admired* means "to marvel," "to be astonished," "to regard with wonder and reverence," "to honor." Truly, Paul's life and labor brought great honor to the Savior he dearly loved.

It is remarkable that our Lord caused many to wonder at and reverence God as the result of His resemblance to the Father in every way. Philip said to Jesus: "'Show us the Father, and it is sufficient for us.' Jesus said, . . . 'He who has seen Me has seen the Father'" (John 14:8–9). By His words and works He resembled the Father. If we desire to know what God is like, we have only to study the New Testament to discover that Jesus came as "the brightness of His glory and the express image of His person" (Heb. 1:3). How Jesus reflected the love, holiness, peace, joy, justice, patience, and power! As God the Son, He was Godlike in all His ways.

Do we so live that others around us believe and marvel at the grace and goodness of God? In Gideon's victorious battle with the princes of Midian, he asked Zebah and Zalmunna what the men were like they defeated at Tabor. They answered: "As you are, so were they; each one resembled the son of a king" (Judg. 8:18).

Do we resemble Him as the King of kings in our daily life? As the world around sees us, do they wonder at the manifestation of Christlike virtues exhibited? Ask the Father to make you a mirror, reflecting His Son to the world.

January 27

[They] worshiped Him who lives forever and ever. REVELATION 5:14

Look in the book of Revelation to find the prophecy and promise of universal adoration of Christ as the Lamb slain before the foundation of the world. All within creation are to be stirred up to worship Him.

The Cross is the grandest fact and event of all time. Without it, Christ would have been in glory alone, and sinners would have had no deliverance from the guilt and government of sin. But the suffering, conquering Lamb of God will have all tongues ascribing praise and honor to His name (see Rev. 5:8–14). Around the throne will be the redeemed of all ages, with the angels forming the outer circle. The seven-sealed book, containing the transferences of authority and government to the Lamb, will be ready. He will be worthy to receive every mark of distinction possible to confer upon Him. He will be praised for the perfection of attributes manifested. Meditate on these attributes noted in Revelation 5:12:

Power—This is first named, for the Lamb is about to exercise power in the widest, most comprehensive character.

Riches—All wealth, whether material, moral, or physical, is His due. As the Lamb who gave His all, He claims our best.

Wisdom—Coming as the personification of divine wisdom and being made unto us wisdom, He will display the highest wisdom when He returns to reign.

Strength—This quality enables Him to carry out His will as He comes as King of kings.

Honor—As the Lamb, He died dishonored by men. Religious leaders caused Him to die as a criminal. Deserved recognition and honor will finally be His.

Glory—Worthy to receive all glory, the Lamb is now glorified with the glory He had with the Father in the dateless past.

Blessing—All forms of blessedness are His. When His completed church is with Him, full contentment will be His.

What exaltation will be His, when the tide of praise gathers force and volume until the whole creation ascribes honor to the Lamb!

January 28

Even so we also should walk in newness of life. ROMANS 6:4

Following the New Testament pattern, we believers have been baptized into Christ's death and raised up from the dead by the glory of the Father. We now walk in the newness of His resurrected life.

Many years ago the ground in central London was cleared of old buildings to make the new kingsway. The cleared site lay exposed for a year to light and air, and a strange sight drew naturalists to the area. The soil had not felt the touch of spring since the day when the Romans sailed up the Thames River and beached upon its strand.

When the sunlight poured its light and life upon this uncovered soil, a host of flowers sprang up, many of which were formerly unknown in England. They were the plants the Romans had brought with them and sown. Hidden away in the darkness, lying dormant under the mass of bricks and mortar, they seemed to have died. But under the new conditions, obeying the law of life, they escaped from seeming death and blossomed into beauty.

Is this not an illustration of what happens in many a life? The term *newness* implies something different, taking the place of an old thing, and not as yet used. So the "new man" is one who differs from the former "old man." As Christians regenerated by the Holy Spirit, we are exhorted to live habitually in the newness of life the Spirit imparted in the hour of our repentance and faith.

After years of wrongdoing, we have discovered the truth that Christ does not deal with us after our sins. He gives us the power of the Resurrection. He awakens and sustains our new life in Him. This resurrection from our dead selves to life is real. Let each new day become one of discovering newness through Christ's powerful example.

January 29

"I will pray the Father, and He will give you another Helper." JOHN 14:16

Among the great and precious promises is the one Jesus made concerning the coming of the Holy Spirit. What a promise of consolation this is for sorrowing hearts in a world of tears!

The term *another* is worth consideration, since it has a twofold significance: (1) someone or something of the same nature, or (2) someone or something of a totally different nature. The word Jesus used implies one of the same nature. So we can read it, "Another like Myself," for the Holy Spirit and Jesus are one in everything. We can think of the promised Helper as Jesus' other self. They are one, even as the Father and Son "are one" (John 10:30).

Helper is another term to examine. It is a word signifying "to soothe," "to take courage," "to take heart," "to speak persuasively and tenderly." It is used of Father, Christ, the Holy Spirit, and Scripture.

The churches Paul visited were edified. These churches, "walking in the fear of the Lord and in the comfort [help] of the Holy Spirit," were multiplied (Acts 9:31).

In the *Book of Common Prayer,* "beside the still waters" (Ps. 23:2) is translated as "beside the waters of comfort." The Holy Spirit is the believer's indwelling advocate to help his ignorance and infirmity and to make intercession.

The final phrase of our Lord's promise of the Holy Spirit must be borne in mind: "That He may abide with you forever" (John 14:16). Although we may be guilty of grieving and quenching the Spirit, He ever remains as the advocate who can never be evicted.

Hover o'er me, Holy Spirit,
Bathe my trembling heart and brow;
Fill me with Thy hallowed presence,
Come, oh, come and fill me now.

January 30

Having disarmed principalities and powers,
He made a public spectacle of them,
triumphing over them in it. COLOSSIANS 2:15

One suggested translation of the end of this verse, "triumphing over them in it," reads "winning the victory through the Cross."

During the dark days of World War II, the *V* sign became the symbol of the faith of free people everywhere. In our country we are accustomed to seeing two triumphant fingers held up in *V* shape, as the token of victory. It was the favorite posture of Winston Churchill, as he indicated the brave assurance he inspired that the Allies would successfully conclude the grim task before them.

But are we not blessed to know that God employs the same sign of victory? A commentator, referring to Jesus bearing His cross, remarked: "The condemned were usually obliged to carry their crosses, the *crossbeams fastened together like the letter V,* their arms bound to the projecting ends." The fastening of those crossbeams like a *V* suggested, in fact and even in form, God's victory sign. Thanks be to God who gives us the victory. The Cross will ever remain as the symbol of present and ultimate victory over all the forces of Satan and sin.

Are we more than conquerors? Are we proving the Pauline assertion: "Sin shall not have dominion over you" (Rom. 6:14)?

A saying of Henry Ward Beecher was: "A victory inside of us is ten thousand times more glorious than one outside of us." The glad message of Calvary is that a constant victory on the inner battlefield of the soul can be ours. Has the day of our personal victory dawned? Is ours the joyful assurance of a blood-bought emancipation? May our lives be open to a victory within.

January 31

"I, even I, am He who comforts you." ISAIAH 51:12

What a precious promise this is for all who are sad and downcast! Again and again God reminds His own that He is able to console them in all their tribulation. In effect, He is saying here: "I, even I, yes, I, the almighty I, the Lord of hosts, I, maker of heaven and earth—I am the One willing to share your sorrows." Beloved, what a gracious God we have! Able to count the myriads of stars studding the sky, He condescends to heal "the brokenhearted" and to bind up "their wounds" (Ps. 147:3). With His majesty there is mercy. Sovereign though He is, He is ever the sympathizer!

In the verse above taken from Isaiah note the contrast, *I—you;* our marvelous God is at one end and a weak, sorrowful, distressed soul is at the other. Have you realized that this great, comforting God is for *you*? Are you appropriating by faith all that He is and has in Himself for your needy heart? His dear Son became a man of sorrows and carried our sorrows. Not only was Jesus sent to heal the brokenhearted but He Himself was compassed by the sorrows of death and died of a broken heart.

Thus, Jesus' personal acquaintance with human grief qualifies Him to be the prince of comforters. He touched our life at every point. His were not the sheltered, unruffled experiences of life. Sorrow was His constant companion. In fact, was there ever sorrow like His? He offered Himself as our comforter, and we realize that His consolation is born of experience.

Are you grief-stricken at this very hour? Has some sorrow struck at your heart or home? Lean hard on Him who walked the dark valley before you, and you will experience a peace passing all understanding. He, whose eyes were wet with tears while among men, knows how to wipe away your tears of anguish.

February 1

Speaking to one another in psalms. EPHESIANS 5:19

What a remarkable volume of promises and prophecies the book of Psalms constitutes! Many of them were set to music and sung by the temple choir. In essence they formed the prayer and praise book of Israel. If for every sigh God has a psalm, then in the 150 psalms forming the Psalter, He is able to banish the manifold sighs escaping the human heart.

The psalms are, indeed, the poets' corner in the Bible. The bards of ancient days thrill our hearts today because their poems are filled with the feeling of their heavenly Father's thoughts. This is why throughout the centuries the poetry of the Bible has fashioned men with true nobility. As we study the poetic works from God's poet laureates, we catch something of the sweetness that inspired their hearts.

Pagan verses celebrating the birth of gods carry pretty compliments and flatteries intended to propitiate. But they do not result from wrestling in prayer with tearful eyes and downcast head, and they do not witness to the full assurance of faith, such as made the psalms for all time the best expression of devotional feelings of men.

Without doubt, David, the sweet psalmist of Israel, was God's chosen poet laureate who, in his day, was unequaled in the expression of truth in poetic form. So the laurel of everlasting remembrance is David's. Since his time, many famous poets have appeared, and the greatest among them paid tribute to Israel's renowned poet. For example, John Milton, when only a lad of fifteen at St. Paul's School in London, wrote a verse based on Psalm 136:

> Let us with a gladsome mind
> Praise the Lord, for He is kind;
> For His mercies aye endure,
> Ever faithful, ever sure.

If today finds you downcast, recite or sing one of the psalms and go on your way rejoicing.

February 2

*Blessed is the man . . . like a tree/
Planted by the rivers of water./The ungodly
are not so,/But are like the chaff.* PSALM 1:1, 3–4

The first psalm (about two contrasting persons) has a distinction all its own. It strikes the keynote for the entire collection of psalms. Psalm 1 can be looked upon as the introduction of the 150 psalms. This initial psalm is the text, so to speak; the rest of the psalms, the sermon or exposition on the text.

The most noticeable feature of this psalm is the way its six verses fall into two natural divisions of three verses each: (1) the reward of the saint (vv. 1–3), and (2) the retribution of the sinner (vv. 4–6). These parallel lines epitomize not only the psalms in their entirety but also the whole of Scripture. They contrast the two classes of people in the world, namely, saints or sinners. The separation between the godly and the ungodly is found in the teaching of Old Testament prophets, in the discourses of Christ, and in the writings of the apostles. The summary is clear: "The Lord knows the way of the righteous,/But the way of the ungodly shall perish" (Ps. 1:6). This scriptural truth is preserved and the reward of each type of person unequivocally declared, no matter where we turn in Scripture.

The opening word of the psalm is a favorite one in the Bible, recurring hundreds of times with its cognates. The Hebrew word for *blessed* is a plural noun and actually means "blessednesses." How bountiful God is in the reward of those who love, obey, and serve!

What a difference there is between the first word and the last word of the psalm: *blessed—perish*! They suggest the chasm between the saved and the lost, the gulf between heaven and hell. How grateful to God we should be if ours is the assurance that we are among the righteous known of Him!

February 3

"Ask of Me, and I will give You/
The nations for Your inheritance." PSALM 2:8

The first two psalms might be treated as one, with Christ as the perfect blessed man in Psalm 1 and as the King's Son in Psalm 2. Let us compare some aspects of the two.

In Psalm 1 we have the contrast between the godly and the ungodly. In Psalm 2 the rage of the godless meets its doom in the reign of the Messiah Prince.

In Psalm 1 the wicked are blown away as chaff. In Psalm 2 they are broken in pieces as a potter's vessel.

In Psalm 1, the righteous are depicted as a stable, ever fruitful tree. In Psalm 2 Christ is forecast as the head of the righteous and as the rewarder of those who trust in Him.

Psalm 2 ends where Psalm 1 begins, namely, with the "blessed . . . who put their trust in Him."

The second psalm was among Martin Luther's favorites. He wrote,

> The second Psalm is one of the best Psalms. I love that Psalm with all my heart. It strikes and flashes valiantly among kings, princes, counsellors and judges. If what this Psalm says be true, then we know the allegations and aims of Papists are stark lies and folly. If I were our Lord God, and had committed the government to my son, as He to His Son, and these vile people were as disobedient as they now be, I would knock the world in pieces.

The New Testament uses the psalm with great effect. Peter, ascribing the psalm to David, applied it to the godless rulers of his own time (see Acts 4:24–28). Paul quoted it in his synagogue sermon on the theme of "justification by faith" (see Acts 13:33). Because of the nature of the psalm, it is applicable to the godless persecutors of any age. How we rejoice in the fact that all the nations of the earth will yet be the inheritance of Christ. "He shall reign forever and ever!" (Rev. 11:15).

February 4

I will not be afraid of ten thousands of people. PSALM 3:6

The background of this psalm is sad. Its title reminds us that David wrote it when he was compelled to flee from his son, Absalom, who was eager to rob his father of the throne and who sought to kill him. Its eight verses can be divided into four sections.

Trouble (vv. 1–2). The godless majority pictured in these two verses claimed that God Himself was against David: "There is no help for him in God." No wonder this first section ends with the exclamation *Selah,* meaning, "Think of that!" Would God refuse help to the man after His own heart?

Trust (vv. 3–4). David may have appeared to be in the minority, but he was with God and therefore had a most blessed majority. Note how the psalmist described his Divine Helper: (1) *a shield for me.* God was his protector, supplying His servant with the whole armor to preserve him from his foes; (2) *my glory.* David's sin had tarnished his kingly glory, yet he aspired to have God as his only glory; (3) *One who lifts up my head.* Because of Absalom's rebellion David was downcast, dejected, and discouraged, but he experienced what it was to have God give him the light of His countenance; and (4) *He heard me from His holy hill.* David called upon God in the day of his trouble and was delivered. He proved God to be a "very present help" (Ps. 46:1) in dark days. The word *present* implies that God was at hand, on the spot as needs arose.

Tranquility (vv. 5–6). Courage became his, for he was not afraid of "ten thousands" of foes. David came to know sublime peacefulness.

Triumph (vv. 7–8). Assurance became David's as he rested in all God is in Himself, the source of salvation and of His continued blessing.

We must trust in God, even when our lives seem threatened.

February 5

"For the oppression of the poor,/
for the sighing of the needy,/
Now I will arise," says the LORD. PSALM 12:5

David, the author of Psalm 12, had great respect for those less privileged than he. In his protection of the oppressed, he reflected the divine character: "He shall stand at the right hand of the poor,/To save him from those who condemn him" (Ps. 109:31). Forcefully, the psalmist described God's arising as the champion of the needy.

We can make a spiritual application from such promised relief. Satan is our oppressor. With accumulated guile he seeks to ensnare us, but our Deliverer is ever near to hear our sigh and to snatch us safely out of the trap of the hunter. A similar emancipation is emphasized by David: "All my bones shall say,/'LORD, who is like You,/Delivering . . . the poor and the needy from him who plunders him?'" (Ps. 35:10).

The bones sometimes stand for a person's whole body: "His bones are full of his youthful vigor" (Job 20:11). Broken bones being made to rejoice is a symbolic description expressing the holy confidence and comfort of mind that restoration to divine favor produces (Ps. 51:8). When David said that all his bones magnified the Lord for His complete deliverance, he was using a figure of speech illustrative of the harmony of all inward powers for the purpose of praise.

Consider this twofold description of the oppressor. He is too strong for the needy to overcome. He is always out to spoil and plunder. All within David rejoiced, however, because in God there is One stronger than the strongest, One who is able to rob the spoiler of his prey. The satanic oppressor must ever bow before Him who destroyed the works of the devil.

May your life be as a platform upon which divine deliverance is displayed!

February 6

The heavens . . . and the firmament . . .
the law of the LORD . . .
the meditation of my heart. PSALM 19:1, 7, 14

This psalm is like a library; it contains three books in its fourteen verses: (1) the book of nature (vv. 1–6); (2) the book of Scripture (vv. 7–11); and (3) the book of the heart (vv. 12–14).

The psalm was used by the master of song in the sanctuary for the use of assembled worshipers. To them, the Lord was the God of the universe, God of Scripture, and God of the human heart.

The opening six verses reveal creation as "the great Natural Bible" made up of three chapters—heaven, earth, and sea. C. H. Spurgeon once said:

> Heaven is the first and the most glorious, and by its aid we are able to see the beauties of the other two. Any book without its first page would be sadly imperfect, and especially the great Natural Bible, since its first pages, the sun, moon, and stars, supply light to the rest of the volume, and are the keys, without which the writing which follows would be dark and undiscerned. Man walking erect was evidently made to scan the skies and begins the book at the right place.

The next section, verses 7–11, brings us to the book of Scripture, designated as the law, the testimony, the statutes, the commandment, the fear, and the judgments. Because of the remarkable contents of Scripture, they are more precious than gold and more nutritious than the finest honey. Thus we have gone from creation to revelation, with the same God as the author of both the physical and spiritual worlds.

The third book, found in the last three verses of the psalm, deals with the human heart. The same God of the skies, and the God of Scripture, is also God of the soul. We should desire Scripture above anything else in the world because by it we are warned of the folly of sinning, from errors, secret faults, and presumptuous sins. The last word of the psalm is *redeemer,* and as such God is able and willing to make us acceptable in His sight.

February 7

My God, My God, why have You forsaken Me? PSALM 22:1

The marked feature of this Calvary psalm is the prophetic image it supplies of our Lord's final, saddest hours. Only the Holy Spirit could have given David such an accurate insight into the Cross, centuries upon centuries before Jesus died. In this forecast of our Lord's life and death, we see Him as the reproached one, the rejected one, the risen one, the rejoicing one, the reigning one, and the righteous one. We can readily understand why this is the most quoted psalm in the New Testament. Further, the details David cites of the particular death Jesus died are remarkable since crucifixion was a Roman invention of some centuries after David's death.

These soul-stirring aspects of Calvary can be noted by the careful Bible student:

1. *The cry of desolation* (v. 1). This fourth cry of the Cross (see Matt. 27:46) reveals the apparent desertion of the Son by His Father. Jesus was forsaken in that lone hour so that He might promise His blood-washed children that He would never forsake them.
2. *Despicable contempt and scorn* (vv. 6–7).
3. *Bones out of joint* (v. 14).
4. *Extreme perspiration; heart affected* (v. 14).
5. *Physical exhaustion and thirst* (v. 15).
6. *Hands and feet pierced* (v. 16). Human minds cannot fully comprehend the agony Christ suffered for our salvation
7. *Lots cast for clothing* (v. 18).
8. *Resurrection accomplished* (vv. 19–20). The borrowed grave could not keep its prey. Satan, who had the power of death, was defeated.
9. *The declaration of the name* (vv. 22–25).
10. *Universal reign* (vv. 27–31).

What a marvelous survey this Calvary psalm provides of the sufferings, death, resurrection, and final triumph of our Lord!

February 8

The LORD is my shepherd;/ I shall not want. PSALM 23:1

This precious psalm came from the inspired pen of David, who as a shepherd lad cared for his father's flock. Among all of the 150 psalms making up the Psalter, none has been read, sung, quoted from, and written about more than this pearl of psalms, Psalm 23.

Because of this psalm's rich poetic beauty and its universal appeal, the saints of succeeding generations have found in it a mirror of the motions of their own soul. Perhaps that is why Saint Augustine chose it as the Hymn of the Martyrs; countless numbers of them quoted it as they perished for Christ's sake. The repetition of the words *my* and *I* indicates that the Lord offers Himself as the shepherd to each and every heart.

The metaphor of the shepherd, expressive of Christ's relationship to His own, is common in Scripture. In beautiful imagery Isaiah depicted the coming Messiah thus: "He will feed His flock like a shepherd" (Is. 40:11). Christ presented Himself as "the good shepherd," willing to die for sinners and able to defend and preserve them once they are within His fold. So the risen, glorified Lord is our "great Shepherd," caring in every way for us as "the Shepherd and Overseer of [our] souls" (1 Pet. 2:25). When He returns in the air, it will be as "the Chief Shepherd" (1 Pet. 5:4) to reward His under-shepherds. Was it not fitting, therefore, that the first to receive the announcement of His birth as the Savior–Shepherd were the lowly shepherds as they watched their flocks by night?

The opening verse of this renowned psalm is an epitome of the entire psalm. The five verses that elaborate upon what we shall never want, as we abide in His will, we might state as: "The Lord is my shepherd, what more do I want?"

As our shepherd, Jesus knows what things we need before we ask Him, and He never fails to meet our every need for life here and hereafter.

February 9

The LORD of hosts,/
He is the King of glory. PSALM 24:10

This psalm provides us with a fourfold revelation of Him who is altogether mighty and worthy to possess all things.

1. *Triumph as the Almighty One* (vv. 1–2). Here we have praise to the Lord as the creator and owner of all things and persons. He is the monarch of all that He surveys. Because He created all, He owns all and uses all as He desires. Although sinful man has conquered the earth by the power of the sword and divided it into nations, he is only a tenant to be evicted when its original owner returns as the great landowner and proprietor of the earth.

2. *Triumph as the Worthy One* (vv. 3–6). The question asked is: Who is able and worthy to rule the earth? The answer is: Only One has all the necessary qualifications. *"He who has clean hands."* This requirement suggests rectitude of character and conduct. Nothing false or unrighteous must be tolerated in any transaction. *"A pure heart."* Christ is worthy to reign because of His holiness of heart. While among men, He could ask: "Which of you convicts Me of sin?" (John 8:46). And none could! *"Who has not lifted up his soul to an idol."* Jesus had sanctification of thought and speech and a life of pureness. The divine benediction became Christ's because of His triumphant worthiness.

3. *Triumph as the Crucified One* (vv. 7–8). Christ was the one here named "King of glory" five times—the one "strong" and "mighty in battle." The Cross opened the door of our Lord's triumphant entry into glory.

4. *Triumph as the Glorified One* (vv. 9–10). The question, "Who is this King of glory?" is answered by thundering voices ringing with admiration as the doors are opened for the Royal Conqueror to enter His heavenly abode.

Have you brought forth the royal diadem and crowned Him as King of your entire life?

February 10

No king is saved by the multitude of an army. PSALM 33:16

Some authorities suggest this unnamed psalm is an extension of Psalm 32 by David. As king of Israel, he knew what he was writing about. As a king, he was severely punished for numbering his soldiers, thinking that deliverance from enemies was wholly dependent upon a host of brave fighters. What a warning is here for kings and rulers of today who advocate large armies and who feel that national security is certain if one country has the strongest fighting force possible!

God, however, has not promised to be on the side of big military forces. No leader is saved by what he has, for ultimately peace and security are ordained of God. Would that we could see less trust put in nuclear weapons, bombs, and armed forces, and a more positive mention of the name of the Lord our God who, by His power, can put any army to flight. The clear testimony of Scripture is that victory is promised to the king and people who are willing to put God first.

In his exhortation as to the scope of intercession, Paul urged the early church to pray "for kings and all who are in authority" that, first of all, "we may lead a quiet and peaceable life in all godliness and reverence" (1 Tim. 2:2).

As a Christian, do you pray for the leaders of your nation, that they might lead the way in the reduction of the most brutal weapons of war and declare that righteousness can exalt a nation? If, out of the millions of Christians, we could gather a million who, believing in the power of prayer, would concentrate upon their elected rulers, interceding for the godliness and divine wisdom in all their deliberations, what a paradise we would have! Pause now to pray, as the Bible commands, for those in authority.

February 11

Why are you cast down, O my soul? PSALM 43:5

This brief psalm is most appropriate for our age of depression. We have no difficulty in identifying David as the author of this psalm. Who but the gifted harpist could write: "On the harp I will praise You,/O God, my God" (Ps. 43:4)? Had not David perfected the art of soliloquy, the habit of speaking in solitude to his own heart about his fears, his foes, and his faith? You can hear David's characteristic voice in this psalm.

Looking at the psalm as a whole, we discover a triad of truth:

1. *Outward,* the oppression of foes (vv. 1–2). David besought God to vindicate and defend his cause against a nation that had lost God. Deliverance was also sought for deceitful and unjust men and from the oppression of soul they caused. The psalmist had a long and bitter experience of being cast down because of the antagonistic position of his enemies. True believers face similar assailants today.

2. *Godward,* the expression of faith (vv. 3–4). In these two verses, David turned his eyes from his enemies to God. While his outlook was oppressive, his uplook was encouraging and heartening. Light and truth would sustain him, although surrounded by ungodliness and injustice. How deep is our need of the light the Spirit imparts and of truth as exemplified in Jesus!

3. *Inward,* temporary depression (v. 5). Continuing and concluding his soliloquy, David, gripped by the feeling of despair, asked himself the question: "Why are you cast down, O my soul?" The *why* of his distress because of oppressing foes led to the *why* of disquietude of soul. Recovery, however, was his through hope. C. H. Spurgeon's paraphrase of this closing verse is most apt: "Come, my heart, look out of the window, borrow the telescopic glass, forecast a little and sweeten the chamber with sprigs of the sweet herb of love."

February 12

I recite my composition concerning the King. PSALM 45:1

The New Testament definitely relates this psalm to Christ. Quoting verses 6 and 7, the writer of Hebrews has it: "To the Son He says: 'Your throne, O God, is forever and ever' " (Heb. 1:8). Thus, without any doubt whatever, the psalm is eloquent with the truth of the mystic union between Christ and His church, given to us in pictorial language of the King in His beauty and of the queen in her glory. The following outline is helpful.

1. *A description of the King* (vv. 1–2). The entire psalm has the King as its subject, even though the latter part is taken up with His family. Everything is the King's, a description occurring seven times. Note the change from *my* in verse 1 to *your* in verse 2.

2. *The dominion of the King* (vv. 3–5). After the introduction of the person of the King, we are brought to consider His power. Perfection of warrior strength is His as well as the perfection of beauty and speech. In these verses before us, we have a powerful sword, a triumphant procession, and a victorious rule.

3. *The deity of the King* (vv. 6–7). Here God addresses God! God the Father is saying to God the Son, "Your throne, O God, is forever and ever." The virtues of deity found in this section are definitely applied to Christ in Hebrews 1:8–9.

4. *The dress of the King* (v. 8). Our Lord's wardrobe, past and present, has a peculiar fragrance all its own. From swaddling clothes to heavenly garments of myrrh, He progresses.

5. *The daughters of the King* (vv. 9–15). The queen in all her glory can be taken as a symbol of the church, the King's bride, all glorious within.

6. *The decree of the King* (vv. 16–17). Here we have the promise that the twofold decree of the King's cause will not fail.

Meditate on the kingly aspects of your Redeemer.

February 13

God is our refuge and strength,/
A very present help in trouble. PSALM 46:1

Known as the "psalm of holy confidence," this psalm inspired Martin Luther's magnificent courage. In moments of trial when the reformer was cast down in soul, he would say to Melanchton, his friend: "Come, Philip, let us sing Psalm 46." This psalm also inspired the words to Luther's battle hymn of the Reformation, "A Mighty Fortress Is Our God."

John Wesley met the approach of death with the language of this stirring psalm on his lips. Bystanders heard Wesley's twice-repeated cry: "The best of all is, God is with us." Through his last night, he was heard attempting to repeat the words: "The Lord of hosts is with us;/The God of Jacob is our refuge" (v. 11).

Prominent features of the psalm are easily discerned, namely, the threefold repetition of God as our refuge (vv. 1, 7, 11) and the threefold Selah (vv. 3, 7, 11). The psalm begins and ends with God. Sung by the sons of Korah in the temple service of song, the psalm may be interpreted as a psalm of the Trinity.

The opening verse portrays God in a threefold way, namely, as our refuge, strength, and present help in trouble. Our shelter from all enemies is not something but *someone*, the almighty, triune God. The phrase, "very present," suggests that He is an actual, real helper, always at hand to protect and provide.

We have not only a Refuge but also a River (vv. 4–7), and we are in desperate need of both. The River must be taken in its symbolic sense as the promise fulfilled by Jesus when He spoke of the rivers of water flowing from Him (see John 4:14).

As for the conclusion of the psalm, the Lord Jesus Christ alone fits into this prophetic section. We live in a troubled world, and we await His coming as the Prince of Peace. Our strength and comfort as we tarry in a sinful world is in the promise: "Be still [relax], and know that I am God" (v. 10).

February 14

God is in the midst of her, . . .
God shall help her. PSALM 46:5

We have New Testament warrant for using "the city of God" as a metaphor for the church, which John saw not only as the bride, the Lamb's wife, but also as a great city, the holy Jerusalem, descending out of heaven from God (see Rev. 21–22).

While the church is not in the Old Testament as a subject of divine revelation, yet we have three thoughts in the verse before us that can apply to her. God *indwells, sustains,* and *helps* her.

Nazism, fascism, and communism, a trinity of brute force, have harassed the church in different parts of the world. Persecution and suffering are still being heaped upon believers in conquered lands, but theirs is the promise of divine help. Soon a despised people will be forever delivered from a groaning creation. The dawn is about to break. Jesus is coming to dry the tears of His own.

The glorious Head of the church Himself once promised: "The gates of Hades shall not prevail against it" (Matt. 16:18). In time of war, bombing destroys public buildings, and churches do not escape the devastation. War is no respecter of sacred edifices. We must remember that the indestructible church of which Jesus prophesied is not one of stained glass windows and ornate stones but of redeemed men and women who form our Lord's body.

Hell could not prevail against Him; hell spends its hate in vain against His blood-bought church. In spite of Satan, sin, and the world, Christ's promise to build His church will be fully realized.

Mid toil and tribulation,
  And tumult of her war,
She waits the consummation
  Of peace forevermore.
Till, with the vision glorious,
  Her longing eyes are blest,
And the great Church victorious
  Shall be the Church at rest.

February 15

Great is the LORD,
and greatly to be praised. PSALM 48:1

Psalm 48 displays the manifold attributes of God. The phrase, "This is God/Our God" (v. 14), provides a fitting climax to such an exultant song. What do we learn about this deity who is perpetually ours?

He is great. How magnificent is the opening phrase, "Great is the LORD"! Everything leaving His hand bears the imprint of His unsearchable greatness. Our salvation is the most wonderful provision of His grace and power.

He is universally praised. Because of His eternal greatness, He is worthy to receive praise "to the ends of the earth" (v. 10). His chosen people in the mountains of His holiness can adore and praise Him as He should be praised.

He is holy. Not all the great people of earth are holy, just as those who are holy in God are not always great in the esteem of others. But the Lord is both great and holy—and great because holy.

He is sovereign. Our great God is often presented as "the great King" (Ps. 48:2; cf. Pss. 47:2; 95:3). Truly, He is greater than the greatest sovereigns that ever reigned. He is higher than the kings of earth. Soon He will fulfill His promise and return to earth as the King of kings.

He is our protection. As our King, he has all preeminence and power. As our refuge, He affords us continual protection. He is our only shield from Satan and sin.

He is supreme. The psalmist gives us a vivid description of God's supremacy over men and nature (vv. 4–8).

God is faithful. Unchangeable in character, all He has been and is, He will ever be! Because of who He is, His manifested virtues cannot change. He remains the same forever. Trust Him.

February 16

Restore to me the joy of Your salvation. PSALM 51:12

The title of this penitential psalm indicates its sad background. Even though he was a man after God's own heart, David was guilty of dark sins. He confessed that he had sinned against God only, but his immediate sin was against Bathsheba and her devoted, patriotic husband, Uriah. Sins of adultery and murder robbed David not of God's salvation but of the joy of it. Peace gave way to pain. Grief took the place of gladness. Instead of the song, there was a sob.

But the promise was that broken bones could be perfectly knit together again (see v. 8). All shadows vanished; the forgiven saint basked in the sunshine of divine favor once again.

Has some sin robbed you of the song of salvation? Then pray David's threefold prayer: *Purge* me! *Wash* me! *Create* in me! God assured His sinning people of old that He would be "the Restorer of Streets to Dwell In" (Is. 58:12). With a trumpet to his lips, the prophet called the people, so signally blessed of the Lord, to consider their transgressions against Him: "Tell My people their transgression, and the house of Jacob their sins" (Is. 58:1). The God of forgivenesses offers encouragement for the wayward to return to Him. It was He who healed David's breach with heaven.

If we are conscious that our feet have strayed from a God-marked path and we have lost the joy of salvation, we need not give up. The promise is that heart strings broken by sin can vibrate with the melody of forgiveness. The divine restorer is able and willing to bring us back to the center of His will. What happy Christians all of us would be if only we could pause and perform the requirements set forth by God!

February 17

Evening and morning and at noon
I will pray. PSALM 55:17

Set times, as well as set places, contribute to the value of our prayer life. David opened the door to heaven three times a day, confident that God would listen to his supplications. As the psalmist started his day, he cried to God for strength and guidance. At noon, David stretched out both hands as he requested further help. As the evening shadows fell, he again sought God, seeking forgiveness and cleansing for any sin committed, and praising God for all His goodness and grace given throughout the day. David would then claim the promise: "He gives His beloved sleep" (Ps. 127:2).

The ideal attitude, however, is concerned less with the *times* of prayer and more with the *spirit* of prayer. In home or business, between morning and noon, noon and evening, unexpected problems may develop. Decisions may be required, necessitating an upward glance to the throne of grace for providential leading and direction. The blessed assurance is that no matter when or why we approach the mercy seat, God's ear is always open to hear our plea. His hand is ready to help. Is it natural and easy for you, even in a shopping mall, without assuming any prayer posture, to look up to God? Anytime during a busy day, can you commune with Him as the friend who sticks closer than a brother? Can you say that prayer is your vital breath, your native air?

Because He is faithful in His promises, we know that God will hear us. The threefold action of God should be noted. God *hears* the desire of the humble, even before it is expressed. God *prepares* the heart not only to pray correctly but to be in a suitable condition to receive His answer. Further, God *inclines* His ear to listen to our petition. All of this results from the work of the Holy Spirit.

> Prayer is the soul's sincere desire,
> Uttered or unexpressed;
> The motion of a hidden fire
> That trembles in the breast

February 18

Do not cast me off
in the time of old age.   PSALM 71:9

David was most likely the author of this psalm. Writing it in the sunset years of his life, David described his varied experiences from his youth to old age (vv. 5–18). Prayer permeates the first section (vv. 1–13) while praise fills the rest of the psalm (vv. 14–24).

The psalm's personal aspect is emphasized in the frequent use of the pronouns *my* and *me*. The psalmist speaks as if he has the exclusive right to all God is and owns. The marvel of grace is that each of us can claim, personally, all the bounty of heaven. Why do so many of us live like paupers, when actually we are spiritual millionaires?

The repeated words, *continually* (vv. 3, 6) and *all the day* (vv. 15, 24), declare God to be the constant, unfailing One. We can, therefore, trust in Him at all times and under all circumstances.

Other significant words and phrases are found here: *strong habitation* (v. 3)—David seems to have borrowed much of the descriptive language of this psalm from Psalm 31. God alone is the true and eternal home, or dwelling place, of all those who love and trust Him; *rock* (v. 3)—Christ, as the rock smitten for us, is able to resist all storms; *fortress* (v. 3)—all satanic and worldly foes assail us in vain as we abide in such a strong, impregnable dwelling; and *strong refuge* (v. 7)—anyone living in the cities of refuge was safe, while the high priest lived. Since Christ is our refuge *and* our great high priest, alive for evermore, continual safety is ours. Such a God offers us hope, and He deserves our continual praise.

Young persons can learn much from this psalm. David proved the value of choosing God as the Lord of his life when he was young, strong, and free. It is also a psalm the aged should treasure; amid failing faculties and increasing infirmities, older persons have the abiding presence of Him who promised: "Even to your old age, I am He, and even to gray hairs I will carry you!" (Is. 46:4).

February 19

Cast your burden on the LORD,/
And He shall sustain you. PSALM 55:22

The changes that come to us each day should always lead us nearer to God. David thought all his adversaries were against him, but he came to see that they were being dealt with by God.

We can learn many lessons from the upheavals in our lives. First of all, there is the sovereignty of God. His purpose runs through all the changes in our lives. All the varied threads are in the hands of the perfect weaver. When severe change comes into our lives—when life seems empty, without treasures, hopes, or ambitions—our first reaction is to blame God. But upon calmer reflection we withdraw our bitter feelings and tell Him that He does all things well.

We must recognize the unchangeableness of God. David recognized that in spite of all the changes in his own life, God was unchanging in His character, purpose, and love. "Jesus Christ is the same yesterday, today, and forever" (Heb. 13:8). Because of a certain sameness in God, people do not fear Him as they should.

If we look at each of our days separately, we often become discouraged. We must learn, however, not to look at one day crowned with abundant success and another shadowed with trial and failure. Instead we must view all our days together and see what a wonderful pageant they make. All our days with all their changes should result in our becoming more like the unchangeable One.

If the world were made up only of those people who have no change or tragedies in their lives and who, consequently, are past feeling, the world would be a cold place to live. Thank God it is otherwise. Those who have experienced the school of grief and have been refined in the crucible of change are therefore able to exercise the ministry of comfort. No hands are so gentle as those that have known affliction. People in sorrow seek out those who have also passed through the shadows. Jesus is able to aid those who are tempted; He was tempted in all points as we are, but He remained without sin.

When sorrow plunges deep into heart and home, we are blessed to have the promise that in all of life's drastic changes, He who changes not is always near to cause all things to work together for good.

February 20

Your servants take pleasure in her stones,/
And show favor to her dust. PSALM 102:14

Several years ago, a friend who had been a member of the church of his conviction for a long time remarked to the writer: "You know, I love every stone in that building. I saw the church go up. We were married in it. Our children grew up and were blessed in it. Through the years we have had godly ministers. It is indeed holy ground."

Doubtless, you feel the same way about your place of worship, if all within it glorifies the Lord. Alas, however, through the intrusion of humanism and worldliness, many places of worship have lost their one-time sanctity. True saints, remaining in such buildings, cannot feel the same way they once did when entering its portals. How imperative it is to have a mighty movement of the Spirit, resulting in more churches wherein God's honor dwells!

From a psalm for the use of the sons of Korah, one or two phrases can be applied to the church: "The LORD loves the gates of Zion/More than all the dwellings of Jacob./Glorious things are spoken of you,/O city of God!" (Ps. 87:2–3). The psalmist's rapturous praise of Jerusalem as the dwelling place of God was justifiable. The history of the city was the joy and pride of Israel. Such a beautiful description of the first temple, however, can be applied to the church. Since her birth at Pentecost, glorious things have been spoken of her achievements. What a history she has! Millions have been born again through her instrumentality!

How her ministries have enriched civilization! In spite of all her blemishes, she remains God's channel of reaching a godless world for Himself. Scriptural and spiritual churches are the conscience of any nation. The promise is that influential and illustrious though her past has been, a still greater future is hers. When the day dawns for her Lord to return to earth as its rightful king, hers is to be the privilege and joy of assisting Him in His governmental control of the world. She is to reign with her Lord.

February 21

The Lord is your keeper. PSALM 121:5

What a bundle of precious promises this psalm, entitled "A Song of Ascents," holds for us as believers to claim! The term *ascents* suggests that the psalm may have been chanted by the people as they climbed to the house of the Lord. The phrase *the Lord* appears here five times, indicating that He is the One to be worshiped and adored for all He is in Himself and for what He is to them who know Him as their keeper.

This psalm assures us of divine security. Within it there is the sigh of the heart for preservation. The word *keeps* occurs twice and its kindred word, *preserve,* three times. The emphasis of the psalm is on the fact that security is the Lord's responsibility. He never fails. We must remember that we do not have to struggle in order to keep ourselves saved: "The Lord is [our] keeper" (v. 5). That He is well able to preserve His own is evidenced by two characteristic features: (1) He made heaven and earth, and (2) He neither slumbers nor sleeps. Count up the realms in which you can expect His keeping power, and you will praise Him anew as the One ever at hand to keep you from falling.

The apostle Jude knew what it was to have the Lord as his keeper and could, therefore, assure the saints that the Lord Jesus Christ was "able to keep you from stumbling, and to present you faultless before the presence of His glory with exceeding joy" (Jude 24). From day to day He is able to keep us from stumbling. At His return, He is to present us without fault.

The possibility of falling, or stumbling, has to do with our daily walk and does not affect our position in Christ. A closer walk with Him cannot make us more secure, but it will bring us a greater reward. While we cannot help Christ to make us eternally secure, we can assist Him to keep us from stumbling.

February 22

It is good for me
that I have been afflicted. PSALM 119:71

We can readily understand why some dear saints who are heavily afflicted may fail to see any beneficial aspect of the sufferings they endure. Yet David, who knew a great deal about affliction, confessed that it had been good for him in every way. Before he was afflicted, he went astray. But in that crucible of suffering he learned to keep God's word (see Ps. 119:67). His trials and sorrows brought him nearer God, in that they were the means of weaning him from the world. They worked submission, produced humility, excited diligence, stirred him up to prayer, and conformed him to the divine image.

Are we proving that our burdens can become beneficial? As we bear them with patience, do we understand God's design in permitting them? Embracing the promises of support, do we gather the blessings they are productive of?

Joseph became fruitful in the land of his affliction. From a pit he found his way to a palace. Had it not been for his slavery he would never have become the savior of Egypt.

Evidently Paul knew something about the divine intention wrapped up in affliction. Writing to the Thessalonians, he could say: "No one should be shaken by these afflictions; for you yourselves know that we are appointed to this" (1 Thess. 3:3). The apostle faced many trials, but grace was his to look at them in the light of glory! He could assure people who felt sympathy for him that God had appointed his afflictions for him.

Over some old established British businesses can be seen the royal crest, bearing the inscription *By Royal Appointment*, implying that such business houses had been commanded by the reigning sovereign to supply the palace with particular goods. Can we describe our affliction as coming to us "By Royal Appointment"? Since our heavenly King appoints our adversities, should we not learn to glory in our tribulations, as Paul could do? Sighs, as well as smiles, are traced upon our lives by a God of love.

February 23

"If it had not been the LORD *who was on our side/. . . the waters would have overwhelmed us."* PSALM 124:2, 4

A verse from the apocryphal book Tobit reads: "God, which dwelleth in Heaven, prosper your journey. And the Angel of God keep you company" (5:16). The central message of Psalm 124 is that the Lord is our ally, our companion, through the varying circumstances of this life. David was a man of many profound experiences, and he knew what it was to have the flood waters dash against his noble soul. Some scholars affirm that this psalm was composed by King David after he and his loyal army returned from the tragic death of his rebellious son, Absalom. If this is its background, it proves that David was not only the recipient of providential deliverance but also that he had God to keep him company.

The repetition of the word *if* is significant, for actually there are no *ifs* with God. He is ever on the side of His own. If we are His, then who can be against us? We can afford to be indifferent as to who is on our side as long as God is our protector and defender from all cunning, malicious foes. We may be tossed about by the swirling waters but never submerged. In this connection, how meaningful are the three *thens* in the psalm! Because we are the Lord's people is no guarantee that we shall not be attacked by foes without and fears within. Some of the saintliest souls are the sorest sufferers. Behind David's symbol of the flood waters and mighty waves threatening to sink a vessel may be a reference to his proud, haughty son, Absalom. For our hearts, the turbulent waters can represent floods of opposition, reproach, temptation, sin, and suffering beating against our frail boat. But our comfort is that the Lord has promised to be always on our side as our helper.

Note the testimony of the just: "The LORD . . . was on our side" (v. 2). Note the triumph of the present: "Our soul has escaped" (v. 7). Note the trust for the future: "Our help is in the name of the LORD" (v. 8). With such a threefold promise we should never yield to defeat or despair. Let the proud waters roar, wicked enemies gnash their teeth, and the satanic hunter do his utmost to trap us, we will not fear what they may do. God is ever our shield and fortress.

February 24

But there is forgiveness with You, / That You may be feared. PSALM 130:4

Out of the depths of David's soul, the cry for redemption reached the ears of the Lord, rich in mercy. To understand correctly the aspect of divine forgiveness extolled by the psalmist, we must give heed to the blessed first word introducing the above verse. An opposite aspect must precede it. How hopeless we would be if we had an unforgiving God to deal with! All sinners, however, are encouraged to confess their sin, because God is the unfailing source of forgiveness. As Alexander Pope expressed it: "To err is human, to forgive divine."

Forgiveness is manifested and freely bestowed that God may be feared—not a cringing fear, as if dealing with a tyrant, but a reverential trust, obedience, and worship. Perhaps no other instance in all the Bible provides a more satisfying revelation of God's character than when He granted Moses the sublime manifestation of His pardoning grace: "The LORD passed before him and proclaimed, 'The LORD, the LORD God, merciful and gracious, long-suffering, and abounding in goodness and truth, keeping mercy for thousands, forgiving iniquity and transgression and sin'" (Exod. 34:6–7).

No wonder Moses bowed his head toward the earth and worshiped! The context reminds us that mercy is kept for an unnumbered host, implying that God has an inexhaustible store of it and can draw on it as sinners need it.

The apostle Paul made it clear that God's forgiveness of us is the inspiration and impetus of our forgiveness of others. We are to be "kind to one another, tenderhearted, forgiving one another, just as God in Christ also forgave you" (Eph. 4:32). The teaching of our Lord Himself in respect to divine and human forgiveness must also be borne in mind.

February 25

LORD, my heart is not haughty. PSALM 131:1

Composed of only three verses, this psalm of humility and hope is among the *multum in parvo* ("much in little") psalms. Actually, it is made up of two triplet stanzas of a personal nature and a final couplet, or postscript, of a national character. An added feature of this brief psalm is that it is one of the group of fifteen psalms, 120–135, known as the "Songs of Ascents." This title means "Songs of the Going Up" and was associated with the fifteen steps of the second temple; the Levites sang a psalm on each step as they ascended. More than likely this psalm and the others were associated with Israel as the people returned from their captivity in Babylon with hearts humbled, weaned from their idols. These ascent psalms have also been connected with the pilgrimage to Jerusalem for the great feasts.

This short psalm has special meaning in these days of human pride and restlessness. Its few words are as a ladder enabling us to climb from deep humility to a fixed and eternal security. Such a distinctive psalm, containing the cry of a childlike heart, is intensely personal. It may be a discourse to be read before others but actually constitutes a private conversation with the Lord. I have named it "The Psalm of Humility and Hope"; the first two verses breathe the air of profoundest humility and submission to God's will, and the last verse encourages the child of God to maintain a lively hope in God. Alas, it is sadly possible for us to be proud of our humility. We need freedom from secret conceit of heart, sincerely confessing along with David: "My heart is not haughty" (v. 1). Pride finds its seat in the heart where it looks forth from the eyes and is expressed in our actions. Pride is destructive of the soul's true happiness.

February 26

How pleasant it is/For brethren to dwell together in unity!

PSALM 133:1

What an exquisite psalm this is! Its three verses praise unity and brotherly harmony. Many writers suggest that this Song of Ascents was composed by David upon the occasion of the union between the tribes when all met to crown him unanimously their king. What joy there must have been in the reuniting of Israel after long disunion, arising from the disruption of captivity.

Various classes of pilgrims, spiritual and secular authorities, the rich and the poor, mingled as the tribes went on a pilgrimage three times a year. Such intercommunion of people fostered a unity of feeling and sentiment; it was good and pleasant to be reunited after their separation. Palestine, both north and south, had been torn by strife, discord, and war. Now David writes as if all the tribes are bound together as one person in the unity of the national and religious life. How happy the heart, home, church, and nation into which such unity comes and abides!

Note the word *brethren.* Who, exactly, is meant by this designation so frequently used in Scripture? Sons of a family are brothers and contribute to a happy home when they strive to live in unity. In one sense, all men and women are brothers and sisters. Therefore, they should seek to live in peace, regardless of their many differences.

But as used by David, *brethren* has a religious connotation equivalent to what Jesus meant when He said: "One is your Teacher, the Christ, and you are all brethren" (Matt. 23:8). Peter had the same significance of the term in mind when he advocated unfeigned or "sincere love of the brethren" (1 Pet. 1:22). Unless Christ is our Savior and master, we are not included in the spiritual brotherhood which He Himself had in mind. Such a relationship only comes as the result of regeneration by the Spirit when we are made children of God and, therefore, spiritual brothers and sisters.

February 27

O LORD, You have searched me. . . . Search me, O God,/and know my heart.

PSALM 139:1, 23

David ended this marvelous psalm by asking God to do that which he said, at the beginning of the psalm, had already been undertaken. Reviewing his outer life in the past, David declared: "O LORD, You have searched me" (v. 1). But as he journeyed with God into the recesses of his hidden, inner life, he prayed that the divine introspection might become more intense: "Search me, O God,/and know my heart" (v. 23).

This truth of invisible omnipresence characterizing the psalm prompted Carolus Linnaeus, the Swedish naturalist (1707–1778), to inscribe over the door of his bedchamber: "Live innocently; God is here." One cannot read this most majestic psalm without the overwhelming sense that God is here, there, and everywhere, and that, consequently, we must live in the order of His will. Ibn Ezra, the great Jewish scholar (1098–1164), spoke of this psalm as the "Crown of All the Psalms."

In this psalm some of the most lofty thoughts of God are couched in the most sublime language ever used to describe the Almighty. It is one of the finest pieces of sacred literature extant because of its masterly conception of the conspicuous attributes of God. The psalm is made up of four stanzas of six verses each, with each section presenting an essential aspect of God's being as well as an element in the soul's experience.

The Omniscient One (vv. 1–6). *Omni* means "all," and *science*, "knowledge." God, as the omniscient one, is perfect in knowledge. Nothing is hid from Him whom the Egyptians called the "Eye of the World."

The Omnipresent One (vv. 7–12). This attribute implies that God is everywhere at one and the same time.

The Omnipotent One (vv. 13–18). All power belongs to Him who is almighty.

The Just and Holy One (vv. 19–24). The last section of this grand psalm breathes the spirit of holy judgment and is related to those forces alien to God's holy will and purpose. Can we say that ours is a God-besieged life?

February 28

The LORD is near to all who call upon Him. PSALM 145:18

Sometimes we forget that we do not have to ask God to be near us and to accompany us over life's highway. We must remember and believe His promise that He is always near, whether we call on Him or not. Yet is it not comforting to know that wherever we have a sense of need or a sense of guilt, He is near, lovingly listening to our cry and graciously willing to help in our distress? *Prayer is an acknowledgment of God's all-sufficiency and of our utter dependence on Him.* Without Him we are nothing.

This great psalm of David emphasizes two important factors in all true prayer. First of all, we don't have to cry as if God were at a distance or deaf. He is "near to all who call upon Him" (v. 18). Whenever need arises, He is at hand. The second aspect is that God only responds to our call if we seek Him "in truth" (v. 18), which implies that our praying must be in accordance with His revealed will.

Our gracious Lord assures that "whatever you ask in prayer, believing, you will receive" (Matt. 21:22). Faith in the willingness of God to hear and answer is essential to prevailing prayer. Did our Lord not emphasize God's power to respond to our faith prayers when He gave us the three key words, *ask, seek,* and *knock?* If we take the first letter from each word, the word *ask* is formed. We will never ask in vain, because all who seek Him, find Him.

God cannot be expected to respond to our asking if doubt lurks in our minds as to the possibility of an answer (see James 1:6–8). Coming to Him, we must believe that He is the rewarder of those who believe and diligently seek Him. George Mueller of Bristol cared for thousands of orphans but never sought a cent from the public to feed them. Prayer, girded with faith, made his great work possible.

February 29 (Leap Year)

Praise Him in His mighty firmament! PSALM 150:1

This concluding psalm of the Psalter is one of exceeding praise to God. The word *praise* appears thirteen times in the six verses. Psalm 150 briefly summarizes the Psalms as a whole in that the subject of its praise is the power of God, who upholds all things by the word of His power.

Before Jesus left His own to return to heaven, He could announce *all* power is "given to Me" (Matt. 28:18). Whenever He speaks, it is done. In the days of His flesh Jesus was the personification of divine power, as His miracles prove. All power was His to enforce His word. His omnipotence extended to every realm. The striking feature of the Gospels, however, is that Jesus never exercised His power to relieve a personal need.

Where the word of a king is, there is power. Our sovereign Lord, who was born a king, holds all the regions of creation, redemption, prophecy, and history, and He is therefore able to care for our personal life, if only we leave our times in His all-powerful hands. We are often despondent when it seems as if His power has been hidden. When we look around the world with its threat of a nuclear war in which millions would perish, we wonder why God is silent. Faith, however, accepts that God not only rules but also overrules and is able to make even our wrath praise Him.

In our personal life, do we believe that God is able to uphold all things by His power, that He is willing to do for us above all we could possibly ask or think? Do we allow Him to make our daily life the platform upon which He visits to manifest His power? He seeks to make His power known in every realm of our personal life.

The greatest manifestation of our Lord's power occurred when He destroyed him that had "the power of death, that is, the devil" (Heb. 2:14). By dying, He slew death. So He raised the dead, effected His own resurrection from the grave, and is alive forever.

March 1

He shall call upon Me,/ and I will answer him PSALM 91:15

Because we feel we have so many personal cares and needs, a majority of our prayers are related to ourselves. Isn't it wonderful that we can enter into a place of solitude and talk with the Lord about all our concerns?

An infant cries to attract attention, to get what he wants, but personal prayer must not be used in that way. We should be grateful that God does not always grant our personal, unworthy requests. Our prayers are too often motivated by a desire to realize our own wishes. In His mercy God listens to these prayers, even though we do not know the ramifications of what we are asking for (see Mark 10:35–45). Prayers said for ourselves must have as their end an increase in the value of the life we would give others. Private prayer should lead to world service.

Many of our prayers are answered through others; therefore, we must pray for others. A person's prayer life is always enriched when he prays for others. Christ exemplified this practice (see Matt. 19:13). We must not only pray with others but also for others. Selfish prayer shuts others out, because it shuts God out. Unselfish prayers are always rich in intercession, adoration, and grace. How blessed we are when we make mention of others in our prayers!

Prayer for others is the noblest type of prayer. Abraham prayed the first prayer of this type in the Bible when he prayed for the cities of the plain. The last words of Christ to His disciples before His crucifixion were a prayer that they might be kept in the truth and from the evil that is in the world.

Intercessory prayer brings us into the company of believers. How privileged we should be to have an association with such a holy group! This is a ministry which many can exercise who are unable to perform other aspects of Christian service, those who may be invalids, infirm, or aged. Eternity alone will reveal what has been accomplished through the prayers of God's shut-in saints.

March 2

The silver-haired head is a crown of glory,/ If it is found in the way of righteousness. PROVERBS 16:31

The *if* in Solomon's proverb must not be forgotten. The tragedy of our modern life is that there are far too many white-haired sinners. A silver-haired head is only a crown of glory if the person is found in the way of righteousness. Dr. Charles Goodell wrote,

> To every true Christian, the life of Indian summer is beautiful with the light that never was on sea or shore. The light of the Son behind the Sun! He feels that he hastens not into the winter but into fairer springtime than earth has ever known. Prophetic voices fill the air and the thought of happy meeting where friends never quarrel and never misunderstand, where the poor become rich and the rich become happy, and the sick are healed, and the old grow young again, makes one almost impatient for the great adventure.

Life's autumn glory can reflect heaven's everlasting glory. The psalmist prayed that God would not cast him off or forsake him "in the time of old age" and that God would uphold and sustain him until he, although old and gray-headed, had fulfilled the divine commission (see Ps. 71:9, 18). These days youth seem to have the monopoly when it comes to positions and pleasures. It is a self-centered society that has little room or sympathy for the aged.

But the glory of grace is that God is ever the friend and protector of those who are nearing the heavenly port. Having weathered many a storm, the Pilot we expect to see when we have crossed the bar will care for our frail craft as we near the haven of eternal safety. Perhaps these lines are being read by one forgotten by those who should have remembered their obligation. Left alone, or relegated to strangers, do you suffer from the ingratitude of those whose duty it was to care for you? Then look up to Him, whose eye is always upon your noble, silver-haired head, and who has promised to care for and carry you until you reach the end of the road. Others may forsake and fail you, but the Provider of the aged offers Himself as your unfailing Companion until life's pilgrimage is over. May we grow old with good grace, found in the way of righteousness!

March 3

God himself is with us for our captain. 2 CHRONICLES 13:12 KJV

The Old Testament word for *captain* is derived or borrowed from a military term signifying "to lead," "to rule," "to have dominion." The Greek word used of Christ in the New Testament means "princely," "leader," "originator." It is the same word given as "author" (Heb. 2:10; 12:2).

Focusing on the Gospel era, when Christ was presented as the captain of our salvation, we should consider the necessary qualifications for captaincy. A captain had to be free and willing to assume the task and office presented and not yield to any force whatever. He also must recognize the necessity of being faithful in all things to his sovereign. Further, not only must he be skillful in the exercise of his office, but he must also manifest a courageous determination, in spite of adverse circumstance, to be true to his calling. Christ as the captain had all the honorable and necessary qualifications to be our leader, and He was thus commissioned by God to function in such a capacity.

In *Richard II,* Shakespeare has the lines: "And there at Venice gave/His body to that pleasant country's earth,/And his pure soul unto his captain Christ,/Under whose colors he had fought so long." How blessed we are if Christ is the captain of our soul! Bishop William W. Howe described Christ: "Thou, Lord, their Captain in the well-fought fight." Valiantly, He met the satanic foe and triumphed gloriously over him, and He now seeks to lead all who are sin-bound into liberty.

With Charles Wesley we must confess:

Captain of the hosts of God,
In the path where Thou hast trod,
Bows my soul in humble awe,
Take command, Thy word is Law.

March 4

"Peace, peace to him who is far off/ and to him who is near." ISAIAH 57:19

As the God of peace, He desires to make all persons the recipients of His bounty. The prophet Isaiah reminds us that there is peace for those "far off," not only geographically but also spiritually. The least privileged and most sinful are called to appropriate God's offered peace. Peace is also for "him who is near." And who are so near as the redeemed of the Lord?

For the sinner, there is peace *with* God. For the saint, it is peace *in* God. But if the wicked are content to remain far off from God, thus retaining their wickedness, they are like the troubled sea, ever restless, casting up mud and dirt.

What we must not forget is that peace is not something but *someone*! As Jesus was about to leave His own, He gave them the promise: "My peace I give to you" (John 14:27). What a loving, beneficial bequest! Dying in poverty, He had nothing of this world's goods to leave His friends. To John, He gave the care of His widowed mother. To His disciples, He bequeathed the legacy of His own peace.

When dealing with those who are estranged from God, we sometimes urge them to make their peace with Him. Since Christ became our peace through the blood of His cross, the sinner doesn't have to plead for his peace with God. By faith he can accept a provided peace through the blood of the Cross. We often sing: "Peace, perfect peace, in this dark world of sin?/The blood of Jesus whispers peace within."

As the result of sin, we are at enmity with God or in a state of war with heaven; so to be delivered from its guilt is called "peace with God." The prophet Isaiah said: "He shall make peace with Me" (Is. 27:5), which is what Jesus accomplished as He died, bearing the sin of the world. True peace is ours when we cease from self, to find our all in Him who came as the Prince of Peace. We have entered into peace with God through faith in Christ's finished work. Thank God for an inner peace, passing all understanding.

March 5

"The LORD *will guide you continually."*

ISAIAH 58:11

Promises of God as a guide and of the guidance He offers are as prolific in Scripture as they are precious. Because efficient guidance depends upon the quality of the guide, let us consider the One who offers Himself to direct our steps continually. We may not know the way ahead, but we do know the Guide.

Among His evident qualifications to be our guide, even unto death, is His *perfection,* assuring us that He cannot err or take a wrong turning in the oversight of our lives. He can never be mistaken in the personal guidance of your future and mine.

Then we have His *patience.* God knows how timid we are to step out after Him on some unknown road. We hesitate as we find ourselves being led into unaccustomed experiences. Our heavenly Guide assures that while we may not understand His leading now, we shall know in the hereafter.

God is *all-powerful* and therefore able to deal with all hellish and human forces set on perverting His benign purposes for our pilgrimage through life. He functions not only as our guide but also as our guard. God guards as He guides. His *insight* and *foresight* enable Him to anticipate and bountifully provide for all needs for the journey. Because of His *omniscience,* He knows the end from the beginning.

How precious is the promise Isaiah has for our hearts: "By the springs of water He will guide them" (Is. 49:10)! While the promise of this verse is related to a preserved and restored Israel, Christ promised to manifest Himself as the One who would be as "a fountain of water springing up into everlasting life" (John 4:14). Is it not gracious of our Guide to provide us with such a source of spiritual refreshment for our journey through life? John seems to have borrowed some of Isaiah's phraseology to describe the bliss of the redeemed once the Guide has safely brought us through the dwelling of death into His own heavenly abode (see Rev. 22:1–4).

Over the perilous and thorny path of life we have the unfailing direction of our unerring Guide. Put your hand in His, and venture forth.

March 6

Be filled with the Spirit. EPHESIANS 5:18

The "filling," or "infilling," is a transaction that can and will be repeated as one lives in the Spirit. The Lord is always the One who fills the earthen vessel. One result of such an infilling is a kind of passive activity, as of one wrought upon and controlled by Another, rather than of one directed by his own efforts. The verb Paul uses here is in the present tense; this "infilling" performed by the Divine Filler is an experience the believer may apprehend and enter into this very moment.

It is true that God alone can fill us with His Spirit, but He never fills us alone. We must observe and fulfill certain conditions if we would be filled fully with the Spirit. What, then, are some of these conditions making real to us all the promised gifts of the Spirit?

We must *acknowledge.* We must frankly and fully confess sin and yield up all doubtful practices. Such a yielding implies the absolute surrender of ourselves to the control of Another.

We must *ask* (see Luke 11:5–13). While it is true the believer in this age does not have to plead with God for the Spirit, there is a sense in which we are to ask, seek, and receive. Too many of us live impoverished lives because we fail to ask and receive. By faith we must claim all we have in the promise of the Spirit.

We must *accept* (see Acts 2:38–39). Faith, apart from strange and strong emotions, high excitement and ecstatic joy, is the only channel of the Spirit's infilling. Believing that there is such a fullness for us, we must accept it by faith and go out and live as filled ones.

We must *act* (see Acts 3:1–6). Action will inevitably follow the filling. As we step out upon the promise and obey instantly and implicitly all the known will of God, the act becomes an attitude.

I take the promised Holy Ghost,
  I take the Gift of Pentecost,
To fill me to the uttermost,
  I take—He undertakes.

March 7

"As Moses lifted up the serpent in the wilderness, even so must the Son of Man be lifted up." JOHN 3:14

When you read the third chapter of John, mark the *musts* of the Master: the must of salvation—"You must be born again" (v. 7); the must of sacrifice—"Even so must the Son of Man be lifted up" (v. 14); and the must of sanctification—"He must increase, but I must decrease" (v. 30).

The people in Moses' day were bitten by fiery serpents and found themselves mortally wounded. Neither Moses nor the Law could cure the people who were serpent-bitten. Their only hope was a look at the brazen serpent lifted up on a tree. Sinners, in a similar manner, are stung with sin—the sting of that old serpent, the devil. No one can cure nor redeem from the sting of sin and death but Christ who was lifted upon the cross.

The serpent Moses displayed was not forged by man's hands and tools but molded in the fire. Fashioned out of gold and brass, it resembled the color of a serpent. It was strong and durable. The parallel is seen in Christ, who was not begotten by man but was conceived by the Holy Spirit in the womb of the Virgin Mary. Further, Jesus came not with outward glory or worldly show but with a poor and humble appearance. Brass, being strong, was the figure of Him who came in the power of God. If the Israelites of old looked only upon their sores and gaping wounds and not to the cure of God's appointment, they died, although a divine remedy was at hand. If they sought earthly physicians for the healing of serpent-bites, or medicines of their own, they perished.

The marvel of grace is that even the greatest of sinners, grievously wounded by their iniquity, can be instantly healed and made the recipients of eternal life. Salvation becomes yours not through any works or reformation of your own but through the blood of Christ. To His cross, you *must* cling.

March 8

Seraphim; each one had six wings. ISAIAH 6:2

The seraphim with their wing-covered forms are one type of angelic host mentioned in Scripture. The ministry of these angelic beings is associated with the manifestation of divine holiness. The highly figurative language Isaiah used in his designation of the seraphim is full of spiritual significance. The term means "the flaming or shining ones," implying that they were unearthly beings who manifested splendor, possessed swift energy, and revealed fiery enthusiasm.

These beings we shall look upon with awe when we reach heaven. They are portrayed in such a way as to suggest that the nearer we are to God, who dwells in inaccessible light, the more we glow and burn. Nothing dull nor icy dwells in His presence. The distinguishing feature of the seraphim is the way they employed their wings—two covered the face, two covered the feet, and two were used for flying. The face represents *worship;* the hands, *work;* the feet, *walk.* Too often we use all our wings for flying, for we are always on the go. We need to cover our faces more than we do. Then we must have wing-covered feet, for arrogant steps hinder spiritual progress. Walking with the Lord produces a joyous, buoyant, unhindered motion. True *worship* regulates our walk and inspires our *work.*

Is your trinity of virtues—faith, hope, and love—intact? May increasing grace be yours to worship the Lord in the beauty of holiness. Magnify Him by your work of faith, your labor of love, and your walk worthy of your vocation!

March 9

In the shadow of Your wings
I will rejoice. PSALM 63:7

The metaphor of God's shadowing wings is often used in Scripture. One cannot study references to wings without observing their double function of speed and of shelter.

Speed. Swift flight through the air is the main purpose of wings. The seraphim had six wings; the cherubim, four wings. The more wings, the greater the speed. "Wings of the wind" and "wings like a dove" represent rapid motion (2 Sam. 22:11; Ps. 55:6).

"I bore you on eagles' wings and brought you to Myself" (Ex. 19:4). How wonderfully the Lord took care of Israel during the rough wilderness days!

The phrase, "the wings of the morning" (Ps. 139:9), depicts the first rays of light in the morning as wings spreading suddenly over the whole earth. "Their wings . . . were full of eyes all around" (Ezek. 10:12); the "eyes" indicate that the wings Ezekiel saw possessed power, speed, and purpose and were guided by the omniscient Holy Spirit. When Daniel described his vision of four beasts, he remarked that the lion and the leopard had the wings of a bird (see Dan. 7:3–6). This feature represents unusual speed in conquest. The prophecy, "The Sun of Righteousness shall arise with healing in His wings" (Mal. 4:2), says that when our blessed Lord appears upon the earth, He will act with speed and suddenness to rid the world of sin.

Shelter. Wings also are symbolic of protection, security, comfort, and rest. "The shadow of Your wings" is a phrase frequently used to indicate our safety in the Lord. We realize, of course, that although we read of His wings, God does not actually possess natural wings. Scripture uses them as the symbol of defense, care, preservation, protection, and rest He provides for His blood-washed children. Did not our Lord have the precious promises above in mind when He used the simile of the hen protecting her brood, allowing them to nestle under her wings?

Because His promise must stand, may we be found sheltering in Him and experiencing His overflowing peace.

March 10

"The fathers have eaten sour grapes,/ And the children's teeth are set on edge." JEREMIAH 31:29

This popular proverb of Jeremiah's time is repeated by the prophet Ezekiel (see 18:2) and is one emphasizing the importance of individuality. "Every one shall die for his own iniquity; every man who eats the sour grapes, his teeth shall be set on edge" (Jer. 31:30). "The soul who sins shall die" (Ezek. 18:4). While heredity is responsible for a great deal of sinning, Scripture reveals that individual choice brings on not only a solemn responsibility but also a glorious promise of undying blessedness. A person is always free to break with a sad and miserable past. Grace can enable that one to overcome inherited tendencies.

As the result of natural generation, we communicate to others our desires, whether they are good or bad. The truth in the expression "like father like son" is one reason why young, unmarried persons should be warned to keep their record clean—to have a life fully yielded to the Savior so that their unborn heirs will be influenced by a godly home. As the young are today, so will their offspring be tomorrow. The stream will correspond to the source.

A striking proof of this principle is in Lot, who miserably failed in his obligation of shaping the character of his children toward righteousness. When parting from Abraham, Lot was prompted by self-gratification to choose the best part of the country; he settled in Sodom because of its position and wealth. Lot came to prove that prosperity and worldly possessions were "sour grapes." His wife and children became immersed in the ways of godless Sodom, and they perished in the ruins of the city when disaster struck. Lot became conscious of his parental responsibility all too late, when he saw disaster ahead. Acting as a father, he sought to warn his children to flee from the wrath to come, but it was a fruitless effort. The sacred record says: "But to his sons-in-law he seemed to be joking" (Gen. 19:14).

May grace be yours so to live and labor that the impact of the fruits of holiness will be seen in your own friends and relatives!

March 11

"I will be to Ephraim like a moth." HOSEA 5:12

Of all the metaphors and descriptions used of God in Scripture, this one of the moth is most instructive. The people who received this strange judgment had rejected God's commands and had followed the wicked counsels of Jeroboam and his princes. From the nature of such a little, despicable creature as the moth, we gather the nature of God's judgments on a rebellious people.

Moths are creatures that devour whatever garment they light upon. Woolen cloth, costly or otherwise, makes no difference to these destructive pests that secretly go about their devouring. God acted in this way when He came in judgment upon Ephraim. Whenever He appears to spoil a nation for its sins, He does not spare the rich more than the poor. He has no respect of persons. Prince and peasant suffer alike. Together they sinned—together they sorrow. Moths give no warning of their coming and devour without noise in their secret destruction. Is this not also the way of God who comes suddenly upon a people and surprises them in a sudden, dreadful confusion and horror?

The Old Testament records other symbolic aspects of the moth. For instance, the book of Job has the phrase: "Who are crushed before a moth" (4:19). This despised insect, weighing so very little, is used as a type of God's wrath in its least and lightest form. The moth is able to crush and wreck mortal man.

David declared that God can "make his beauty melt away like a moth" (Ps. 39:11). A moth is easily and quickly destroyed, and natural human beauty, which man prides himself on having, can be as easily crushed and lost. Isaiah assures us that our foes will be consumed just as "the moth will eat up" an old garment (Is. 50:9). God delights in using little things to remove great things, just as a small moth can destroy a large, costly garment.

Our Lord's inclusion of the moth in the destruction of stored up riches should be noted (see Matt. 6:19–21). The ruin of earthly possessions comes from three sources: the animal kingdom from the moth; the mineral kingdom by the rust; and the human kingdom by the thieves.

March 12

He also brought me up out of a horrible pit,/ Out of the miry clay,/And set my feet upon a rock,/And established my steps. PSALM 40:2

In this great psalm of praise, David magnifies God for answering prayer in his rescue from a severe illness or some other cause in which death seemed imminent. The psalmist's language, however, fittingly describes our deliverance from the pit of corruption and the miry clay of iniquity and portrays our establishment in Him who became the smitten rock. So we sing:

> O safe to the Rock that is higher than I,
> My soul in its conflicts and sorrows would fly;
> So sinful, so weary, Thine, Thine would I be;
> Thou blest Rock of Ages, I'm hiding in Thee.

When Job cried, "He has cast me into the mire" (Job 30:19), he compared his sorrow, trouble, and poverty to mud or slime. Why? Because they are all so unpleasant and difficult to emerge from once anyone is submerged in them. David also wrote of sinking "in deep mire,/Where there is no standing" (Ps. 69:2). These images bespeak the deep sorrow and the anguish of heart the Lord Jesus experienced as He journeyed from Gethsemane to Calvary.

A captive in a dungeon, Jeremiah experienced what it was like to sink in the mire but to be delivered (see Jer. 38:6–22). The prophet's situation typified the crisis Israel encountered because of her iniquity and sin.

Multitudes today prefer the pits of godless pleasures and pursuits and the miry clay of sinful practices; they scorn the security and satisfaction of the Rock of their salvation. In the far-off country, the prodigal son was reduced to feeding swine and feeding on swine's food, but he returned to feasting on a fatted calf in his father's home.

Oh for a mighty revival with multitudes turning from the horrible pit to the heavenly palace, and from the slimy mire to mansions above!

March 13

"These people refused/
The waters of Shiloah that flow softly." ISAIAH 8:6

In Isaiah 8 the distinction between the quiet, little brook of Shiloah and the strong, turbulent rivers of the Euphrates points to the eventual consequences of Israel's actions. Israel refused the more gentle waters in order to "rejoice in" the torrents in the kingdom of Rezin, which God allowed to overwhelm Judah as divine retribution for forsaking Him. Such a comparison is discussed by Alexander Maclaren, the renowned English preacher:

> The waters of Shiloah that go softly stand as an emblem of the Davidic monarchy as God meant it to be, since the monarchy was itself a prophecy. They therefore represent the Kingdom of God or the Messianic King. The little brooklet slipping quietly along suggests the character of the King, the meek and lowly in heart. It suggests the manner of His rule, wielded in gentleness and exercising no compulsion but that of love. . . . The soul that rejects Christ's gentle sway is harried and laid waste by a mob of base-born tyrants. We have to make our choice—either Christ or these: Shiloah or Euphrates.

Too many people are guilty of refusing to pitch their tents alongside the calm flow of those streams making glad the city of God; instead they choose the raging torrents of sin, passion, and judgment. What tranquility is ours if we can sing: "No earthly joy can lure my quiet soul from Thee;/This deep delight, so pure, is Heaven to me." The gentle, healing spring in Jerusalem symbolizes the reign of God in the yielded heart of the believer and the rest of soul Jesus promised His own when He invited them to appropriate His own peace of heart.

Jesus knew all about the beneficent value of the waters of Shiloah. He anointed the eyes of a blind man with clay softened by His spittle and then said, "'Go, wash in the pool of Siloam [Shiloah].' . . . he went and washed, and came back seeing" (John 9:7).

Blinded by the god of this world, sinful, sightless people all around us can only receive their spiritual sight through Him who is the Living Water.

March 14

"Behold, your King is coming to you,/ Lowly, and sitting on a donkey." MATTHEW 21:5

An impressive aspect of our Lord's ministry is that while He went about doing good, He discouraged any acclaim to popular adulation. Those He healed were commanded not to make Him known. Although born a king, He resisted efforts to proclaim Him king, declaring that His kingdom was not of this world. However, in His triumphal entry into Jerusalem, He not only accepted the acclamation of the populace but also helped to further it. He instructed His disciples to go to a neighboring village, where He knew there was a bound donkey, and to commandeer it for His use. Such acquisition was no last desperate bid for recognition because His enemies were closing in upon Him on every side; neither was it a display of hysteria. The life of Jesus was characterized by a calm serenity. His planned entry into the city was free from any panic on His part.

His choice of a donkey held significance for the orthodox Jew, because it was the fulfillment of a promise dear to the heart of a son of Abraham (see Zech. 9:9). Jesus had come to be the Messiah foretold by the Old Testament prophets. Judges and seers also used the donkey as the symbol of their divine commission. To those who looked for redemption in Israel, the regal Man on that donkey was a return to the time when He Himself was the monarch and guardian of His people.

But when He returns to earth to usher in His kingly reign, His kingdom will stretch from shore to shore. He will not be found riding on a donkey, but on a majestic white horse, riding prosperously because He is called "Faithful and True" (Rev. 19:11). May we ever be found in the company of those who proclaim Christ the King of kings.

March 15

The LORD will strengthen him on his bed of illness. PSALM 41:3

Experience has taught many of us that nurses are especially trained in the art of bed-making. Without undue discomfort or inconvenience to a sufferer unable to leave the bed, a careful nurse can change the bedclothes. And to one forced to stay in bed, it means a lot to have the sheets changed and the pillows turned and thumped up. What a precious glimpse into the heart of the Eternal One it is to realize that He can act more tenderly than any devoted nurse! Surely this precious promise is a constant reminder that our loving Lord will never forget or neglect us. The rustle of His seamless robe can be heard by the bed of languishing and pain. In every sickroom He is present, seeking to ease the afflicted and impart strength and courage to the sufferer. He has promised never to leave His own but to uphold and sustain sufferers through long and difficult days. If, as you read these lines, yours is a bed of sickness, trust your Divine Nurse to do the very best for you.

It seems as if the entire world is like a vast sickchamber; hospitals are becoming more numerous with the passage of time. In every community, afflicted minds and bodies can be found. We have never had so many physicians, surgeons, nurses, and agencies to alleviate pain-stricken humanity. Sickness is sometimes related to Satan, but the Gospels make it clear that God anointed His Son, Jesus of Nazareth, to heal all afflicted by the devil.

"At evening, when the sun had set, they brought to Him all who were sick and those who were demon-possessed. . . . Then He healed many who were sick with various diseases" (Mark 1:32, 34). It is encouraging to remember that all sicknesses were known by their Master, to whom the afflicted gathered. He was able to dispel their woes.

At even, ere the sun was set,
  The sick, O Lord, around thee lay;
Oh in what divers pains they met!
  Oh with what joy they went away!

March 16

"As one whom his mother comforts/ So I will comfort you." ISAIAH 66:13

Among the manifold promises of God for His children, none is more intimate, tender, and heart-warming than the one depicting the "God of all comfort" (2 Cor. 1:3) consoling His own in a motherlike way. Isaiah gives us a precious insight into the heart of God, portraying it as the mother to whom a needy child turns when there are tears to be kissed away. Rest and sleep are found on a mother's breast.

The question is: How does a worthy mother comfort? One of the original words for *comfort* means "speaking to anyone near, kindly, soothingly, tenderly, and with persuasive influence." Such a quality expressed in the humming of lullabies, a loving kiss, a hug to the breast, or a gentle rocking in embracing arms provides an immediate cure for distressed baby hearts. Is it not condescending and gracious for the Lord God Almighty to promise to act a mother's part to bounce us upon His knees and carry us on His side (see Is. 66:12)? Has He not also promised to take His handkerchief and dry our tear-stained faces, like a mother kisses away the sobs of her crying child (see Is. 25:8)?

A good mother is never weary of her child's coming for consolation. In like manner, the ear of God is always open to our cry. His heart is always tender toward us. His hand is always strong to meet our need. The tragedy of life is that there are so many sorrow-laden hearts all around us who meet their trials without a knowledge of Him who offers Himself as a comforter, dearer than the best of mothers.

Balancing the truth of the motherhood of God with His fatherhood must not be neglected, for He not only promised to comfort like a mother but to pity like a father. "Male and female He created them," the opening of Scripture declares (Gen. 1:27), and the characteristic features of both are resident in the Creator's loving heart. All that is best and gracious in a noble father and also in a pure-hearted mother can be found in Him who is the source of all womanly graces and manly virtues.

March 17

She came and worshiped Him, saying, "LORD, help me!" MATTHEW 15:25

Entering Tyre and Sidon, Jesus sought much-needed rest and seclusion in the home of a disciple. But He could not remain hidden. Somehow, a woman of Canaan found her way to the house where Jesus was staying. Discovering Him, she worshiped Him and urgently requested His help in the deliverance of her daughter from demon-possession. However, "He answered her not a word" (Matt. 15:23).

The distressed mother's appeal for the cure of her daughter seemed to fall on deaf ears. But the silence of Jesus to the woman's plea was not the silence of rejection. His delay in answering her heart-moving appeal was not a denial. When trials, sorrows, and adversities overtake us, we cry to God to help us, but the trying silence of heaven perplexes our minds. Chrysostom's comment on Christ's silence is worthy of note: "The Lord knew that there was a hidden jewel, which He would not conceal from us, but delayed His answer, that the woman's sedulity or diligence, might become an example and doctrine to posterity."

The dialogue that eventually took place between Jesus and the mother centered on *lost sheep, children,* and *dogs.* The woman of Canaan was a Gentile. Gentiles, false teachers, and sinners often received the term of derision, *dogs.* The woman affirmed that she was a dog—not a wild, vicious, starved dog of the streets but a little dog, a playful, harmless puppy, that loved to eat crumbs falling from its masters' table. This reply captured the heart of Jesus and prompted His statement: "O woman, great is your faith!" Her remarks, coupled with her threefold recognition of Him as Lord, obtained for her the miraculous cure of her demon-possessed daughter.

Study the silences of Jesus; meditate on His so-called sharp answers. Appreciate His understanding of the human heart.

March 18

When you roam, they will lead you;
When you sleep, they will keep you;
And when you awake,
they will speak with you. PROVERBS 6:22

One cannot read the biblical books Solomon wrote without being impressed with his gifted use of expressing truth in triadic form. In the verse before us, we have a striking illustration of this method of presenting Scripture. The word *they* in this verse refers to the law and the commandment of verse 23. Divine commands are able to *lead, keep,* and *speak.*

They will lead you. Whenever we face the need of direction or decision in any circumstance and prayerfully seek guidance, the Holy Spirit seems to say: "This is the way, walk in it." Safe and sure is the leading of the commands of God, which He offers us. Amid any encircling gloom, we have the kindly light of Scripture to direct us. The Holy Spirit not only guides us *into* all truth but also *to* a particular portion of the Word He inspired which will be helpful in time of need.

They will keep you. This aspect of the triad affirms that the Word is able to guard us as well as guide us. But how does it keep us when we sleep through the silent hours of the night? If the promises dwell in us richly in all wisdom, then the dreams of night will be pure and good. If through the night we cannot sleep, the precious truths of Scripture will steady the heart and keep it calm. This could be the best rest of all.

They will speak with you. When we awake, how comforting it is to be reminded of some verse of Scripture. There can be no better beginning to a day than that of a few moments with our Bible, praying that God will grant us a message that will take us through the day ahead. We do not know what crossroads and difficulties await us, but God does. Through His Word, He prepares and strengthens us to meet any trials, temptations, duties, and problems the day may hold for us.

May grace be ours to make the Bible the map by which we daily walk; the perfect balance by which all actions must be weighed; the one clear light shining across the sea.

March 19

"The waters. . . . buy wine and milk without money." ISAIAH 55:1

Each of the three liquids the prophet urges to the thirsty to secure without payment has a spiritual significance all its own. Taken together they imply that in God's cup of salvation is all that needy hearts require. The gifts of His love have no price tags attached to them.

The waters. If spiritual refreshment is to be ours, we must first of all feel our need. We must have thirst and then the willingness to partake of the living waters. In other words, we must repent and show faith toward Christ. In Scripture, water is symbolic of the ministry of the Holy Spirit in and through the believer and also of the Word of God as it cleanses and quickens the soul. Although the waters of the world leave us thirsty, only the life-giving stream out of the smitten Rock imparts new life.

The milk. A sure sign of salvation is the ever-deepening desire we have for the sincere milk of the Word. As newborn babes, we grow and thrive by living upon the precepts and promises of God. Milk symbolizes the nourishing quality of Scripture. Paul used the metaphor of milk to illustrate the simpler truths of Scripture which can be grasped without deep study. These truths are contrasted with the deeper and more difficult truths compared to strong meat (see 1 Cor. 3:2; Heb. 5:13). May we be found living in the land of milk and honey!

The wine. The psalmist would have us know that wine "makes glad the heart of man" (Ps. 104:15). Applied to Scripture, wine illustrates the cheering and invigorating effect within the believer's heart. God does not desire any child of His to walk through life with lagging steps, a hanging head, and cheerless heart, but to experience a buoyancy and "all joy in believing." C. H. Spurgeon used to contrast "sour saints and sweet sinners." As saints, may we be found "rejoicing in the Lord always"! Joy is the fruit of the Holy Spirit.

March 20

All Your garments are scented with myrrh and aloes and cassia. PSALM 45:8

This great psalm of the King occupies a prominent position among the Christ-exalting psalms. No other than the King of Glory can lay claim to the honor and holiness, glory and grace, fame and fragrance described in this psalm. The garments in this triad of fragrance indicate all Christ is and has.

Myrrh. Herbs and spices, highly esteemed in the East, were distributed by spice caravans traveling over trade routes. Solomon enforced tolls upon those caravans trading in and passing through his realm. Myrrh was one of the ingredients making up the holy anointing oil, and it was also highly prized for its aromatic assets. It was among the gifts the wise men brought to Jesus; it was offered to Him on the cross; and it was used at His burial. Myrrh represents not only the love of our heart for the Savior but also the fragrance of Christ to God in His sacrificial death—a sweet-smelling aroma to both God and man.

Aloes. Herbs and spices were used in biblical times for perfuming garments and beds and also for embalming the dead, as seen in the spices Nicodemus used in embalming the body of Jesus (see John 19:39). Perfumes represent the worship, praise, and adoration emanating from the heart filled with the love of God. Aloes, a fragrant herb, can also represent holiness of life.

Cassia. This aromatic, somewhat bitter substance was also found in the mixture of the anointing oil (see Ex. 30:24) and was largely used at Roman funerals. Paul called the gift sent from Philippi "a sweet-smelling aroma, an acceptable sacrifice, well pleasing to God" (Phil. 4:18). Cassia can symbolize the service of our hands and the sweet worship and praise of our hearts, ever pleasing to God.

March 21

The faith of Abraham. . . .
He . . . was strengthened in faith,
giving glory to God. ROMANS 4:16, 20

The kindred terms, *faith, terms, belief,* along with their derivatives, appear hundreds of times in Scripture. They express the twofold application of the body of truth as given by God to the church and as a principle of life and living by the individual. We are exhorted to "keep the faith" and to live, personally, "by faith." Some people argue that it does not matter what a person believes as long as he believes something. But such a premise is false because belief influences behavior. What we believe shapes our character and determines our eternal destiny; therefore, the right object of faith is essential.

Jesus gave us the perfect object of faith when He said to His own, "Have faith in God" (Mark 11:22). Having God as the center and circumference of such a faith means that power can be ours to remove mountains of doubt, difficulty, and despair. Our object of faith either enriches or impoverishes life. The faith that pleases God is that which laughs at every impossibility and proclaims: "It shall be done." Under hopeless circumstances, Abraham hopefully believed, and strong in faith, the ancient patriarch glorified God and was enabled to do daring acts. Our forefathers often said, "Act faith," which was the attitude of Abraham who had God as his sole object of truth.

The slogan of General Booth as he sought to encourage his soldiers in the Salvation Army was: "Keep up with your repeated acts of faith." An elderly Methodist preacher gave us practical wisdom when he wrote: "If the devil puts up a stone wall in front of us, we are to believe right through it!" But only *strong* faith can secure such dominion. Lowell said of such acting faith: "He who keeps his faith, he only cannot be discrowned."

By faith we are saved, justified, and sanctified. Whether we think of faith as the bridge spanning the chasm between God and the soul, as the opening of a beggar's hand to receive the gold of heaven, or as an active energy in devotion, such faith is always the fruit of the Holy Spirit.

March 22

Everyone went to his own house. But Jesus went to the Mount of Olives. JOHN 7:53; 8:1

The poet Coleridge, in *The Ancient Mariner,* wrote of being "Like one that on a lonesome road/Doth walk in fear and dread." Our Lord traveled over a lonesome road, but He never walked in fear and dread. His was indeed a lonesome life, but He was never lonely. He knew what it was to be homeless although surrounded by a thousand homes. The people He ministered to went to their own homes but He went to the Mount of Olives where, with the darkness of the night as a blanket to cover Him through the silent hours, He found a refuge in communion with His Father.

If, as the proverb has it, "Solitude is the mother-country of the strong," then Jesus gathered a deep, inner strength from His lonely prayer vigils. The question may be asked: Why did Jesus not go to His own home in which He was born and lived for thirty years? The stark fact is that He was never *at home* when home. He once declared: "A man's foes will be those of his own household" (Matt. 10:36). A characteristic feature of our Lord's teaching is that it came out of the crucible of experience. Truth is effective when wrung out of one's own heart.

Jesus experienced difficulties with His family members in Nazareth. At the early age of twelve, He rebuked His parents for their failure to recognize His divine mission. His brothers and sisters did not believe in Him. To them He was an alien and a stranger. His foes were of His own household, and the rejection of His claims by His own friends and relatives was His deepest wound (see Mark 6:3–4; John 7:5). Often we pay a similar price for discipleship. Our love and devotion for Jesus are not understood or shared by those dearest and nearest to us. When lonely in our witness for Him, we should be consoled to know that as the man of sorrows, He had a share in such grief. He is ever our abiding companion.

March 23

Jacob made a vow, saying,
"If God will be with me, . . .
then the LORD shall be my God." GENESIS 28:20–21

Jacob was forced to flee from home because his brother Esau threatened to kill him for his deceit in stealing Esau's birthright. A solitary, friendless exile, Jacob, heavy-hearted and sorrowful, faced a dark and uncertain future. At the close of his first day's flight from Beersheba, he came weary, sad, and lonely to a place called Luz. Having only the cold earth as his bed and a stone for his pillow, he received a divine revelation. God promised him guidance and provision through all the unknown future. Such a challenging revelation caused Jacob to say, "How awesome is this place!", and he renamed Luz *Bethel*, meaning "God's house" (Gen. 28:17, 19).

Jacob set up a stone pillar to mark the holy spot where he entered into a covenant with God, and he confirmed it with a solemn vow. Jacob was strong in his love when he had made his vow, but he was thinking small with his wishes. All he humbly asked for was to be kept in the way and to have bread to eat and raiment to put on.

The ensuing experiences of the fugitive prove how graciously and generously God responded to Jacob's vow. Some twenty years later when, richly laden he returned to "his father's house in peace," he kept to his vow for the rest of his days honoring the Lord whom he loved.

The question of paramount, personal importance is: Have we covenanted with God and dedicated ourselves to Him to honor Him in the unknown path ahead? How tragic it is to set out as a traveler through the desert of the world without a guide, without a friend to keep us along the way and give us bread to eat and clothes to wear! All who can say from the heart, "The Lord shall be my God," are honored by Him. Because of all He is, Jesus cannot fail.

March 24

"The rainbow shall be in the cloud, and I will look on it." GENESIS 9:16

How overcome with wonder we are as we gaze at the magnificent sight of a rainbow encircling the heavens with its varied hues! Wordsworth, musing upon the rainbow hanging in the skies, wrote: "My heart leaps up when I behold/A rainbow in the sky." Shelley expressed a similar sentiment in the lines: "When the cloud is scattered/The rainbow's glory is shed."

Exhibiting all the colors of the spectrum, it is called the *rain*bow, because it is produced by the sun shining on the rain during a heavy shower. The rainbow was originally given to inspire grateful emotions in the hearts of those who saw it. God called Noah to gaze upon it as a witness to His promise never to deluge the earth again. Every rainbow, then, appearing on a wet day is fresh evidence that: "Never again shall there be a flood to destroy the earth" (Gen. 9:11). God Himself, looking upon the rainbow in the cloud, remembers His everlasting covenant.

Our human eyes have never seen a complete rainbow but one always broken at the bottom. We have the promise, however, of a complete rainbow with no break and with only the color green. An emerald rich in green is prized as a very precious gem. "There was a rainbow around the throne, in appearance like an emerald" (Rev. 4:3). This complete vow assures that God's grace and goodness in eternity will inspire our unceasing, adoring praise and worship. Here below, the rainbow is an impressive symbol of spiritual blessing as well as temporal mercies. Jesus is our "rainbow in the cloud" of heaven's wrath, assuring us who have been saved from it that fiercer storms than any that have devastated the world have passed forever. As we see Jesus appearing in the spiritual firmament, all fear is dispelled.

He is our hope of eternity's calm brightness, the reality of God, deserving our love and faithfulness.

March 25

*"Dwell in the depths. . . .
dwells securely . . . dwelling alone."* JEREMIAH 49:30–31

We live in a superficial age. Deep is not calling unto deep (see Ps. 42:7). In the religious world we live too much on the surface. We prefer a dwelling place on Easy Street and shun the more difficult road. Light reading appeals to us more than hard thinking. Ours is not an unchanging love.

Charles Kingsley, to the daughter of Earl Haldan, wrote:

> Be good, sweet maid, and let who will be clever;
> Do noble things, not dream them, all day long;
> And so make Life, and Death, and that For Ever
> One grand sweet song.

Alas, too many of us love to be *dreamers* rather than *doers*. In *Faustus*, a sixteenth-century poem by Christopher Marlowe, Helen is extolled for having a face that launched a thousand ships, and Mephistopheles is made to say: "There will I dwell, for Heaven be in these lips." We know, however, that ours is the assurance of dwelling in heaven because of the promise of the Savior. Here and now we have the superb dwelling place Jeremiah wrote of where we can dwell deeply and securely—a city the villagers were urged to flee to so that they could be at rest, and dwell safely.

The Lord would have us live without unnecessary care. But such a carefree life is only ours as we dwell deeply in Him in whom there is peace. Having such an impregnable dwelling place deep in His heart, we are safe from calamities that would overtake us. We must also be determined to dwell alone if we would dwell securely. Our failure is that we live too much with the world and are too laden with its cares and anxieties. Alone with Him who trod the winepress alone, we are guarded against finding ourselves in "a dwelling for jackals, a desolation forever" (Jer. 49:33).

Ask for deliverance from fear, worry, remorse, and superficiality.

> We bless Thee for Thy peace, O God,
> Deep as the soundless sea,
> Which falls like sunshine on the road
> Of those who trust in Thee.

March 26

He runneth upon me like a giant. JOB 16:14 KJV

In this verse Job refers to the Divine Being as a giant. Used of a person, the term implies one of abnormal size and strength. In biblical times, there were many giants, the most prominent among them being the Philistine Goliath, whose height was around nine feet. Heavily armored and flashing a mighty sword, he struck fear and terror into the hearts of Philistines and Israelites alike. But a small pebble from David's bag, directed by God, was sufficient to slay the proud, defiant giant.

The powerful giant Job describes is mightier than any person of extraordinary size and power, in that He is the almighty, invincible God no stone can destroy. The Most High is praised, extolled, and honored as the king of heaven, leader of the army of heaven.

Under the heavy pressure of his trials and afflictions, Job made the bitter complaint that God was running upon him as a giant, a symbol of the terror and strength with which He is able to clothe Himself. God not only afflicts those He loves but often afflicts swiftly. A giant is no mere ordinary person, but one of unusual strength. What can a poor, weak person do if he is in the hands of a giant? When God puts forth His giantlike power, how helpless man is! In His judgments, God is fierce, terrible, acting with great speed. Job felt that God would break him in pieces and destroy him immediately, giving his flesh to the fowls of heaven.

The question is often asked: Why does God hasten like a giant and act furiously upon those He loves? The answer is that He is greatly provoked by sin and acts quickly to remove it. "You only have I known of all the families of the earth;/Therefore I will punish you for all your iniquities" (Amos 3:2). Although God came forth quickly and fiercely upon Job, He did not act to injure him in any way. Rather He came to act for his spiritual advantage. "You have heard of the perseverance of Job and seen the end intended by the Lord—that the Lord is very compassionate and merciful" (James 5:11).

March 27

*"Watch and pray,
lest you enter into temptation."* MATTHEW 26:41

We often fail because we are not watching constantly for the beginnings of evil. Surprise attack is one of the principle methods used by the devil, and because we are not always on guard, he breaks through easily. How we need to have our eyes open to detect his faintest approach!

Prayerfulness is essential. Satan trembles when he sees a saint upon his or her knees. If we are constantly praying that temptation may not overtake us, it will be difficult for him to catch us unaware.

Resistance is another avenue of victory. James 4:7 reminds us: "Resist the devil and he will flee from you." How can we successfully resist this persistent foe? One very effective method is simply to remember those who care for us and uphold us in their prayers.

Our memory of Christ's love for us should be our conscious thought at all times. When we are under His divine control, we have a strong force to keep us from temptation. Each of us has exhausting struggles that are secretly fought and won. The world has no knowledge of our battles, but God records them in His book of honors.

If our hearts are constantly drawn to God and His Word, the devil's temptings will hold little interest for us. David sought to hide God's Word in his heart that he might not sin against the Lord. A mind steeped in God's Word and a life filled with God's Spirit are effective weapons against temptation.

The mightiest weapon we have to wield against our archenemy is the blood of the Lamb. Through the death of Christ on the cross we have forgiveness of sins and the power to withstand temptation.

Are you being tempted right now? Then use the weapons God has given you for battle against the devil and claim the victory Christ gave you at the cross.

Robert Browning asks:

> Why comes temptation, but for man to meet
> And master, and make crouch beneath his feet,
> And so be pedestalled in triumph.

March 28

I lay down and slept;/I awoke,
for the LORD sustained me. PSALM 3:5

A concordance reveals that the Bible has much to say about sleep. All kinds of beds, even the latest water beds, are advertised to give us sound, relaxing sleep. But what is the use of the best of beds if a person has a bad conscience? In his affirmation, "Your sleep will be sweet" (Prov. 3:24), Solomon emphasized the thought that sleep is only sweet and beneficial if the person seeking it walks in wisdom's ways and loves her counsel. Many martyrs have slept soundly on bare boards because their sustaining Lord had power to make them sleep as comfortably as if stretched out on inner springs.

The ultimate source of "Care-charmer Sleep," the easer of all woes, is not the most modern bed calculated to induce necessary and rejuvenating power but the Creator of the human body who knew all that it would require once fashioned by His power. Thus the psalmist declared: "He gives His beloved sleep" (Ps. 127:2). It is in such a mental state, when the mind is not corroded by worldly cares, that God's gifts and revelations come to His own. Moffatt's translation reads: "God's gifts come to His loved ones as they sleep." A double thought is emphasized here, namely, that God is the creator and giver of the sleep that mind and body require and that as we sleep His communications as gifts prepare us for our waking hours with their tasks and responsibilities. Who else but the One who never sleeps or slumbers is qualified to give us undisturbed and refreshing sleep?

If sleep is sweet to us, may we remember to intercede for those in strife-plagued parts of the world to whom natural sleep comes hard because of terrorist attacks. Also pray for those who, because of physical affliction or personal cares, are robbed of beneficial, natural sleep and seek forced slumber by recourse to an ever-increasing quantity of drugs to numb the mind. In the name of Him who prayed all night, let us pray for the removal of those terrors forbidding natural sleep.

March 29

As a father pities his children,/So the LORD pities those who fear Him. PSALM 103:13

Although Scripture abounds with the truth of the fatherhood of God, we do not remember as often as we should that we have a Father in heaven who loves us and cares for us. He has given His word that He is always ready to do us good. Fatherhood is attributed to God in a fourfold way. He is (1) the eternal Father of the Lord Jesus Christ, who is His only begotten Son; (2) the Father of Adam and all his natural offspring in respect to creation; (3) the Father of all mercies flowing from His bountiful hand to His creatures; and (4) the Father of all those regenerated by the power of His Spirit, manifesting His grace.

Our Lord taught us to address and trust God as our "heavenly Father" (Matt. 6:32), who knows what we need and provides all we need. What a mercy and a privilege to have such a Father for whom nothing is too hard to effect, nothing too great to provide, and nothing too good to bestow upon those redeemed by the blood of His beloved Son! In such an inhospitable world like ours, we should rejoice in having such a loving, merciful, and bountiful Father.

The tender heart of God knows how to pity His children in their sins and sorrows. While never winking at their shortcomings and lapses, He upbraids with love. Remembering their frailty, a wise father never imposes too heavy a load on his children. Thus the pitying God, mighty as He is, stoops to our weakness. He never condones sin in any child of His. Transgression is more grievous in His own than in the godless who are of their father, the devil. Over a century ago an unidentified poet penned the lines:

Father, on me the grace bestow,
To call Thee mine while here below,
To love Thee as Thy law requires,
To this my longing soul aspires.
May every word and action prove
My soul is fill'd with heavenly love.

March 30

"I will see you again and your heart will rejoice." JOHN 16:22

Notice the sadness in the conversation of Jesus as recorded in this narrative (see 16:16–23). He had just announced: "A little while, and you will not see Me" (v. 16). His disciples were distressed over the thought of His departure, and He sought to ease their pain by the revelation of what was before Him and before them. The phrase "a little while" occurs seven times in verses 16–19. The Wycliffe Commentary says,

> This refers to the short interval that remained before his burial, when the disciples would no longer *see* him with eyes of physical sight. The second *little while* designates the interval between his burial and his resurrection, after which they would see him again. Here the word *see* is not the same as in the first occurrence. It conveys the thought of perception as well as of observation.

In His previous forecast of His betrayal, Jesus used the same phrase, "I shall be with you a little while longer. . . . Where I am going, you cannot come" (John 13:33). Peter and the rest of the disciples were distressed over the impending absence of the Master, but He consoled their troubled hearts by the assurance: "If I go and prepare a place for you, I will come again and receive you to Myself; that where I am, there you may be also" (John 14:3). We are in this "little while," which will end with the Rapture.

The "little while" of John 14:19 is associated with Christ's promise of the advent of the Holy Spirit, whom He bestowed upon His church after His ascension. As Christ was God's representative in the days of His flesh, so in this age of grace—the little while between His ascension and second advent—the Holy Spirit is the Savior's representative. Although our eyes have never seen the radiant face of Jesus, we endure the little while of His absence as seeing Him who is presently invisible. In this we rest and know that our adorable Lord will redeem His promises.

As we await such a glorious manifestation of our Redeemer, may He unite us ever closer to Himself.

March 31

Consider Him . . . lest you become weary and discouraged. HEBREWS 12:3

The term *consider,* used over eighty times in Scripture, affords a profitable study. In the epistle to the Hebrews the word provides several lessons.

"Consider the Apostle and High Priest . . . Christ Jesus" (3:1). Here the word *consider* means "to perceive clearly or understand"; "to examine closely," as though the observer had to bend down for the purpose. We are urged to bend low in our meditation of Jesus in His twofold office—one past, "the Apostle," the other present, the "High Priest."

"Consider how great this man [Melchizedek] was" (7:4). The term *consider* (both here and in Heb. 12:3) implies more than a mere superficial observation. It suggests concentration or very close attention upon a subject; it suggests contemplation with the idea of wonder and admiration. This should be our attitude as we think of this mystic person, the King of righteousness and peace, who so fittingly typifies the Lord as king and priest (see 7:26; Rev. 19:16).

"Let us consider one another in order to stir up love and good works" (10:24). Too often we criticize instead of considering one another. But the more we observe closely to help one another, the less criticism we will have. The more we strive to help others, the less we will hinder them. Alas, we are near weeping, when we think of the lamentable absence of love among professing Christians who declare their faith is the love of God.

"Consider Him who endured such hostility from sinners against Himself, lest you become weary and discouraged" (12:3). This particular word means "to consider thoroughly or count up or weigh in the balances." The direct application, then, is the counting up of our sufferings to discover how they tally with all Jesus endured in the days of His flesh. This is our safeguard against weariness and discouragement.

Remember the true teaching we have received and imitate the faith and godliness of our Christian teachers.

April 1

Will You not revive us again? PSALM 85:6

In these critical times, the church is not as awe-inspiring as she should be. Her heartfelt prayer should express her pressing need for a mighty quickening of the Holy Spirit, making her, thereby, the channel of spiritual power throughout the world. In the revival psalm before us, the church is encouraged to pray for revival, because she has a God who is willing to forgive her lapses.

The psalmist also makes it clear that once the people of God are forgiven and restored to His favor, they must have no more relapses. "Let them not turn back to folly" (v.8). Further, revival is related to the redeemed of the Lord, where there is still life within. Anything totally dead cannot be revived. The impartation of new life—a resurrection—is required. Life, then, no matter how low, must be present in believers if they are to experience spiritual quickening. Sinners cannot be revived, because they are dead in sins. The word and experience for them is not *revival* but *regeneration*.

Those who have been born again by the Holy Spirit, but who have permitted the sinister influences of the world to rob them of spiritual power, desperately need the reviving grace of the Lord. Do *you*, as a Christian, have need to pray: "Will You not revive *me* again?" Does the spark within need to be fanned into a glowing flame? If civilization is to be saved from catastrophe, a worldwide spiritual revival must take place. Church history reveals that in the midst of the darkest years, God breaks out in marvelous ways as the God of salvation.

Some people discredit all hope of revival, arguing that the terrible condition of things in our fragmented world precludes a spiritual upheaval. How can we concentrate upon the vital truths of the soul, when we are either locked in a death-struggle or are laboring incessantly to provide the necessities of life? Pagan forces predominate, and civilization seems to be crumbling. Yet God waits to manifest, in a remarkable way, His power to make the church a wonderful, triumphant, spiritual force in our world.

April 2

*Blessed are you who sow
beside all waters.* ISAIAH 32:20

All who are called as ministers of the Word need to pray constantly that the good Lord will deliver them from mere professionalism. Although the Lord's Day is the great day for sowing the seeds of eternal life, Isaiah reminds us that all who are truly saved by grace are thrice blessed if they grasp every opportunity for telling others about Jesus and His love. The true sower will not save his seed for special occasions. He will, with a full, prepared basket, have a handful of seed ready to scatter over the soil of any soul he touches day in and day out, in public witness, in visitation, or in conversation. The diligent pastor and Christian worker will drop a seed here and there, trusting the Lord of all harvest to guard the sown seed and make it fruitful.

Daniel encouraged sowers by reminding them that those turning many to righteousness will shine as "the stars forever and ever" (Dan. 12:3). This entire verse is a promise for all soul winners, but it provides a special incentive to pastors, who have the greatest opportunity for turning souls to God. Paul knew that if he were wise in the winning of the lost, he would shine as the brightness of the firmament. That is why he rejoiced over the conversion of the Thessalonians: "What is our hope, or joy, or crown of rejoicing? Is it not even you in the presence of our Lord Jesus Christ at His coming? For you are our glory and joy" (1 Thess. 2:19–20).

Brilliance may not be yours, but be patient and faithful, my fellow sower. Serve God to the limit of your capacity, and eternal brilliance will be yours. Many ministerial and media stars will fade. They are now having all the shine they will ever possess. Your unnoticed sowing of the seed will yet have its glorious harvest.

> Sowing in the morning, sowing seeds of kindness,
> Sowing in the noontide and the dewy eve;
> Waiting for the harvest, and the time of reaping,
> We shall come rejoicing, bringing in the sheaves.

Open your life to the leadership of the Holy Spirit, asking Him to put a specific soul on your heart.

April 3

"I will be a Father to you." 2 CORINTHIANS 6:18

That God holds a sacred estimation of fatherhood is evidenced by His frequent use of the relationship to illustrate His feelings toward His own. Further, when an earthly father dies, God offers to take his place and care for those who are orphaned; He speaks of Himself as the "father of the fatherless" (Ps. 68:5).

The best fathers in the world are those who are fully separated from the world and who, endeavoring to be free from an unequal yoke of unbelievers, know what it is to have the Lord Almighty as a Father. Life is ever fragrant in a home when a father, loving his heavenly Father and striving to please Him in all his ways, so orders his home life as to give his children a beautiful conception of the love, sympathy, and protection of the heavenly Father above. The greatest responsibility of any father is to reflect the character of God.

A father mirroring the father-heart of God is different from one with a heart of stone. David reminds us: "As a father pities his children,/So the LORD pities those who fear Him" (Ps. 103:13).

God knows how to pity His children in their sins and sorrows. While never condoning their shortcomings and lapses, He upbraids with love. And, remembering their frailty, a wise father never imposes too heavy a load on his children. Thus it is that God stoops to our weakness, mighty as He is. Knowing our frame and remembering that we are but dust, our Father above makes all necessary and just allowances and showers His pity where it is deserved. To merit His pity, however, we must fear Him. That means we are not to cringe before Him as a tyrannical Father but to exhibit reverential trust and holy confidence in Him.

Eternal Father, Who didst all create,
In whom we live and to whose bosom move,
To all men be Thy name known, which is Love,
Till its loud praises sound at heaven's gate.

April 4

You have the dew of Your youth. PSALM 110:3

Without doubt this psalm sets forth the high-priestly and kingly prerogatives of the Messiah. Christ recited the psalm as referring to Himself (see Mark 12:36). The epistle to the Hebrews also quotes this psalm, interpreting it messianically. By the *dew,* we are to understand freshness. In a very real sense Christ retains the dew of His youth. He did not come to the end of His earthly sojourn an old, decrepit man. He was just thirty-three years of age when He returned to glory. He was a vigorous personality.

Thirty-three! The glory of a young man is his strength, and our blessed Lord, as "the young Prince of Glory," as Isaac Watts named Him, retains the dew of His youth. The Ancient of Days, He yet has the freshness and vigor of eternal youth. No wrinkles will ever gather on His brow. Time produces no change in His glorified body. His strength will never diminish. And, glory be, when we see Him, we shall be like Him, youthful forevermore.

None of us is as youthful as we once were. Our steps falter, and our strength wanes. Physical deterioration has set in. Grace, however, can keep us youthful in spirit. It is Christ "Who satisfies your mouth with good things,/So that your youth is renewed like the eagle's" (Ps. 103:5).

Spiritual vigor and buoyancy can be ours all through the days of our life. The Creator who remembered us in the days of our youth will not forsake us when our hair is gray and we have little pleasure in the years as they pass by. The secret of perpetual youthfulness of spirit is habitual fellowship with Him who is the source of eternal life. Alas, sin is producing too many old, young people. How refreshing it is to meet so many young, old persons in the service of Christ! Too often people feel old because they are aging or because their fellowship with the Lord is intermittent. May we ever be found asking Him for new strength!

April 5

Power of death, . . . fear of death. HEBREWS 2:14–15

What great power Satan must have possessed before Calvary! He certainly exercises great power still, but the Cross was his Waterloo. The keys of death and hell are not his any longer. They dangle at Christ's side. The question is: If Christ has destroyed the *power* of death, why do we not let Him deliver us from the *fear* of death? If its power has gone, why do we dread it? Many people, all their lives, are subject to such bondage. We have been taught to sing that we should fear the grave as little as our bed. To the Christian such a fear is sinful and has no foundation. Having destroyed the power of death by His death, Christ is able to deliver us from any lurking fear of the grave.

The psalmist declares that the future of the upright person is peace, not fear (Ps. 37:37). If our sin is forgiven, then death is not a leap into the dark but a falling into the embrace of the Savior. A peaceful end likewise comes to those who have not been idle in the marketplace but who have appropriated every opportunity of witnessing for Him. Christ destroyed the one who had the power of death. What else can a believer do but die happy and victorious when he knows that his heart and life are to be entirely emancipated from evil and that the society of the holy, the sight of Christ's face, and the full enjoyment of God's presence in all eternity await him?

But to have a fearless, peaceful end we must have Christ as our peace as we journey over the rough and rugged highway of life. David makes it clear that only the perfect or upright one has a peaceful end and can sing with full assurance that the fear of death has gone forever. The apostle Paul, in 1 Corinthians 15:55, quoted Hosea, saying, "O Death, where is your sting?/O Hades, where is your victory?"

Give thanks to God for His glorious victory over death.

April 6

"I give them eternal life,
and they shall never perish." JOHN 10:28

Evidently the saved-today-and-lost-tomorrow adherents underestimate the power of Christ not only to save but also to keep safe. Sheep do not have to struggle to keep the Shepherd. Our salvation is not something but Someone. Therefore, it is an impossible task, is it not, for the creature to strive to keep the Creator? People who speak about losing their salvation treat such a provision as a mere *it.* To them it is an intangible, impersonal something that one has to be very careful to retain. Eternal life is salvation in Christ Himself, who is our life within the soul. Thus when He declares that He gives His sheep eternal life, He actually affirms that He gives them Himself. What a gift! And once ours, He is ours forever. Nothing can ever rob us of Him nor sever us from Him.

Further on in the Gospel of John, we find Christ saying to His own: "Because I live, you will live also" (John 14:19). The word *also* in this memorable chapter should be noted: the *also* of faith (14:1); the *also* of presence (14:3); the *also* of knowledge (14:7); the *also* of power (14:12); and the *also* of life (14:19). He bases these promises not on His earthly life but on His present, glorified throne life.

Paul reminded the Romans that they were "saved by His life," implying Christ's present life in glory (Rom. 5:10). The particular phase of salvation the ascended, reigning Christ makes possible is freedom from sin's power and dominion. Alive forevermore, we live in Him; and being in Him, we have a more glorious life awaiting us. Those who are of this world speak about seeing life. The child of God, however, is the only one who really sees and possesses life, and who has the promise of a life abundant and unending. Are we not lost in wonder and praise as we contemplate the glorious life awaiting us beyond a death-laden earth?

Praise God for the confidence Christ gives you that He will never withdraw Himself or His gift of salvation from you.

April 7

"Put in the sickle,
for the harvest is ripe." JOEL 3:13

The Bible compares a people ripened by sin for destruction to a harvest ready for the sickle of God's vengeance. What a bloody harvest awaits a guilty, godless earth! The vision of Armageddon is terrible to contemplate. What destruction will overtake the multitudes when "the harvest of the earth is ripe" (Rev. 14:15)! The sickle of judgment will be in the pierced hands of the Son of man. Rejecting Him, sinners once thrust a reed into His hands and then pounded cruel nails through them. But when those sacred hands lay hold of the sickle, woe betide the rejecters thronging the earth. None will escape the dread vengeance, as Christ sends forth "the reapers . . . to burn" (Matt. 13:30). Blessed be God, the saved will not participate in such a horrible harvest! Already they have been reaped in grace and thus realize they will not experience the sickle of slaughter.

Jeremiah lamented: "The harvest is past . . . and we are not saved!" (8:20). This prophet of tears had a unique way of employing forceful metaphors as he endeavored to bring a backsliding nation back to God. His was a fruitless task, however. Ceaselessly he cried that if the people but repent, God would save them from the aggression of the Babylonians. But hopelessly and fanatically attached to their idols, the people were doomed. Their harvest of grace and summer of acceptance were ended, and those to whom the prophet addressed his tear-drenched messages were not saved from their idolatry and consequent destruction.

In our gospel age, let us be spurred on by the fact that the harvest is not past nor the summer ended. Souls can still be gathered in. Our solemn responsibility is to rescue the perishing, care for the dying, weep over the erring one, tell the lost of Jesus who yearns to gather them to Himself. The tragedy is imminent, but the possibilities are glorious: "The harvest truly is plentiful, but the laborers are few. Therefore pray the Lord of the harvest to send out laborers into His harvest" (Matt. 9:37–38).

Will you volunteer to work His fields and bring the sheaves to Him?

April 8

Be watchful in all things . . .
fulfill your ministry. 2 TIMOTHY 4:5

Next to the Lord, Paul is the most ideal preacher the New Testament presents. The apostle was no professional. He found himself in the ministry because he could not help it. On that Damascus road, his dramatic and dynamic experience transformed him from a persecutor of Christians into a person whose life and service were for the Christ loved and served by the ones he had persecuted. As soon as he was saved, Paul asked: "Lord, what do you want me to do?" Then came the revelation of the great ministry as "a chosen vessel" he was to exercise (see Acts 9:6, 15).

At the end of a long, faithful, fruitful, and honored career, the veteran minister gave young Timothy some very practical advice as he faced his life's task. All who are called to preach the Word can easily discover by reading 2 Timothy 4 how they can successfully fulfill their ministry. Being true to God and His Word, laboring in the light of eternity, remaining alert for lost souls—these are among the secrets of a God-honoring ministry.

Peter, in harmony with Paul, urged all who are called to witness to "shepherd the flock of God . . . when the Chief Shepherd appears, you will receive the crown of glory" (1 Pet. 5:2, 4). If pastoral counsels are to be obeyed and pastors themselves to be held in reputation and honor, pastors must remember the qualifications they must have in their ministry. The crown of unfailing glory is only for those shepherds who are examples to the flock. If they act "as being lords" in their office (1 Pet. 5:3), what do they expect to receive from the Lord? Crowned with self-glory, they forfeit the right to receive a crown of divine glory at the judgment seat of Christ.

Intercede for your pastor, and pray that the Great Shepherd will call a younger generation of under-shepherds.

April 9

Though war should rise against me. . . .
He shall hide me. PSALM 27:3, 5

Our Lord told us that among the signs of His reappearing would be the hearing of "wars and rumors of wars" (Matt. 24:6). Since the last two world wars, we have witnessed several international and national conflicts. In this twentieth century the nations are multiplying nuclear weapons of mutual destruction at a frightful pace. Today the instruments of war have become more deadly than ever before, until misdirected ingenuity and science have succeeded in creating the most fearful implements of destruction. We think of the enormous toll of human life that tanks, bombs, submarines, and powerful guns have taken. But we know the discovery of nuclear power and weapons indicates the possibility of a nuclear war destroying millions in a brief space of time.

Divine promises of protection in war-laden days do not imply immunity from the sorrows of war. Rather they mean that if war should come, we have a source of consolation and hope of which the world is ignorant. The promise is: "He shall redeem you . . . in war from the power of the sword" (Job 5:20).

As believers we are not to fear those who are able to starve or kill the body. Engines of destruction have claimed many of God's people as well as non-Christians. Although war claimed them, Christians had the assurance that warring forces were not able to kill the soul. When the sword fell upon them, it only liberated them from the sordidness of earth. Many of the early martyrs could kiss the flames encircling them, seeing they only hastened their entrance into heaven. Theirs was the assurance that "no weapon formed against you shall prosper" (Is. 54:17). Having created those who have developed a warlike nature, God is able to deal effectively with anyone to whom He has given life. Weapons of warfare are indeed terrible, but when levelled against the saints, God knows how to bring them to nothing. Often He rallies the forces of nature to combat the cruelty of men. Thus God used the snow against Napoleon and the mists at Dunkirk against the Germans.

Praise God for the peace He puts within the believer's heart.

April 10

"I will set your prisoners free./. . .
You prisoners of hope." ZECHARIAH 9:11–12

Scripture uses the words *prison* and *prisoners* in various ways. A prison is the figure used of Christ's grave. Those who are in bondage by reasons of their own lusts are the prisoners the Lord came to "bring out" of the prison house of sin (Is. 42:7). God's power over Satan is proved by the latter's presence in prison for "the thousand years" (Rev. 20:7). Paul spoke of himself not as the prisoner of Nero but as "the prisoner of Jesus Christ" (Eph. 3:1). Those of Smyrna who were cast into prison because of their allegiance to Christ were likewise His prisoners. Those persons received the promise that the Lord would not despise them. They would not be left to die and rot unforgotten. He always hears the groaning of His prisoners and has His own way of delivering them, as Peter experienced when he was delivered from prison (see Acts 12:5–18).

In Zechariah's portrait of "prisoners of hope," the narrative is directly related to the regathering of the Jews and their re-establishment as a nation. Scattered as they still are among the nations, the Jews are upheld by the hope that they will all be brought into the stronghold of their promised land. For their tears, God is to give them triumph. Glory is to compensate their grief. Thus as prisoners, they continue to hope.

The saints are also "prisoners of hope," for their redeemed spirits within the prison of their bodies yearn for freedom. Restrained by the world and the flesh, they cannot serve the Lord as they should and would like to. But theirs is the blessed hope that at the coming of the Lord, they will leap out of their bodily prison and leave all their chains behind. Meantime, as "spirits in prison," they have the presence and ministry of the Lord Jesus (1 Pet. 3:19).

Listen to the words of Jesus as He explains one basis of future rewards: "I was naked and you clothed Me; I was sick and you visited Me; I was in prison and you came to Me" (Matt. 25:36).

Keep your heart sensitive to the needs of those who do not have His freedom.

April 11

This is my comfort in my affliction,/
For Your word has given me life. PSALM 119:50

Affliction is a most prominent term in Scripture, appearing some two hundred times in its related forms. The word can signify (1) adversity, trouble, or distress (Job 5:6); (2) outward and public oppression (Mark 4:17); or (3) necessary divine correction (Ps. 119:75).

Francis Bacon in his volume, *Of Adversity,* stated, "The pencil of the Holy Ghost hath laboured more in describing the affliction of Job than the felicities of Solomon."

David, having had his share of adversity, gave the world a little of his own experience when he wrote, "Many are the afflictions of the righteous,/But the LORD delivers him out of them all" (Ps. 34:19). Yet in all his crises, the psalmist had recourse to the Word of comfort. Just how did the Word he loved quicken him? Amid all his cares and calamities he knew from the sacred commandments that afflictions would not last forever. The glorious hope of cessation from the tears and trials of life upheld the psalmist in the woes he bore with peace and patience.

David's greater Son revealed to the saints of all ages how He provided through His afflictions "the patience and comfort of the Scriptures" (Rom. 15:4). Jesus was tested in the furnace of affliction. He experienced what it was to feed upon the bread and water of affliction.

The apostle James was no visionary, but he approached the problem of life in a most practical way. He urged his readers to pray if in pain, to supplicate God when in suffering, sickness, or sin (see James 5:13–18). Prayer is a wonderful relief when affliction is heavy upon us; thus is the testimony of many a suffering saint. Too often, adversity finds us irritable rather than prayerful. We complain instead of communing with the Lord, who knows what is best for every child of His. Prayer strengthens us to suffer, lightens our load, fashions pain into a pulpit, and interprets our baffling infirmities.

Has affliction overtaken you? Then pray for perseverance and victory.

April 12

First learn to show piety at home. 1 TIMOTHY 5:4

What a different world ours would be if only the entrance of every home bore the message, *Here is the place where I sit best!* The poet Longfellow in "Stay at Home" has the couplet: "Stay, stay at home, my heart, and rest./Home-making hearts are happiest." In "Home, Sweet Home," J. H. Payne would have us remember: "'Mid pleasures and palaces though we may roam,/Be it ever so humble, there's no place like home." As for William Cowper, in "The Task," his estimation of the value of true home life is expressed in the lines: "I crown thee king of intimate delights/Fireside enjoyments, home-born happiness."

Pious homes, made possible by those who love God and His Word, form a nation's greatest asset. Surely it is not glorifying to God for a Christian to be always on the run. What value is running to meetings, if outside activities mean negligence of home duties and ties? Many a family has gone to pieces simply because the parents neglected their children or left them to the care of others.

Parenthood involves sacrifices so that young lives might be shaped and molded right. A good deal of public life, even if one is fitted for it, must be maintained in proper perspective. Tragic results accrue from keeping other vineyards and forgetting our own. Keeping faith and showing piety at home may not carry the notice or popularity of social or club life, but they work together to produce young lives well-guarded to face the temptations and trials of the world. Although public life may seem to have more variety and glamor than the humdrum duties of the home, the house of which Christ is the Head is never lacking in spiritual and mental refreshment, and in peace and pleasure.

God, give us Christian homes!

April 13

"God will wipe away every tear from their eyes." REVELATION 7:17

These words, unequalled in their depth and tenderness, also appear in Revelation 21:4 and relate to the same people. Yet the application of each passage is different, for each is speaking of a different period of time.

In our world today, however, tears are common to all. The strongest, most joyful, or seemingly hard and thoughtless have times when their faces are wet with tears. Surely there is nothing unmanly or unwomanly in the shedding of tears. Tears relieve burdened hearts and crushed spirits. Often we feel better after a crisis when we have had a good cry. Jesus wept! And His tears make Him sacred to our memory and have forever sanctified our tears and anguish.

When John penned these beautiful lines, he doubtlessly was thinking of Isaiah's description of a tearless world: "The Lord GOD will wipe away tears from all faces" (Is. 25:8). John does not tell us in this passage what heaven is like, but the apostle does contrast it with our lives here on earth. He cites an array of occasions for shedding tears as a contrast to the positive peace of God's people in eternity.

Here we have tears, misery, sickness, pain, and graves. God did not promise us freedom from such sorrows, but His keeping power draws us to Himself. In heaven we will be in intimate and constant communion with Him. There we will experience the absence of all the causes of anguish, as well as the addition of a glorious provision of unending bliss. In eternity there will be no more death, no more sorrow, no more pain, and no more crying.

Whether physical or spiritual death causes our tears, we can say with Christina Rossetti:

All tears are done away
  with the bitter unquiet sea;
Death done away from among the living
  at last;
Man shall say of sorrow—
  Love granted it to thee and me!—
At last—It is past.

April 14

"The LORD *. . . rested the seventh day. Therefore the* LORD *blessed the Sabbath day and hallowed it."* EXODUS 20:11

Originally the Sabbath was a day of worship in memory of God's work in creation. Then it was recognized as a day of repose for man and beast, that they might not have their bodily strength exhausted by uninterrupted labor. The Sabbath was made for man, being ordained for his welfare.

Modern life has turned this day of rest into one of restlessness. The ceaseless whirl of cars on the highways, tens of thousands at sporting events, moving picture shows offering entertainment, and countless ways of robbing the Sabbath of its restful value prove the decadent life of the nation.

If the Creator rested on the seventh day, surely the creature has greater need of a day's cessation from the labor, legitimate and exacting, monopolizing the other six days of the week. Do you keep the Lord's Day free from all unnecessary work and employ it for worship and rest? If you do, then you have His benediction. Isaiah says that the Lord blesses the person "who keeps from defiling the Sabbath, and keeps his hand from doing any evil" (Is. 56:2).

Such ethical instructions laid down for Israel hold an application for us today. Nothing can contribute to our personal happiness, which is what the term *blessed* implies, like a Sunday kept free from worldly pollution. Spiritual, physical, and mental reward is ever ours if we remember the Sabbath to keep it holy. What a benediction is ours if our Sundays are as oases in this desert-world! A tender, Spirit-inspired conscience enables us to determine how we should keep the Sabbath.

Read the reward of Sabbath-keeping (and the alternative) offered the citizens of Jerusalem: "This city shall remain forever. . . . then I will kindle a fire in its gates, and it shall devour the palaces of Jerusalem" (Jer. 17:25, 27).

Praise God for the happy, joyful recurrence of the Lord's Day and the resurrected Savior it honors.

April 15

"I will correct you in justice." JEREMIAH 30:11

The constant remembrance that God, because of His mercy, does not reward us according to our iniquities but inspires us to walk humbly before Him. If we received what we deserve, we would not be able to survive. Sin merits correction, and love sends it, but we are corrected only in justice and not according to the just deserts for our sin.

Earlier in his prophecy Jeremiah prayed: "O LORD, correct me . . . not in Your anger, lest You bring me to nothing [or diminish me]" (Jer. 10:24). Later on the Lord said to Jeremiah: "I will make a complete end of all the nations . . . but I will not make a complete end of you. I will rightly correct you, for I will not leave you wholly unpunished" (Jer. 46:28).

The discipline of God as the righteous judge is at once retributive and reformative. David prayed: "O LORD, do not rebuke me in Your anger,/Nor chasten me in Your hot displeasure./Have mercy on me, O LORD" (Ps. 6:1–2). So great is God's mercy toward us that He does not deal with us in anger but in love. With His Father's heart He pities and corrects us in measure. "You our God have punished us less than our iniquities deserve" (Ezra 9:13). "Through the LORD's mercies we are not consumed, because His compassions fail not" (Lam. 3:22).

As our Father, He chastens us, not in full but in measure; not in wrath but in love; not to destroy us but to save us. As His children, we are in constant need of His correction, and it would not be right for Him never to reprove us. Because God loves us, He rebukes and chastises us. He wants us to learn from discipline and grow in grace.

An unknown writer would have us pray:

Father, if Thou must reprove
For all that I have done,
Not in anger, but in love.
Chastise Thy wayward son;
Correct with kind severity,
And bring me home to Thee.

April 16

"I seek out My sheep and deliver them from . . . where they were scattered on a cloudy and dark day." EZEKIEL 34:12

The Jews have experienced numberless cloudy and dark days. In different parts of today's world much anguish is theirs. Nazism initiated a bloody purge of Jews and communistic states offer them scarce refuge, but they live on.

The ancient Jews saw Rome, the mighty heart of nations, sending its own ceaseless life's throb through all the arteries of its vast empire. The Jew, too, has seen that heart cold and still in death, but he lives on—the same silent, mysterious, unbeaten being. Neither country nor climate changes him, for the world is his home. Scattered among the nations, the Jews believe that their regathering will come as foretold by their glorious prophets (see Ezek. 37; Hos. 1:10–11; 3:4–5). Because of this divine purpose we can speak of "the indestructible Jew."

Zechariah prophesied of the Jews: "No longer shall there be utter destruction,/But Jerusalem shall be safely inhabited" (14:11). Jerusalem is sacred to the heart of every true Jew, in spite of countless efforts to keep the city from them. Wandering as a captive in the streets of his own once beautiful Jerusalem, meditating sadly and gloomily upon the relics of ancient power, the Jew is yet inspired by the promise of a safe habitation. Although he has been trampled and exiled, his name made a badge of deceit and disgrace, his city surrounded by foes, the Jew continues to have ancestral pride. The Jew loves the land that is his by divine right and gift. Although subject to Gentile dominion and persecution, he is assured that some day the enemies will be scattered: "Jerusalem will be trampled by Gentiles until the times of the Gentiles are fulfilled" (Luke 21:24). The Jew and his ancient home are to be reconciled, but meantime the responsibility of the Christian is to "pray for the peace of Jerusalem" (Ps. 122:6), the city whose sins Jesus wept over.

April 17

"The Lord will open to you His good treasure." DEUTERONOMY 28:12

Through the goodness of God, Israel was productive in goods so that she might be able to "lend to many nations," but borrow from none (Deut. 28:12). The work of her hands was blessed not only because God delighted in her but also because she would be able to become the medium of blessing to others. Treasure was hers, not to save but to scatter. On January 21, 1835, George Muller, the apostle of faith, wrote in his journal: "The Lord pours in, while we seek to pour out." Basil Miller, Muller's biographer, remarked: "He had struck a partnership with God, and had promised to dispense whatever the Almighty provided." Israel was to function in this manner. What the Lord poured into her, she had, in turn, to pour out! Have we learned this lesson?

Jeremiah records the sorrow of God over Israel's adverse reaction in the day of prosperity: "I spoke to you in your prosperity, but you said, 'I will not hear'" (Jer. 22:21). In a notable way, Israel possessed the "good treasure" of God. The nation, however, committed the folly of glorying in its prosperity, rather than in the One who sent it. Divine warnings passed unheeded. Prosperity resulted in pride. The goodness of God should have begotten humility and repentance. But the people, puffed up with conceit over their divinely bestowed possessions, lived to see their treasures plundered by ruthless hands.

Is not Israel's tragedy that of many professed believers? God was good in blessing them with much, but affluence, instead of being used for God, withered up their spirituality. Gains were not dedicated to the Lord who permitted them to accumulate but were used for the gratification of selfish desires. God lovingly warned Israel, but her ears were deliberately closed to the divine appeal. Let each of us beware of making a god of prosperity, thereby losing the prosperity of our bountiful God.

April 18

A haughty look, a proud heart . . .
are sin.

PROVERBS 21:4

While the commendable virtue of humility is praised, it is seldom practiced. The majority of us find it hard to believe that the best way *up* is *down,* or as Jesus promised, the humble will be exalted. Left to ourselves we are nothing, know nothing, and can do nothing. Only in the Lord do we live, move, and have our being.

Although the word *humility* does not appear in the Gospels, its close relative, *humbles,* occurs four times and means "to make low." As John Bunyan reminds us,

> He that is down needs fear no fall,
> He that is low no pride.
> He that is humble ever shall
> Have God to be his guide.

Solomon affirmed, "Better to be of humble spirit/with the lowly,/Than to divide the spoil/with the proud" (Prov. 16:19). The proud person finds it hard to believe that the only true independence is in humility, seeing that the humble expects nothing and therefore is not disappointed. Humility has also a healing attribute in that it will cauterize a thousand wounds which pride would keep open. But no person, except Jesus, meek and lowly in heart, will remain the perfect model of the grace of humility.

As Thomas Dekker of the seventeenth century described Jesus:

> The best of men
> That e'er wore earth about him, was a sufferer,
> A soft, meek, patient, humble, tranquil spirit,
> The first true gentleman that ever breathed.

Of those who are proud of their humility, Coleridge warned: "And the Devil did grin, for his darling sin/Is pride that apes humility."

Lord Jesus, teach me the danger of false meekness but the beauty of Your own true humility.

April 19

His fame went throughout all Syria. MATTHEW 4:24

One cannot read the Gospels without being fascinated by the fame of Jesus which gained widespread momentum during His public ministry. He was acclaimed king of the Jews, yet His sphere of work was limited to a radius of some forty to fifty miles; such was a limited, national sovereignty. But His forecast was: "I, if I am lifted up from the earth, will draw all peoples to Myself" (John 12:32). His death by crucifixion gave Him universality as the Savior of the world. Isaiah not only predicted Christ's coming as a child but also the increase of His government and peace, of which there will be no end. "The glory of the LORD shall be revealed,/And all flesh shall see it together" (Is. 40:5).

After our Lord's ascension, "when the Day of Pentecost had fully come . . . devout men, from every nation under heaven" were gathered together, and everyone heard the Spirit-inspired message "in his own language" (Acts 2:1, 5–6). The story of the book of Acts is that of the rapidity with which the fame of Jesus spread from a national boundary to an international outlook.

Here are we today, almost two thousand years away from the days of His flesh, and what universal honor and glory are His! No one can dispute that Jesus is the character in human history of whom more has been written and spoken than any other person. Friends and foes alike have uttered widely differing opinions about Jesus, who never ceases to be the center of universal attraction. There has never been another like Him, nor will there ever be, seeing He ever remains man's perfect God and God's perfect Man.

When He returns to earth, He will not be a limited sovereign as the king of a certain group of people; instead, He will be as *the* King of all other kings and rulers. Then blessings will abound.

> Jesus shall reign where'er the sun
> Does his successive journeys run;
> His kingdom spread from shore to shore,
> Till moons shall wax and wane no more.

Thank the Father for sending a universal Savior.

April 20

"If anyone keeps My word he shall never see death." JOHN 8:51

This declaration caused the Jews to say that Christ was demon-possessed. Evidently, they did not discern the difference between physical and eternal death. Our Lord, of course, was simply emphasizing what He had already said about unbelievers dying in their sins (see John 8:24).

Certainly, we shall see physical death, that is, if Christ does not come in our lifetime. A grave awaits each of us, if He tarries. But death in our sins, the second death or eternal death, will never be ours, because we are in Him who is alive forevermore. He promised, "Because I live, you will live also" (John 14:19). The death, then, which Jesus had in mind when He affirmed that no child of His should see death, was the second death or the eternal separation of the spirit from the presence of God. Paul agreed with this glorious heritage when he affirmed that nothing can separate believers "from the love of God which is in Christ Jesus our Lord" (Rom. 8:39).

As for actual, physical death Paul said that Christ is magnified "by death" and that to "depart and be with Christ . . . is far better" (Phil. 1:20, 23). As the apostle meditated upon the restraining influence of the flesh, all his hardships, trials, sorrows, and disappointments, he realized that death would be a positive gain since it would be the door ushering him into the presence of his Lord, where tears and affliction are unknown. Yet Paul knew, as we must learn, that death is only gain as we live in Christ. Our passion must be to know Christ, our longing to serve Him, our ambition to follow Him, and our joy to witness for Him, if we would experience the blessed advantage death brings. If when He calls me, I shall go to Him with gladness, then I must have Him and His will as the center and circumference of my life.

Can you say with Paul, "For to me, to live is Christ, and to die is gain" (Phil. 1:21)?

April 21

"I will not remember your sins." ISAIAH 43:25

Is it not wonderful to realize that the God who freely offers to forgive is the One so constantly sinned against? Turn to Isaiah 43 and read the last phrase of verse 24, "You have wearied Me with your iniquities." Then continue to verse 25, "I, even I, am He who blots out your transgressions for My own sake; and I will not remember your sins." These two verses offer a most blessed glimpse of God. The One despised, outraged, scorned, and deserted for idols was the very One Israel was urged to return to. God further declares His willingness to forgive for His own name's sake. Such a statement implies that because of His loving, righteous character, expressed in many of His names, His actions must correspond to His attributes.

Isaiah 44:22 records these words of the Lord: "I have blotted out, like a thick cloud, your transgressions,/And like a cloud, your sins. . . . I have redeemed you." The basis of divine forgiveness is the redemption work of the Cross. Because righteousness and truth kissed each other at Calvary, a vindicated justice is now able to blot out our confessed sins. By His death, Christ purchased redemption for all persons. Few in comparison, however, have appropriated by faith such a redemption. Although Christ paid their ransom, they are not healed, restored, or forgiven. Are we among the redeemed who know that God will remember sin against us no more?

The familiar proverb has it: "To err is human, to forgive, divine." When our divine Father forgives, He forgets. He said, "Their sin I will remember no more" (Jer. 31:34) Imagine that! We may be sincere in our forgiveness of others, but we find it difficult to forget. The nail may be drawn from the hand, but the scar remains. God, however, removes both the nail and the scar. If God has forgotten our past, should we not endeavor to do the same? What a comfort are the words of Daniel 9:9: "To the Lord our God belong mercy and forgiveness, though we have rebelled against Him"!

Praise God that He forgets your sin but remembers to care for you.

April 22

"Of all He has given Me I should lose nothing, but should raise it up at the last day." JOHN 6:39

Several truths describing the relationship of Jesus to the Father are found in this verse. We were given to Christ by the Father. His will is that, surrendered to His Son, we should never be lost. We are Christ's own, and our security rests with Him who will raise us up on the last day. How impressive are the words *lose nothing*! We belong to Christ, and He will see to it that not one of His chosen ones will perish. God wills our security, and Christ provides it. Thus, when Satan would cast doubt upon our eternal salvation, we remind him that Christ has declared He will lose nothing. All His people will be raised up to meet Him at the day of His appearing.

Later on, Christ elaborated on our security by declaring, "I give them eternal life, and they shall never perish; neither shall anyone snatch them out of My hand. . . . No one is able to snatch them out of My Father's hand" (John 10:28–29). We might call this the double grip: "My hand. . . . My Father's hand." Thus, we are doubly secure, for the Father and the Son are one in their purpose to preserve their own. We must also note that no condition is attached to this charter of security. Christ did not say that we can only be eternally safe if we strive to keep ourselves in His hands. "Whatever God does, it shall be forever" (Eccl. 3:14). Once union with Christ has been established, it can never be severed. Communion may be ruptured, but union is eternal. If we could receive life from Christ today and lose it tomorrow, then how could it be eternal? Paul, the apostle of assurance, had no doubt as to his standing in grace. He wrote, "I know whom I have believed and am persuaded that He is able to keep what I have committed to Him until that Day" (2 Tim. 1:12). Like the rest of us, Paul had no doubt as far as his security was concerned. But he clearly taught it is the work of the Holy Spirit to translate position into practice. In his positive declaration we have the double commitment and the double security. Rest confident, today and every day, that your salvation is secure.

"Salvation is of the Jews." JOHN 4:22

The Jew is the world's greatest benefactor. Let us think for a moment what we owe the Jew. The literature of the ancient Hebrews triumphs over all creeds, schools, and sects. Jewish hands wrote the priceless, incomparable original Scriptures. Today we worship in the sacred songs of David.

Christianity bows to and follows the divine teachings of Christ, who came as a Son of Abraham. Jewish blood flowed in His sacred veins: "You, being a Jew" (John 4:9). He was born and died as the king of the Jews for the salvation of both Jews and Gentiles. This salvation, in a very real way, is of the Jews. Then, let it not be forgotten, the promise is that the Jews, strange and solitary as they may seem to be with a drama of a long and mournful history, will yet become the media of salvation to a troubled world. Prophecy depicts them as the evangelists of the coming kingdom.

The exalted position of the Jew was emphasized by Paul, when he declared that the gospel is the power of God unto salvation, "for the Jew first" (Rom. 1:16). Often when quoting this great text of Scripture, we end with "believes." But the apostle did not stop there because he knew that the last part of the idea is just as authoritative as the rest of it. "For the Jew first and also for the Greek [the Gentile]."

Maligned and rejected though he is, the Jew has yet the first claim upon the prayers and efforts of Christians. Our responsibility is to deal with the Jew from God's standpoint of superiority; the divine blessing is always ours when we place the Jew first, knowing God still seeks his faithful obedience. The Abrahamic covenant has never been revoked: "I will bless those who bless you, and I will curse him who curses you; and in you all the families of the earth shall be blessed" (Gen. 12:3).

April 24

"He who rules over men must be just,/
Ruling in the fear of God." 2 SAMUEL 23:3–4

Scripture has much to say about the integrity and responsibility of kings and rulers. The above quotation is among the last words of David, whose reign as a king had been an honored one. Blemishes there were; but for the most part, David's life and rule were Godward, earning for him the commendation, "a man after God's own heart." As he expresses himself for the last time, Israel's illustrious king leaves a promise for those who follow him, that they too will rule as unto God:

> "And he shall be like the light of the morning
> when the sun rises,
> A morning without clouds,
> Like the tender grass springing out of the earth,
> By clear shining after rain" (2 Sam. 23:4).

Think of what civilization would have been spared if Adolf Hitler had been a God-fearing man! In contrast, when Jesus returns to earth and exercises His universal rule, peace will cover the earth as the waters cover the sea.

The psalmist, in no uncertain terms, describes the unworthy rule of those who have authority and power: "The kings of the earth set themselves,/And the rulers take counsel together,/Against the LORD and against His Anointed" (Ps. 2:2). Here we find deliberate and planned hostility to God and to Christ on the part of earthly rulers, unified in their determination to abolish all religious worship. Prophetically, before Christ returns to earth as the King of kings, earth rulers are to be joined into a godless confederacy with their every action leveled against Christ. But as He appears on earth, He will destroy the scepter of rulers, taking unto Himself His power as the prince of the kings of earth. He will fashion the kingdoms the earthly rulers failed to govern in a Godlike way into His own world kingdom and rule as the perfect world emperor. What a magnificent and glorious era the millennium will be!

April 25

"The captive exile hastens, that he may be loosed,/ That he should not die in the pit." ISAIAH 51:14

The pit as a prison was prevalent in the East. Prisoners were let down through a hole into a narrow pit, where they were confined at the pleasure of tyrannical masters. Many years ago when visiting St. Andrews, Scotland, I shuddered on viewing the Bottle Dungeon, in which saintly Samuel Rutherford had been forced to suffer.

The prophet Isaiah makes it clear that no captive wants to die in such a prison but hastens to be loosed "that his bread should not fail." How multitudes suffered in European camps in past years! How pitiable and painful was their condition! But both psalmist and prophet proclaim relief for the singing prisoner: "But I am the LORD your God" (Is. 51:15). He whose eye is on the sparrow is not deaf to the cry of the prisoner.

Our Lord said, "I was in prison and you came to Me" (Matt. 25:36). His was a sorrowful prison experience. Pilate sought to release the innocent prisoner, but the chief priests and elders insisted on the release of Barabbas, the guilty, notorious prisoner. In His Olivet discourse, Jesus affirmed that in caring for the needy in and out of prison, we are actually caring for Him: "You did it to Me" (Matt. 25:40). Do we remember to pray for those prison chaplains and workers who visit prisoners in the name and spirit of Christ? Let us never cease to pray that God will use His Word for the transformation of criminals.

Jesus went from His prison to Calvary, to die for all bound with the fetters of sin. The first to receive Him as the crucified Savior was the dying thief, who recognized the sinless One, dying for the sins of others.

Look at Psalm 107:13–14 for a picture of release:

They cried out to the LORD in their trouble,
And He saved them out of their distresses.
He brought them out of darkness and the shadow of death,
And broke their chains in pieces.

What an exhilarating feeling—to be released from bondage!

April 26

"When I send against them the terrible arrows of famine." EZEKIEL 5:16

Ezekiel confirms that famine is one of the divine judgments for sin. For numbering the people, David was given a choice of punishment for his sin: "Three things [famine, flight, pestilence]; choose one of them" (2 Sam. 24:12). The aspect of famine, however, that Ezekiel mentions is its terrible arrows. What are these arrows that God calls "terrible"? They are the gnawing of the bowels resulting from unappeased hunger, the wasting of the body, loss of sleep, the torture of the mind in its anguish over others similarly situated, and extreme inertia—all part of a living death. What a quiver of arrows! May they never pierce your body or mine. It is far better to be slain than starve; to die suddenly than gradually, as the famine-stricken do. As long as we have a loaf of bread, let us never deny a beggar a slice. Hungry people get desperate, but by feeding them, we may save them from a criminal act, which is often one of the terrible arrows of famine. God's ability to care for His own in days of famine is promised often in Scripture. Crops may fail, but God's storehouse is never empty.

Amos affirms that there is a worse famine than scarcity of food to eat: "I will send a famine . . . of hearing the words of the LORD" (Amos 8:11). Surely these are days when there is a famine in our land, not of bread but of hearing the Word of the Lord! Multitudes of Bibles are in circulation and churches are in abundance; yet there is widespread spiritual famine. We have pleasing, inoffensive sermonettes, book reviews, political and topical talks, religious homilies, but a famine of scriptural expositions. People receive stones instead of bread. What a nation of spiritually starved souls ours is! We have an abundance of material goods but an empty spiritual cupboard. Multitudes gather on the Lord's Day in dire need of the Bread of Life but leave His house empty-handed. Where a spiritual feast is provided, there is never any lack of guests who hunger and thirst after righteousness that they may be filled.

Show your appreciation to the Lord by setting aside a daily time to pray for the Holy Spirit's guidance and to feast on His Word.

April 27

"He Himself took our infirmities and bore our sicknesses." MATTHEW 8:17

Much misunderstanding has arisen over the identification of Christ with our human life. Advocates of what is known as "divine healing" (all healing, with or without medical aid, is divine; physicians may prescribe, but only God can heal) affirm that there is healing as well as salvation in the Atonement. At Calvary, Christ bore our sicknesses as well as our sins, they claim; therefore, we have no right to be ill. If sickness does overtake us, then we can claim healing in virtue of the Cross. But such an interpretation is not scriptural.

What Christ bore on the tree was our sins; He healed us from the destruction of iniquity. Thus, interpreted in the light of the context, taking our infirmities and bearing our sicknesses indicate Christ's perfect sympathy with all who suffer. The sight of the fever-stricken mother and of the demon-possessed souls brought to Him drew forth the compassion of His loving, sympathetic heart. Deeper still, in taking upon Himself the likeness of our flesh, He knew something of our weariness, hunger, thirst, and pain. But there is no record of His suffering from sickness of any kind. More or less, sickness is a fruit of sin. Had there been no sin, there would have been no sickness. Jesus was without sin. As a true representative, He carried many of our sorrows and the pain tearing our hearts. He is ever touched with the feeling of our infirmities (see Heb. 4:15). We find Jesus saying: "I was sick and you visited Me" (Matt. 25:36). But such a statement does not imply that Jesus was on a sickbed during His ministry and that His disciples sat by His bed to comfort Him. As the context proves, He was identifying Himself with His afflicted brethren: "Inasmuch as you did it to one of the least of these My brethren, you did it to Me" (Matt. 25:40). Are we not enjoined to weep with those who weep?

Whenever we shed a sympathetic tear over another's sorrow in Christ's name, we are actually ministering to Him, because He and His are one.

April 28

Behold, children are a heritage from the LORD. . . . Like arrows in the hand of a warrior. PSALM 127:3–4

Jacob replied to Esau's question regarding the young people accompanying him by saying, "[They are] the children whom God has graciously given your servant" (Gen. 33:5). Bible-loving parents agree with both Jacob and the psalmist that children are gifts from heaven. But they are as arrows in the hand of a mighty man, bringing happiness to those whose quiver is full of them, only as they live for the Lord. While children may come from God, the author of all life, the tragedy is that sometimes they grow up utterly godless in life. Only those who are reborn as children of God are a happy heritage. If you were born of God-fearing parents, who prayed for you before you saw the light of day, are you living in a way to please God who gave you life and gladden those who nurtured that life through early years? Children given of the Lord should be godly.

Isaiah could exclaim: "Here am I and the children whom the LORD has given me!" (Is. 8:18). What unbounded joy will be the portion of completed circles as they gather around the Lord! To realize that no member is missing will result in eternal praise. The sorrow is that so many family circles are presently broken. Parents are saved, children unsaved. The old-fashioned religion of mother and father is not good enough for worldly sons and daughters, who feel they have outgrown the faith of their parents. If you are a parent heartbroken over the lack of spiritual desires on the part of your offspring, remember that God hears and answers prayer. Plead on for that boy or girl still out of the fold. Sooner than you expect, the wayward one may turn to the Lord and give you, thereby, a family circle complete in grace. There is, of course, the larger application of Isaiah's statement, for at the Rapture when all Christ's redeemed ones are with Him, He will be able to say to His Father: "Here am I and the children whom God has given me" (Heb. 2:13).

Have you remembered to thank God for your children and to intercede for their spiritual growth?

April 29

You are the helper of the fatherless. PSALM 10:14

Approximately forty references to the fatherless appear in Scripture. The designation of God as the helper of the fatherless is comforting to all who have had an earthly father taken from them and now face life without the care, protection, and counsel they came to depend upon. If this is your experience, the One who promised to help the fatherless can cover all the personal needs of a child bereaved of its father. Also as the Judge, He stands ready to defend the fatherless against those who would take unjust advantage of them.

What must be made clear, however, is that God can only be expected to function toward the fatherless as they, themselves, commit their ways to Him. The Father in heaven must be loved and obeyed if those without earthly fathers expect His provision and protection. Only if we seek His grace and guidance through His beloved Son can any of us, fatherless or otherwise, lay claim to the sympathy and sustenance of Him who is the God and Father of our Lord Jesus Christ.

David assures us that God is indeed "a father of the fatherless" (Ps. 68:5). Jesus reminds us, in Luke 12:6–7, that the death of a lonely sparrow is witnessed by our heavenly Father in whom "the fatherless finds mercy" (Hos. 14:3). Responsible as He is, as the source of all life for all fathers, surely He is able to care for those who are without father or mother!

What is the function of a true father? Do not his children rejoice in his companionship? What a refuge his love and companionship are! When others misunderstand, an earthly father understands! When others grieve us, he throws his strong arms around us and soothes our heart. In our perplexities he is at hand to guide us. How able and ready he is to straighten out our problems! When a father dies, light fades, and life becomes vacant. But God, our Father in heaven, stands ready to fill the vacant place and to be all and more than the one we have loved. Communicate with your eternal, heavenly Father—adore Him.

April 30

They shall still bear fruit in old age;/ They shall be fresh and flourishing.

PSALM 92:14

Benjamin Disraeli in his *Coningsbey* (1868) moaned, "Youth is a blunder; manhood a struggle; old age a regret." But history and experience verify the psalmist's declaration that old age can be fruitful and flourishing, not a regret.

"Grow old along with me!/The best is yet to be," said Robert Browning. John Wesley was past eighty when he traveled England as a highway evangelist with a smile on his face, saying: "Tis time to live if I grow old." Moses also was eighty when God called him from Midian to free the Israelites and establish them as a nation. At sixty-three, Cicero wrote his *Cato* and reminded his readers that Plato died at his desk at eighty-one. Michelangelo was active in his eighties. Titian, at sixty-five, painted two masterpieces. At eighty Victor Hugo astonished the world with *Torquemada.* When just seventy, a bankrupt Handel wrote the glorious *Messiah* which so moved the audience when it was first presented and continues to move us today. If advancing toward the eventide of life in spiritual fulfillment is yours, then heed the verse for today. Is your old age charming because of your saintliness of character (see Ps. 71:18)?

Job could write of coming to the grave at a full age: "As a sheaf of grain ripens in its season" (Job 5:26). Truly there is nothing to compare to autumn glory. The ripened golden shower is the evidence of God's promise to send seedtime and harvest, while the earth lasts. Life, too, has its autumn glory. Years that have been lived for Christ and His cause bring a harvest of grace, resignation, and contentment. The faith of the aged is crowned in virtue and assurance. Long tuition in the school of experience means a disciplined life, and the soul flowers into Christlikeness. If you are on the sunset slope, is Indian Summer yours, with its harvest of Christian testimony and godliness of life? If a full age is yours, let God grant you a beautiful autumn glory!

Thank the Father for the years He has given you; pledge Him your remaining years as opportunities of praise and service.

May 1

"Since that time the kingdom of God has been preached, and everyone is pressing into it."

LUKE 16:16

A store where I often shop has a complete glass front, so that from the outside you can see the varied merchandise displayed. The door of the store has printed on it in distinctive letters the word *push*. The door does not open of itself, nor is there anyone standing by to open it for you. You can stand outside all day, but if you are to reach the inside and purchase what you need, there is only one necessary action you must take—*push*! Then when you are ready to leave the store, you cannot leave unless you obey the injunction on the door—*pull*! Push and pull! Is not this double requirement implied in the Master's statement about everyone pressing into the kingdom? What are the pushing and pulling but *pressing*, or earnestness in our efforts to possess the riches of the kingdom. Just as there is no easy road to learning, so on the doors of scriptural knowledge there is the commanding term *push*!

We should not have to wait to be asked to enter or wait for someone to take us by the hand to lead us into the kingdom. We must push the door open for ourselves. We cannot be crowned unless we strive lawfully, according to rules. Such a decisive, personal action is described in many ways. Our salvation must be worked out "with fear and trembling" (Phil. 2:12). If we are to wrestle victoriously against Satan and his power, we must put on "the whole armor of God." It is only then that we can fight "the good fight" (2 Tim. 4:7). The weapons in such a conflict are not "according to the flesh" (2 Cor. 10:3), but mighty in God for pulling down strongholds. It is only then that we can "wage the good warfare" (1 Tim. 1:18). The devil and his forces must be "resisted to bloodshed" (Heb. 12:4). James 4:7 states: "Resist the devil and he will flee from you." How forcefully this pressing into the kingdom is illustrated for us in the great multitude of joyful saints before the throne! They are there because they "washed their robes and made them white in the blood of the Lamb" and were thus able to emerge from "great tribulation" into God's temple (Rev. 7:14).

May 2

The love of money is a root of all kinds of evil. 1 TIMOTHY 6:10

Scripture affords at least three forceful illustrations of this illicit love. By the Spirit of the Lord, Micah condemned those in Zion who perverted all equity: "Her heads judge for a bribe, her priests teach for pay, and her prophets divine for money" (Mic. 3:11). Micah anticipated the New Testament that speaks of those who, coveting money, have strayed from the faith. Micah asked: How can the Lord work among us, if we judge for reward, teach for hire, and preach for money? If we are in the ministry as pastor, teacher, or evangelist, our solemn responsibility is to minister the Word to all without due concern of the cash value of opportunities. We know that as the laborer is worthy of his hire, the Lord will provide all necessary remuneration. He is ever a good paymaster.

The second warning against love of money is associated with Judas who, as treasurer of the small band of disciples, kept what they had accumulated. He was chosen by Jesus to handle money matters because of his administrative ability, but his gift was his downfall. Disgusted over Mary's expression of love, Judas could only think of her anointing gift in terms of money. His greed reached its tragic climax when he betrayed his Lord for thirty pieces of silver.

Simon, the sorcerer, further illustrates an illicit love of money. Accustomed to receiving payment for his sorceries, he evidently thought Peter was a dealer in the peculiar power of the Holy Spirit. He wanted to buy the gift. But whatever faults Peter might have had, a craving for money was not one of them. Thus Simon could not buy him or what he had. The incident of the silver piece in the mouth of the fish had taught Peter earlier that his Master could supply all the money he needed. The important lesson is that there are treasures money cannot buy. A pauper can enjoy as much of the sun as a prince. Thus, is it with salvation and the Spirit's power.

Each and all must exercise faith, for nothing is sold over heaven's counter.

May 3

"LORD, make me to know . . .
what is the measure of my days./
You have made my days as handbreadths,/
And my age is as nothing before You." PSALM 39:4–5

A handbreadth was a measure of about four inches, or the width of the four fingers, and is thus used to signify the brevity of life. The measure of our days, the psalmist declares, is as nothing in God's sight. Man at his best state is altogether vanity. David reminds us that it is not the length of our life that counts but its quality. One may live to an old age and yet have lived in vain. Others may have gathered fame, position, and wealth with the passing years and yet, at their best state, have nothing at all as far as heaven's values are concerned. What we pack into our years for Christ and His cause makes life precious in God's sight. We live in vain if we live merely to live. The humanist speaks of "really living," but we never really begin to live until we die.

Moses is a notable example of living a long life for God and for God only. Addressing Israel, he said, "I am one hundred and twenty years old today. I can no longer go out and come in" (Deut. 31:2). What a physical marvel Moses was! When he came to die, his eye was not dim nor his natural force abated. When he reached his last birthday, he must have said, "Well, I feel as fresh as ever." What a young, old man he must have been! After such a long pilgrimage, Moses witnesses to the fact that no enemy is able to outwit God, no emergency finds Him unprepared, no urgent call goes unanswered by Him, and no necessity fails to elicit sufficient help from the Father's heart. Year after year in the palace, in the desert, and in the wilderness, Moses had seen his fears disappear. He had seen darkness turned to light and his prayers answered. Now the everlasting arms, which had borne Moses up, were about him to carry him into heaven itself. May his testimony be ours if God spares us to become old and gray-headed! Then life will be valuable before Him.

Although life seems short, every day is an occasion to discover a new blessing that the Creator has for you.

May 4

"You are My friends. . . .
I have called you friends." JOHN 15:14–15

Do you have enough friends? The matchless treasure of friendship is seen in its highest and best estate in Christ, who not only taught it but practiced it in His noble and winning life. Lord Byron wrote, "Friendship is Love without his wings." Such is the character of the friendship Christ offers His own.

Scripture is our most valuable handbook when it comes to the subject of friendship, because it depicts the lives of those who experienced it. The Bible also lists the various attributes of those described as friends. Because of his close relationship with God and his faithfulness, Abraham earned the title, "the friend of God" (see 2 Chron. 20:7). As for Moses, such was his intimate fellowship with God that God could speak to Moses "face to face, as a man speaks to his friend" (Ex. 33:11). Our Lord who spoke of Lazarus as our friend, assured all His disciples that they were His friends—friends of the bridegroom. Such divine friendship is so unparalleled that the human mind cannot fully explore it. How spontaneous it is! The Lord also takes the initiative in such love, since there is little in us to join us with Him in unbreakable bonds. Is He not gracious even in being the friend of publicans and sinners?

While in the days of His flesh, He gave His own evidences of friendship. He triumphantly ratified it when He died for our sin: "Greater love has no one than this, than to lay down one's life for his friends" (John 15:13). The greatness of His sacrificial love, however, is seen in that Jesus died for His enemies as well as His friends. Thus His administrated friendship comes to us signed and sealed with His own blood and is carried to our hearts by His pierced hands. How we praise Him as the friend who loves us at all times! He is the One who sticks closer than a brother and whose wounds are ever faithful. Says the Apocrypha: "A faithful friend is the medicine of life." Truly He is the friend who never changes, whose love will never die.

May 5

"Bind this line of scarlet cord in the window." JOSHUA 2:18

What lesson can you discover in this strange verse? See in it something of what Christ was to accomplish when He came to lay down His life for our salvation. The window as the way of escape for the two spies befriended by Rahab is one of the symbolic forecasts of Christ. After hiding the spies at the peril of her life, Rahab let them down by a cord through the window. The scarlet thread from the same window was to be a true token that when Joshua invaded Jericho, Rahab and all her relatives would be delivered from death. What an appropriate illustration this provision suggests of an alarmed and repentant sinner, saved by grace through promise, relying on the scarlet sign because of the declared Word! Calvary is the scarlet thread in God's window assuring us of safety when His righteous judgments are abroad. John Milton wrote, "At my window bid good morrow." But there can only be a good morrow for each of us if the scarlet thread hangs from the window of our hearts. If God does not see His Son's blood upon us, then He cannot pass over us.

One provision the spies made was that no soldier would attack Rahab's house when Jericho was under siege, assuring her that no relative of hers would be taken captive and killed if he or she were under the token of the scarlet thread. What zest must have been Rahab's as she gathered her loved ones and servants, bringing them to the house of safety! All were saved from death for Rahab's sake. When Joshua finally entered and conquered Jericho, light broke through Rahab's window for all who were behind it, with its scarlet token dangling.

We are extremely happy if all the members of our family are in the house of safety, free from condemnation because they are in Christ Jesus. Can it be that you still have a dear, unsaved loved one? Then by divine grace, may you be enabled to bring that one behind the shelter of Calvary's scarlet thread before it is too late.

Intercede today for loved ones who haven't turned over their lives to Christ the victorious.

May 6

My God shall supply all your need according to His riches in glory by Christ Jesus. PHILIPPIANS 4:19

Paul wrote the epistle to the Philippians while he was in a prison. Exposed to insult and assault, the members of the Philippian church were encouraged by his words to them. Hidden with Christ in God, they were free from the tyranny of time and circumstances.

The epistle to the Philippians contains doctrinal passages revealing truth of the first magnitude and vital precepts for Christian life and conduct. Most noticeable of all is the spirit breathing through the entire epistle. The joy of a heart that knew the secret of the Lord is indicated in the ringing and victorious words cited above, which close the epistle. Nobly beginning with the words *my God,* Paul thought of God as his own personal possession from the hour of his dramatic and dynamic encounter with Him on the road to Damascus. Amid all his experiences, Paul proved that his God was able to supply all his needs—not his own desires and wishes, but imperative needs—according to His riches in glory.

The grace and goodness of the Lord are the storehouse of every blessing we require. What a sublime standard is embodied in the phrase, "His riches in glory"! How happy are the souls who have such a treasure! What gracious help, unfailing wisdom, strength of character, peace of heart, and all immortal hopes await those willing to appropriate heaven's wealth! The core and center of the verse is the promise to supply *all* our need. Our weaknesses, our longings, our continuous and recurring needs have a divine remedy. God's affluence brings a definite deliverance. Following the apostle's counsel we arrive at his goal; we find a sweet and heavenly peace fortifying our inmost being—a peace destroying all depression and worry.

Let us relax in a peace that enables us to be anxious for nothing.

May 7

"Lo, I am with you always, even to the end of the age." MATTHEW 28:20

When it was time for Jesus to leave the earth and ascend to heaven, He gave His disciples one of the most precious promises to leave His sacred lips. This was Christ's promise of His perpetual presence, found only in Matthew in the last verse of his gospel. The pronoun *I* emphasizes the identity of the Promiser Himself. He is none other than the great *I am* of Exodus 3:14 and Revelation 1:18. It is wonderful to realize that the almighty Creator condescends to become our abiding Companion, the everlasting Father, our ever-present Friend! "He Himself has said; *'I will never leave you nor forsake you'* " (Heb. 13:5). A comforting aspect of this royal promise is that such a privileged, never-failing companionship is ours to the end of the gospel age. "The LORD your God is with you" (Deut 20:1), even though He is currently invisible.

The term *always* is also suggestive of the Companion who is never absent from the presence of His redeemed children. And because He is always with us, He hears our prayers *always* (see Job 22:27; Acts 10:31); we rejoice in Him *always* (see Phil. 4:4); we keep His commands and fear Him *always* (see Deut. 11:1; 14:23). In our pilgrimage on earth we know not what awaits us but because our divine Companion is the omniscient Lord, knowing the end from the beginning, no sudden circumstance or event takes Him by surprise. As need arises He is always at hand to meet it.

Shakespeare in *Henry IV* has this interchange:

> CHIEF JUSTICE: God send the prince a better companion!
> FALSTAFF: God send the companion a better prince!

As princes, "Whom You shall make princes in all the earth" (Ps. 45:16), it is impossible to have a better Companion than the Prince of glory. May God grant that we may become better princes of such a perfect Companion!

May 8

"I will send Him to you." JOHN 16:7
"I will build My church." MATTHEW 16:18
"I will come again." JOHN 14:3

In His teaching our Lord frequently used the words *I will.* This is a very positive declaration of His authority and power to fulfill His holy will and purpose. Let us look at three of these statements that present a wonderful trinity of truth.

I will send Him to you. This promise is placed first because the coming of the Holy Spirit was a prerequisite to the fulfillment of the next promise of the building of the church. At Pentecost, the Spirit came as promised by the Father and by His Son, who, as soon as He was glorified, sent His precious gift with us to dwell. We live in the age of the Spirit.

I will build my church. Such a church bearing the name of God and of Christ is composed solely of those who have experienced the saving grace and power of the Lord. It is described as Christ's body, into which we are baptized by the Spirit (see 1 Cor. 3:1–11), and as "the habitation of God in the Spirit" (Eph. 2:22). A person may be a member of a visible church, yet not be a member of the church which is of Christ's building and is His body.

I will come again. The promise of building His church was initial and progressive. Christ's return for his church will terminate her sojourn on earth as His channel of expression through the Holy Spirit. As the first promise already has been fulfilled and the second promise is being daily fulfilled, so the third one ultimately will be fulfilled by Christ, who as the Truth cannot lie.

Are we redeemed by the precious blood of Christ, living and laboring in the light of His glorious appearing, possible at any moment?

May 9

I trust in Your word. PSALM 119:42

People who say one thing and do another cannot be trusted. Those whose word cannot be relied on are characterized by comments such as, "He's not a man of his word," "He's a double-dealer, promising one thing and doing another," "He never says what he means," or "His deeds contradict his promises."

Shakespeare in *Hamlet* said: "Suit the action to the word,/the word to the action." One can be trusted only when words and actions harmonize. With God, His word is His bond. He spoke, and it was done. "He who calls you is faithful, who also will do it" (1 Thess. 5:24). Emerson would have us remember: "Words and deeds are quite indifferent modes of energy. Words are also actions, and actions are a kind of words."

David could trust what God had declared because he knew that what God had promised, He was able to fulfill. God was not a man that He should lie. Over and over again the psalmist had proved that not one word of God would fail to be realized; that God was not only in His words most wonderful but also most sure in all His ways; that any promise of His was His bond, and He would keep it.

Believing, then, that God is as good as His word, we fear no foe. We dread no trial because we know that His word will be fulfilled in caring for us, as He said He would. Confidence is ours that promises are suited to our need. As we quote them and rely on them, we will experience their fulfillment.

If we cannot take God's word and depend upon it, what can we trust? Our comfort and encouragement are that His promises have been tried by multitudes of saints down the ages and proved faithful. Trusting in God's unalterable Word brought them, as it brings us, peace of mind, joy of soul, and all that is necessary wherever need arises. Our responsibility is, finally, to act on His mighty promises. "Whatever God has said to you, do it" (Gen. 31:16).

May 10

"A son of Jonathan who is lame in his feet."

2 SAMUEL 9:3

The permanent crippled condition of Mephibosheth commenced when he was five years old and fell from the arms of his nurse. Receiving news of the deaths of Saul and Jonathan, "she made haste to flee, . . . he fell and became lame" (2 Sam. 4:4).

The chapter revolving around David and Mephibosheth is rich in the virtues of loyalty, kindness, and love. What a struggle Jonathan's lame son must have had for existence! The famed biologist, Herbert Spencer, gives words of "this survival of the fittest." But God sometimes plans that the forgotten shall survive; that when the physically strong pass away, no one remains but a Mephibosheth.

The day came when David reigned undisputed over Israel. Remembering his covenant with Jonathan, he inquired about Saul's family. He discovered that the crippled son of his dear friend was alive, and he arranged for him to eat at the royal table (see 2 Sam. 9:1–7). David took no notice of the boy's distorted legs and feet, but generously received this handicapped remaining member of Saul's family and heaped upon him lovingkindness for his father's sake.

Years before, when David and Jonathan were close friends, David had pledged that he would care for his friend's family if he were slain in battle. True to his vow, David blessed Mephibosheth, giving him all the possessions that had been his father's.

Throughout the narrative, we have the refrain *for Jonathan's sake*. Is not this kindness for another's sake a parable of the love of God, who blesses and enriches us for the sake of His only begotten Son? Sinners are spiritually lame, poor, and forgotten, but One greater than David, through His marvelous grace, restores a lost inheritance and takes the helpless into a rich fellowship with Himself. David was kind to Mephibosheth not only because of his lameness but also for the sake of his father. Does not God deal with those crippled by sin? Through His matchless grace, He restores them for the sake of His Son. "Be kind to one another, tenderhearted, forgiving one another, just as God in Christ also forgave you" (Eph. 4:32).

Accept the Father's lovingkindness, and be sensitive to others in their needs.

May 11

I am not ashamed
of the gospel of Christ. ROMANS 1:16

An eminent personality in the New Testament is Paul, who never considered himself inferior in any way to the chiefest of the apostles (see 2 Cor. 11:5; 12:11). When God wants a person for a specific work, He knows where that person can be found. Thus when He desired to fashion the teachers of the gospel of Christ into a systematic form, He chose Saul of Tarsus. Saul graduated from the university of Jerusalem, where he was brought up at the feet of Gamaliel. Versed in rabbinical lore and in Greek philosophy, Paul is conspicuous as the most skillful dialectician of his time. The wonderful letters he wrote have survived the test of time throughout the centuries and point to Christ as the Way, the Truth and the Life. In his ringing avowal as a servant of Christ, Paul declared that he was not ashamed to preach His gospel.

Moffatt's translation of the opening phrase of the apostle's affirmation reads: "I am proud of the Gospel." He was never ashamed of it. Much that he had been proud of before he met Christ, he came to treat as rubbish. His boasting was not in himself. Dealing with his birth, zeal, culture, and Roman citizenship, Paul treated them as something to be cast out (see Phil. 3:4–8). To know or gain Christ and be found in Him was not only his heavenly privilege but also his unfailing river of joy.

When I survey the wondrous cross
  On which the Prince of Glory died,
My richest gain I count but loss,
  And pour contempt on all my pride.

Forbid it, Lord, that I should boast,
  Save in the death of Christ, my God;
All the vain things that charm me most,
  I sacrifice them to his blood.

Do your friends know that you are proud of the gospel of Christ?

May 12

[Jairus] had an only daughter about twelve years of age, and she was dying. LUKE 8:42

Parents can imagine how Jairus and his wife knelt beside a bed in the Jewish quarter of Capernaum, hoping against hope that their child would not die. This dying girl was their *only* daughter. Often one thing or one person stands at the center of a gospel scene or story. The shepherd lost *one* sheep; the woman lost *one* coin; the widow of Nain had *one* son; and in the grief-stricken home of Jairus was *one* daughter. While it is thrilling to know that around the throne of God in heaven thousands of children stand, we magnify Him for His personal love and grace. "The Son of God, who loved me" (Gal. 2:20).

When his precious, solitary child was at the point of death, at the break of day Jairus sought Jesus and in all humility implored Him to spare his daughter. Love for his only child forced his plea, but many impulses lead us to kneel before the compassionate Jesus for help. Reaching the house of sorrow, Jesus emptied it of those who had rudely invaded it, especially the professional mourners who were paid to weep in death chambers. Having perfect sincerity, Jesus hates all deception. As the Lord of life, Jesus raised the young daughter from the dead

An aspect of the miracle that we must not overlook is the unfailing thoughtfulness of Jesus as He commented that the resurrected child should be given food. Although Jairus and his wife dearly loved their daughter, in their joy they had not noticed that she was hungry. An abiding lesson of this miracle is that all spiritual awakening is the work of the Holy Spirit. Because the young are the most easily awakened, we should strive to bring them to Jesus before the grave clothes bind them.

Ask the Holy Spirit to make you sensitive to a young person's needs.

Though He giveth or He taketh,
  God His children ne'er forsaketh;
His the loving purpose solely
  To preserve them pure and holy.

May 13

Now to appear. . . . He has appeared. . . . He will appear a second time. HEBREWS 9:24, 26, 28

Among the many wonderful promises the Lord Jesus gave directly and indirectly through His apostles, we have the three related ones in the above verses. They form a divine trinity of truth, namely, incarnation, intercession, and imminent return. What a marvelous, unbreakable, threefold cord!

Past appearing, "He has appeared to put away sin" (Heb. 9:26). Such an appearing is permanent, representing salvation from the penalty of sin. *To put away* actually means to "set aside," or "to displace," and all sin, outward and inward, is displaced as a sinner receives the Savior. Jesus made such a cancellation of sin possible through the sacrifice of Himself. Because of all He accomplished the first time He appeared, our sin is cast behind His back, cast into the depths of the sea, removed as far as the east is from the west, and forgiven and forgotten.

Present appearing, "Now to appear" (Heb. 9:24). This appearing is present and progressive and represents salvation from the power and tyranny of sin, as Christ pleads the merits of His perfect sacrifice. "He ever lives to make intercession" (Heb. 7:25) for those He is able to save to the uttermost. So, although I have *been* saved, I am *being* saved. How comforting and assuring it is to know that Jesus constantly appears before God as our advocate, or intercessor, pleading His efficacious blood on our behalf that we might not sin! If we do sin, His spirit can restore a broken fellowship.

Prospective appearing, "He will appear a second time" (Heb. 9:28). The epistle to the Hebrews is heavy with the truth of our Lord's return for His true church. This aspect of His appearing is related to our salvation from the entire presence of sin within and around. This is the advent when the church will be saved to sin no more. If she lives and labors in the light of His glorious appearing, a special reward will be hers for keeping the advent hope alive in her heart. Presently, her earnest plea is, "Even so, come, Lord Jesus" (Rev. 22:20).

May 14

"He came to himself. . . .
and came to his father." LUKE 15:17, 20

In this familiar chapter of Luke we have a group of three parables: the lost sheep, the lost silver, and the lost son. In one sense there is only a single story in three sections, for Luke says of Jesus: "He spoke this parable to them" (15:3). And in it the charge against the Lord, "This man receives sinners," is answered in the three illustrations of God's interest in saving the lost. More than likely the parable of the prodigal son has been used more than any other part of Scripture to restore prodigals the world over to fellowship with God. We will concentrate on it here.

He came to himself. These words of our Lord imply that the profligate son was repentant of his sin against heaven and also against his forsaken home of love. He was at a dead end. Penniless, homeless, reduced to feeding swine, almost dying from hunger, and ready to eat swine's food, he remembered his old home in which there was bread enough and to spare. Acutely conscious of his dilapidated condition, he decided, "I will arise and go to my father" (15:18).

He came to his father. Repentance led to return. When those who are out in the far country of sin become conscious that they are hell-deserving sinners, they are likely to return to the heavenly Father, who is plenteous in mercy and ready to forgive.

From the time the prodigal left home, his father would daily scan the horizon for his return. One day the miracle happened. Knowing all too well the walk of his dear son, he saw in the distance his son coming and compassionately ran, fell on his neck, and repeatedly kissed him. The prodigal started to make his prepared confession, but those warm kisses prevented its completion. What a gripping story this is of rags to riches, of poverty to plentitude, of famine to feast, of misery to merriment! In all three stories Jesus told, *joy* was that of the finder, and that is the celebration of grace, for there is always joy in heaven over the return and recovery of sinners.

With one hand they worked at construction, and with the other held a weapon. NEHEMIAH 4:17

In the divine gallery of saints, Nehemiah, cupbearer to the king of Persia, is one of the godliest and bravest characters of Scripture. The good hand of the Lord was upon him in his honorable palace position, but his noble soul was burdened to see Jerusalem in ruins. Surrendering his lucrative sphere, he set out to face the hardships and peril of repairing the city walls.

The narrative records the trials and difficulties Nehemiah confronted in his patriotic task. Enemies surrounded him, but slowly and surely the great work was accomplished in the face of all opposition. A most practical man, renowned for his deeds, Nehemiah was pre-eminently a man of prayer, for behind the hand holding the sword and trowel was the beating heart of prayer. His men were both soldiers and builders. As they toiled with trowels, their swords were ever ready for battle. As they labored, their ears were alert, and at the sound of the trumpet, they would leave their work for war. Actually, their work was a warfare in disguise.

What blessed truths are enshrined in this stirring record for your heart and mine! What are we but builders, and the wall is rising from a sure foundation. But as we build we battle, clad in the whole armor of God. Let us never forget that the trowel of service must always be accompanied by the sword of the Spirit. We are able to fight the good fight of faith with all our might and assist in the building of His church. Charles Wesley wrote:

Stand then, in his great might,
With all his strength endured;
But take, to arm you for the fight,
  The panoply of God:
That, having all things done,
And all your conflicts passed,
Ye may o'ercome through Christ alone,
  And stand entire at last.

May 16

"LORD, it is good for us to be here." MATTHEW 17:4

The account Luke gives us of our Lord's transfiguration on the mount focuses on Peter. Dazed and dazzled by the outflashing of our Lord's inherent glory and by the appearance of Moses and Elijah, the glorified saints, Peter said that he desired them to remain. He blurted out that he would build a tabernacle for each, "not knowing what he said" (Luke 9:33). As for Peter and the other disciples who saw Christ's glory, in later years it was written: "We beheld His glory" (John 1:14). Peter erred when he spoke of retaining all three glorified ones: Moses, the law-giver; Elijah, the fiery prophet; and Jesus, the promised Messiah. Jesus is not to be looked upon as one among others. In Him, law and prophecy are combined. So when Peter opened his eyes, he saw *Jesus only.* The forerunners had departed, and Jesus was left as the author and finisher of our faith. He superseded all who prepared His way.

Peter's expressed pleasure, "Lord, it is good . . . to be here," can be applied in other ways. When we come to the trials and burdens of life or to a bed of affliction, can we say, "Lord, it is good to be here"? Do we honor Him by our loving submission and patient suffering? In our daily task, no matter what our occupation as long as it is legitimate, do we say, "Lord, it is good to be here, for I have opportunities of showing patience and witnessing to Thy matchless grace and power"? If we are truly the Lord's, it is always good to be anywhere, to do anything, as long as He is being glorified by our life and labors. If our chief aim is to glorify God and to enjoy Him forever, then no matter where we are, our hearts will say, "Lord, it is good to be here!"

When ultimately we reach heaven, from which Moses and Elijah traveled to the mount and returned again, and find ourselves in their majestic company as well as with the redeemed of all ages, with perfect delight our response will be: "Lord, it is good to be here!"

May 17

My people will dwell in a peaceful habitation. ISAIAH 32:18

All who are not at peace with God do not experience the inner rest of which Isaiah wrote. Their hearts are like the waters of a troubled sea that cannot rest. Jonah found a temporary resting place beneath his vine until it withered away, and the runaway prophet was without shelter. But those who are the Lord's have enduring shrines and sanctuaries. Foremost is the Savior, who makes Himself a quiet resting place for all redeemed by His precious blood. In Him they are safe and sheltered forever. Nothing can destroy Him who is our hiding place, the Most High our habitation. How peaceable is our home in Him!

Paul spoke of "our earthly house, this tent" (2 Cor. 5:1). Our body is a brief and fragile habitation. It is earthly; it perishes. Jesus, however, has redeemed it and makes it His own pure and peaceable home as long as life is in it.

Job reminds us that the grave is the body's long and gloomy habitation: "The grave as my house . . . my bed in the darkness" (Job 17:13). But this is, by no means, a peaceful habitation, for its silence is that of death. Yet this is the resting place of our body, and over it the Lord watches until the resurrection morn.

The sure, perfect, and perpetual dwelling place for both soul and body is "My Father's house" (John 14:2). No plague can come near this blessed habitation, within which is room for an unnumbered multitude of the redeemed. Robert Browning could write of "the sanctuary within the holier blue." Here on earth help is always ours out of such a glorious sanctuary. The reality of our heavenly, eternal habitation of rest is confirmed by the assertion of Jesus: "If it were not so, I would have told you" (John 14:2).

John Bunyan described his longing for this peaceful abode thus, "Now, just as the gates were opened to let in the men, I looked in after them, and behold, the city shone like the sun, which I had seen, and I wished myself among them."

Praise God, someday—it may be sooner than we expect—we shall hear a voice proclaiming our eternal happiness and arise to be at home with our Redeemer forever.

May 18

May the God of peace Himself sanctify you completely; and may your whole spirit, soul, and body be preserved blameless at the coming of our LORD Jesus Christ. 1 THESSALONIANS 5:23

What an impressive triad of Scripture! Surely there is no more comprehensive prayer to offer for ourselves than this one Paul offered for his Thessalonian converts. No experience is comparable to that of being sanctified wholly and having every part of our threefold nature in complete harmony with the will of God. When you are sanctified in thought, feeling, imagination, ambition, speech, and life, then your entire personality is indeed a holy temple for His praise.

A person is a threefold being, a trinity in unity, consisting, as Paul says, of spirit, soul, and body—not separately but whole only when the three are together. At creation, the Trinity of God formed the trinity of man, as the first reference to man's threefold nature reveals (see Gen. 2:7). The *body* of man was created out of the dust of the ground; the *spirit* of man came as the result of the inbreathing of the Creator's breath; the *soul* of man, "a living soul," a mixture of dust and deity, became the medium between body and spirit.

We can think of these three in terms of a temple. The body is connected with the material world, without and around the outer court, open to the sky. Through the medium of the body, we are connected with the world around us. We have a *world consciousness.* The spirit reaches out after and responds to God, within and above. This holy of holies represents *God consciousness.* The soul, compared to the holy place, contains all the powers that make up personality and, therefore, represents *self-consciousness.* All we are and have must be brought into a complete and glad uniformity to the divine will, a task God Himself can accomplish "who also will do it" (1 Thess. 5:24).

Our spirit, soul, and body, Lord,
We offer up with one accord,
And pray that these may blameless be,
Until Thy presence we shall see.

Have mercy upon me, O God. PSALM 51:1

Since the term *mercy* and its cognates appear some three hundred times in Scripture, we can well name the Bible "God's Dictionary on Mercy." Used of both God and man, mercy represents compassion and pity for the undeserving and the guilty. The word is frequently translated "lovingkindness." Mercy is indeed an outflowing of God's love. It is for "all the days of our lives" (Ps. 23:6), "new every morning" (Lam. 3:23), and "abundant" (1 Pet. 1:3).

The epitaph of William Carey, the renowned missionary, reads:

WILLIAM CAREY, Born August 17th, 1761; Died—
A wretched, poor, and helpless worm,
On Thy kind arms I fall.

Whether this epitaph had any influence on Frederick William Faber, we cannot tell. His dying prayer was, "God most high, have mercy on us worms of earth." When Carey faced a critical illness in India, he was asked what passage he would select as a text for his funeral sermon. He replied, "Oh, I feel that such a poor sinful creature is unworthy to have anything said about him; but if a funeral sermon must be preached, let it be from the words, 'Have mercy upon me, O God.'" At his death, his wish was fulfilled.

In the Apocrypha we find the confession: "We will fall into the hands of the Lord, and not into the hands of men; for as His majesty is, so is His mercy." Robert Browning exalts mercy thus: "Mercy every way is Infinite." Such a blessed attribute seasons justice. Those who seek to serve the Lord best are most conscious of sin within. I am thankful that God has forgiven my sins and given me the privilege of preaching His inexhaustible mercy to a world of sinners, lost and ruined by the Fall.

Chance and change are busy ever,
Man decays, and ages move,
But his mercy waneth never;
God is wisdom, God is love.

May 20

A place called Gethsemane. MATTHEW 26:36

Many places noted in Scripture have sacred associations and have been revered by saints in succeeding generations. Gethsemane, a garden east of Jerusalem and near the Mount of Olives, was one of these places. It was a favorite retreat of Christ and His disciples. In this garden Jesus agonized in prayer while the disciples slept. Three times He went to them for assurance that they were praying along with Him, but He found them sleeping. Judas, who knew the garden only too well, made it the place of his betrayal of the Master. Luke reminds us that Jesus knelt in prayer while in Gethsemane, and it was this attitude that gave rise to the Christian custom of kneeling in prayer.

In this garden Jesus, as our substitute, prepared to receive divine wrath intended for us and make it His own. The name *Gethsemane* means "wine- or oil-press"; there wine and oil were produced by the crushing of grapes and olives. For Jesus, no human hand touched Him, no human voice consoled Him as great drops of His blood fell on the ground. The sorrows of death encircled Him. Here God's Olive was being crushed. What groans and heart-breaking sighs were His! From the garden He went to Calvary, there to pay our debt, redeem our souls, and purchase our peace. Jesus came to Gethsemane that we might not go to hell (see Matt. 5:22, 30).

Let none of the ransomed forget that Jesus bore all the pain and anguish of Gethsemane and Calvary that they might be redeemed and glorified! By faith, let us visit the sacred garden often and experience fellowship in Christ's sufferings.

> Go to dark Gethsemane,
> Ye that feel the tempter's power;
> Your Redeemer's conflict see,
> Watch with Him one bitter hour;
> Turn not from His griefs away—
> Learn from Jesus Christ to pray.

May 21

"As I was with Moses,
so I will be with you." JOSHUA 1:5

Edmund Spenser, gifted poet of the sixteenth century, writing of "the ever-whirling wheel of Change," left us the lines: "For all that moveth doth in change delight;/But henceforth all shall rest eternally."

The truth of divine constancy runs like a golden thread through Scripture. How conspicuous is the Lord as the unchanging and unchangeable companion on life's highway! "I am the LORD, I do not change" (Mal. 3:6). Joshua was assured that God's presence and protection promised to Moses would also be his as he assumed command of Israel. The courageous leader proved that God unalterably adhered to all His promises. He is the same yesterday, today, and forever. We may change, but Jesus never changes. Glory to His name!

When James wrote of God as "the Father of lights," he affirmed that in Him "there is no variation or shadow of turning" (James 1:17). Because of all He is in Himself, He cannot vary or change between shadow and substance. All He has been, He is and will ever be. As Jean Ingelow expressed it: "The course of God is one. It likes not us/To think of Him as being acquaint with Change;/It were beneath Him!" Said Saint Theresa of Avila: "All things are passing! God never changeth."

How grateful we are that God, having been our help in ages past, will continue to be our hope for years to come! His love is unchanging. As we retrace the path of the past, we bless Him because His goodness has never failed. Cheerfully we lay our hands in His, believing that all He has been, He will be until we enter His presence above. What a sweet anchor in the storms of life is God's unchangeableness! Earth's joys may grow dim and its glories pass away, but as Henry F. Lyte would have us sing: "Change and decay in all around I see;/O thou who changest not, abide with me."

May 22

The grace of the LORD *Jesus Christ, and the love of God, and the communion of the Holy Spirit be with you all.* 2 CORINTHIANS 13:14

Among all the benedictions, as well as the other triads of Scripture, none is as prominent as this one Paul gave to the church at Corinth. Christian pastors have used it throughout the centuries to conclude the hour of sanctuary service. In this trinity of truth, we have the most comprehensive and compact statement of the fullness of divinity to be found in Scripture.

From earliest times, the pronouncing of a benediction, or the giving of a blessing, has been a common practice among saints. Its origin can be traced to the tabernacle of the Old Testament, where Moses gave Israel the first priestly blessing recorded in Scripture. Priests would bless the people with uplifted hands. Later we read, Jesus "lifted up His hands and blessed them" (Luke 24:50).

Paul's second epistle to the Corinthians is the most agitated, stormy letter he wrote. It is full of rebuke and condemnation of the unspiritual condition of the church at Corinth. Yet it closes with the most beautiful benediction ever composed. The close of such a letter is like the calm of a subdued evening after a day of tempest and storm. It contains Paul's heart longing for the carnal church to experience the grace, love, and fellowship which the Trinity represents and which alone could correct the unworthy life of the church.

Paul addressed each member of the Trinity as a person worthy to be worshiped. All three divine persons are presented in equality, each having a distinct and different attribute: *grace* from Christ, *love* from God, *fellowship* from the Holy Spirit. It is fitting that Paul gave God the Father the central place in his benediction, for it is from Him that the grace of Christ and the fellowship of the Spirit flow.

All we need here on earth to carry us through the varied experiences of life can be found in this most precious apostolic benediction.

May 23

"Man, who is a maggot,
And a son of man, who is a worm." JOB 25:6

A proud person may shudder when he is reminded that the body upon which he spends so much time and money will come to be the companion and food of worms—those small, creeping, repulsive creatures conveying contempt. Yet such is the testimony of Scripture. "The worm should feed sweetly on him" (Job 24:20).

In many references to worms in Scripture, the repugnant creature is used metaphorically to describe how man, naturally proud, is stripped and humbled in the dust. The lowly cry of David was, "I am a worm, and no man" (Ps. 22:6). Because of his grievous sin, David felt what he said of himself with the force of his great and emotional nature. His was not a false modesty when he named himself as one who was contemptible in the sight of God and man. He showed no pretended humility when he described himself to be like a worm.

Do we feel ourselves to be poor, weak, and worthless worms in the sight of a thrice-holy God? If we do, there is grace for each of us at our worst. Isaac Watts would have us sing:

Alas! and did my Savior bleed,
And did my Sovereign die?
Would he devote that sacred head
For sinners such as I?

"Fear not, you worm Jacob. . . . I will help you" (Is. 41:14).

Think of David's words in Psalm 22:6 as messianic. There the brightness of God's glory was compared to a low organism. The express image of His Father was treated with the greatest contempt. What a mystery of mercy it was for Jesus to be reduced to the level of a worm, that we might be raised higher than angels!

Out of the depths I cry to thee;
Lord, hear me, I implore thee!
Bend down thy gracious ear to me;
I lay my sins before thee.

Proper humility, without going to the extreme of self-loathing, is the goal of Christ's followers.

May 24

But Jesus went to the Mount of Olives. JOHN 8:1

As we read the four Gospels, we discover the prominent place the Mount of Olives occupied in the life of Jesus. It was the scene of His periodical solitude, His habitual haunt as He detached Himself from the crowds to be alone with God the Father. When the day was over, people went to their own homes (see John 7:53), but Jesus ascended the sacred mount to be alone and pray. With the daily pressures of preaching, teaching, and miracle working, Jesus sometimes "did not even have time to eat" (Mark 6:31). The seasons of His solitude preserved the poise and power of His life. Even He could not live continually in public view, and thus He sought solitude.

Poets have ever praised the virtue of solitude. Edward FitzGerald wrote: "The thoughtful Soul to Solitude retires." John Milton said: "And Wisdom's self/Oft seeks to sweet retired solitude." He also felt that solitude is sometimes the best society. Shelley confessed: "I love tranquil solitude." Wordsworth, in "A Poet's Epitaph," declared: "Impulses of deeper birth have come to him in solitude. . . . the self-sufficing power of solitude." Alas, some persons are so fond of the constant round of company that they find a season of solitude somewhat irksome and uninviting.

We often sing, "Faith has still its Olivet and love its Galilee." Galilee shared with Olivet the honor of being a frequent resort of Jesus. When He came into busy Jerusalem, the people asked: "Who is this?" The reply came: "This is Jesus, the prophet from Nazareth of Galilee" (Matt. 21:10–11). Can we say that our faith has an Olivet and a Galilee? Have we learned that seasons of solitude are the sanity and sanctity of our life and living, that periods of retirement to be alone with God and His Word are an imperative necessity? If so, at all cost, let us keep such sacred meetings with Him on *our* mount, no matter where it is. Go there often in order to be still and know that He is God.

May 25

I called him,
but he gave me no answer. SONG OF SOLOMON 5:6

We can couple with the deaf ear that Solomon wrote about, the apparent silence of Jesus to the cry of the woman of Canaan for the relief of her severely demon-possessed daughter. "He answered her not a word" (Matt. 15:23). Shakespeare may affirm that "delays have dangerous ends," but this is never so with divine delays, which are always beneficial. They develop trust and patience in the soul that waits for heaven's response. The Canaanite woman proved this when Jesus broke His silence and said: "'O woman, great is your faith! Let it be to you as you desire.' And her daugher was healed from that very hour" (Matt. 15:28).

Delay of answer to a prayer must not be thought of as denial. Though God appears to tarry, He will surely come to our aid. There are times when our needs are pressing and help is urgent, but our prayers seem to rebound in our ears as if from a brazen sky. God is not dead or indifferent to our cry. But often when He gives great faith, He tests it by long delays. We may feel like Jeremiah who said of the God who hears and answers prayer in His good time, "You have covered Yourself with a cloud,/That prayer should not pass through" (Lam. 3:44). But all prayers inspired by the Holy Spirit and offered by sincere hearts reach divine ears and, although not answered immediately, ultimately receive response.

Let us be encouraged by the fact that God keeps a file of our prayers and that seemingly long awaited pleas will be punctually honored by the God of truth. Are your prayers for the salvation of some dear one still unanswered? Do not mistake delay for denial. God is the sovereign Lord who gives according to His own good pleasure. Therefore, if He is exercising your patience by not opening His gate at once, remember He can do as He wills for His own. Rest assured that He will answer at the right moment. The voice the woman heard saying, "great is your faith," will sound more musically in our ears because for awhile He answered us not a word. Remember that His silence is as eloquent as His speech.

May 26

"LORD, be my helper!" PSALM 30:10

David was not long in receiving an answer to his request, for he went on to write: "Behold, God is my helper" (Ps. 54:4). Scripture mentions those who had no helper (see 2 Kin. 14:26; Job 30:13; Ps. 72:12). But how encouraged we are to know that God presents Himself as our unfailing helper! He *can* help for He is omnipotent. So we raise our *Ebenezer,* which means "Stone of Help," and say: "Thus far the LORD has helped us" (1 Sam. 7:12). With the psalmist we, too, can confess: "You are my help and my deliverer" (Ps. 40:17). "From whence comes my help?/My help comes from the LORD,/Who made heaven and earth" (Ps. 121:1–2).

Sometimes we feel our weakness is too much for us. Then His hand is stretched out to us for our assistance, and by faith we lay hold of His hand and proceed, confident of His powerful help. "God shall help her,/just at the break of dawn" (Ps. 46:5). The Lord *must* also help us, for left to ourselves we are helpless and weak. But we are assured that God is "a very present help in trouble" (Ps. 46:1). The term *present* signifies that He is right there on the spot, as the God-at-hand to cope with any need arising. He is always near those who fear Him. The arm of His power is the protection of His saints in danger.

Has any kind of trouble or difficulty overtaken you? Then plead His promise of help; it is plain, positive, and sure. God cannot lie. He will not deceive. His strength is made perfect and is glorified in your weakness. In Him, as the Lord Jehovah, is everlasting strength, and such strength becomes yours in answer to prayer. Why, then, should you be fearful or cast down? John Newton would have you sing:

> He who has helped me hitherto
> Will help me all my journey through,
> And give daily cause to raise
> New Ebenezers in His praise.

May 27

This I recall to my mind,/
Therefore I have hope. LAMENTATIONS 3:21

Scripture has much to say about the function of memory and the art of remembrance. Of saints it is said: "They shall utter the memory of Your great goodness" (Ps. 145:7). "The memory of the righteous is blessed/But the name of the wicked will rot" (Prov. 10:7). Of the dead, Solomon wrote, "The memory of them is forgotten" (Eccl. 9:5). But this is not always so, for the righteous dead are ever remembered. In instituting His Supper, our Lord said: "Do this in remembrance of Me" (Luke 22:19). Paul's injunction to the Corinthians was to "hold fast that word which I preached to you" (1 Cor. 15:2).

Memory has been described in many ways. We are prone to forget, hence, the promise that the Holy Spirit would bring all things "to your remembrance" (John 14:26). Shakespeare wrote of memory as "the warder [wonder] of the brain." As for Coleridge he called it, "the bosom-spring of joy." The rich man in hell, however, found memory to be the source of eternal anguish (see Luke 16:19–31). Tennyson's estimation is expressed in the line: "A sorrow's crown of sorrow is remembering happier things." Jeremiah recalled that the Lord's mercy and compassion had not failed him through all past affliction and misery. This recollection stimulated his hope and trust in his compassionate Lord. Memory can become the bond servant of despondency of the mind as it feeds on the dark foreboding of past sin. Although Jeremiah remembered the cup of mingled gall and wormwood of former days, he transformed the cup into comfort. Therefore he had hope. Like a two-edged sword, the prophet's memory first killed his pride, then slew his despair.

Sir James Barrie once said, "God gave us memory that we might have roses in December." One of the marvels and miracles of grace is that God is able to erase from His memory all thought of our past sin against Him. Praise His name and remember His providential care.

May 28

"Yet, I am not alone, because the Father is with Me." JOHN 16:32

Recognizing that the end of His time on earth was coming soon, Jesus told his disciples of the blessed assurance of God's presence with Him. This assurance should be ours as believers also. It is the blessed privilege of every follower of Christ to abide in loving union with Him. We can rejoice, knowing that we have the joy of sharing heaven's companionship together.

We will never experience the isolation that Christ experienced when He cried on the cross: "My God, My God, why have You forsaken Me?" We have the promise of Hebrews 13:5: "I will never leave you nor forsake you."

We have the company of the Father: "My Father will love him, and We will come to him and make Our home with him" (John 14:23). We have the fellowship of the Son: "I am with you always" (Matt. 28:20). We have the presence of the Holy Spirit: "He may abide with you forever" (John 14:16). With such a threefold companion, why should we be lonely or need other friendship? If our circle of friends seems to be narrowing because of our witness to the greatness and goodness of God, let us not mourn over our solitude. Victory can be ours if we can sing with May Grimes:

A little sanctuary art Thou to me!
I am always "at home" on land or sea:
Alone, yet never lonely now, I prove
The "hundredfold," Lord Jesus, in Thy Love.

God's keeping power over solitude is also described:

Alone, yet not alone am I
Though in this solitude so drear;
I feel my Savior always nigh,
He comes the weary hour to cheer;
I am with Him, and He with me
Even here alone I cannot be.

May 29

"LORD, you delivered to me five talents; look, I have gained five more talents besides them." MATTHEW 25:20

The parable of the talents tells us that unequal gifts, if used with equal fruitfulness, will be equally rewarded. The parables of the ten virgins and the ten talents, if not spoken by Jesus at the same time, were likely intentionally placed together because of the light one throws on the other. The virgins is a parable of *watching,* while the talents is a parable of *working.*

As watchers, Christians are meant to work, and as workers, they must watch. In the parable of the talents the man with five of them certainly worked hard and doubled their worth. The man with only one talent was of moderate ability, yet failed through lack of industry to multiply what he had. The evident lesson of this parable is "use it or lose it." The question is: Are we gainers or hoarders, and consequently losers? In a lecture to the students of the Royal Academy, London, Sir Joshua Reynolds, the famous artist, said, "If you have great talents, industry will prove them, but if you have but moderate abilities, industry will supply their deficiency."

The five virgins failed because they were overconfident. The one talent man failed because he was overcareful and afraid. A further lesson to be learned from the talents is that our gifts are proportioned to our ability to use them. If we are faithful in the least and over a few things, the Lord will make us rulers over many things. It is not enough to have a gift or gifts. What we have must be used, for God is disappointed not only when we misuse a talent but also when we do nothing with it.

Shakespeare gave us the verse:

> Heaven doth with us as we with torches do;
> Not light them for themselves; for if our virtues
> Did not go forth of us, 'twere all alike
> As if we had them not.

May 30

In nothing was I behind the most eminent apostles, though I am nothing. 2 CORINTHIANS 12:11

The virtue of self-depreciation seems unattractive to proud souls in the world. Instead of singing with the Christian, "O to be nothing, nothing," they shout, "O to be something, something." The philosophy of humanism exalts the individual by telling him that he is all-sufficient in himself to achieve what he desires. The humanist despises the attribute of self-denial and rejects the Pauline doctrine that no good thing dwells in the flesh. Carlyle wrote of "The golden-calf of self-love—the idol of all lovers of self-worship." Shakespeare in *Henry V* affirmed: "Nothing so becomes a man/As modest stillness and humility." Solomon would have us remember that "before honor is humility" (Prov. 18:12).

The greatest figure in the New Testament, next to our Lord, is the apostle Paul who never thought too highly of himself. To the Corinthians he could write: "Though I am nothing." The Ephesians read of him as "less than the least of all the saints" (Eph. 3:8). He described himself to Timothy as the chief of sinners (see 1 Tim. 1:15) and to the Romans as the one in whom "nothing good dwells" (Rom. 7:18). Paul was blissfully content in exalting the Master he dearly loved and sacrificially served. The more he knew and saw of himself, the more humbled he became before a thrice-holy God. As believers we are willing to be nothing that Christ may be everything, for apart from Him we are less than nothing.

All we are in grace is *by* Christ; all we have is *from* Christ; all we shall be is *through* Christ. We are empty but He fills us; lost and ruined by the Fall, but He saves us; naked, but He clothes us; helpless, but He strengthens and sustains us.

Coleridge in "The Devil's Thoughts" has this couplet: "And the Devil did grin, for his darling sin/Is pride that apes humility." The Lord deliver us from all such false humility and from imagining we deserve more than we receive, either from God or other persons. "Lower and lower, yet higher we rise,/Lifted in Jesus, led on to the skies."

Learn humility from the Master Teacher.

Get up into the high mountain. ISAIAH 40:9

The record of mountains in the Bible confirms the lines of William Blake: "Great things are done when men and mountains meet;/This is not done by jostling in the street."

Our Lord and mountains often met. How Christ loved their solitude and serenity (see Matt. 5:1; 17:1)! E. F. Blakeney in *Peaks and Glaciers* remarked, "In all times and among all people the mystery and majesty of the hills have, it may be unconsciously, exercised some benignant influence; there is something in the preternatural calm, their august purity, and their solitude that, while humbling the earth-bound spirit, at the same time lifts it near Heaven from whence it came." One version of Psalm 84:5 reads: "Blessed is the man who, nerved by Thee, hath set his heart on ascents."

Because there is a certain security of elevation about divine purity, Isaiah called to Zion: "Get up into the high mountain" (Is. 40:9). David could say of the Lord: "Your righteousness is like the great mountains" (Ps. 36:6). The native name for Mount Everest was *Diva Dlunga,* "God's seat." The saints of old lifted up their eyes to the hills to learn their mystic secret. The higher one climbs, the more one is thrilled with the widening prospect, which is also true spiritually. The higher we ascend, the clearer the view we have of the glory and beauty of Him who called the mountains into being.

The peaks of many Bible mountains were the stepping stones of deity upon which God and man met. John Ruskin, a fervent lover of hill climbing, wrote: "My most intense happinesses have been amongst the mountains." As the apostle Paul neared his end, death seemed like gaining the summit of a mountain, from which he could view the whole of the faithfulness and love of Jesus to whom he had committed his entire life: "I know whom I have believed" (2 Tim. 1:12). As we think of the hymn, "Nearer, My God, to Thee," may we prove the blessedness of those who set their hearts on ascents.

June 1

"When its branch . . . puts forth leaves, you know that summer is near." MATTHEW 24:32

Our Lord used a day in late spring, heralding the approach of summer, to typify the various events forecasting the coming of His glorious kingdom. As these events are so ominous today, how near must His coming be.

What are these events, or signs, of His return in glory? Christ Himself enumerated them in His unveiling of the future. Describing the course of this age, He declared that antichrists, wars, earthquakes, famines, and persecution of the saints would be among the "fearful sights and great signs" as His coming draws near (see Luke 21:7–19).

Then, foretelling the destruction of Jerusalem brought about by Gentile dominion, Christ went on to depict signs in the heavens, the powers of which are to be shaken. He spoke of international distress as nations perceive no way out of the problems confronting them. He told of persons' hearts failing them with fear, as His coming with power and great glory is at hand. In view of all these predicted events, His exhortation is *look up*! Do not look down and around on a troubled world but look up to the throne where God reigns. Christ also said to "lift up your heads because your redemption draws near" (Luke 21:28). Our manner of life, as we await Christ's return, is also to be consecrated, as described in Luke 21:34–36.

The question we must ask ourselves is: Are we living and laboring in the light of Christ's sudden return? As ones washed in the blood He shed for our salvation, we cannot live just any kind of life.

Bring near Thy great salvation,
  Thou Lamb for sinners slain;
Fill up the roll of Thine elect,
  Then take Thy power and reign.

May we be found among those who live pure lives and are eager to hail His arrival!

June 2

"I have inscribed you on the palms of My hands." ISAIAH 49:16

If you tattooed your name on the palms of your hands, no amount of washing could erase the ink. Every moment of the day, you would see the engraving. It is so with the inscription of your name upon the loving, powerful hands of the Lord! You are never out of His sight. Perpetual and personal remembrance is His. As Isaiah illustrated, a woman would sooner forget a child she bore; the Lord said, "I will not forget you" (Is. 49:15).

Another thought associated with our name inscribed upon the Lord's sacred palms is that all the provision and power of His hands is at our disposal. It is as if the continual sight of the inscription prompts the Lord to say, "All that I am and have is ready for your appropriation." Ezekiel could affirm, "The hand of the LORD came upon me" (Ezek. 37:1). Our difficulty is that although we are His and are weak and helpless apart from Him, we fail to use the resources at our disposal. God reminded Jeremiah that His people would be satisfied with His goodness. Alas, we fail to receive all that those bountiful hands wait to bestow.

Zechariah predicted that those divine hands would be wounded, and at Calvary brutal men pierced His hands and His feet. Our names, written across those nail-prints, can speak of our fellowship in His suffering and of our identification with Christ in His death. With Paul we can say, "I have been crucified with Christ" (Gal. 2:20). Our name inscribed over those indelible wounds bids us to crucify "the flesh with its passions and desires" (Gal. 5:24). Our name woven into His nail-prints reminds us that "the world has been crucified to me, and I to the world" (Gal. 6:14). How comforting are the lines of Augustus M. Toplady:

My name from the palms of His hands
  Eternity will not erase!
Impressed on His heart it remains,
  In marks of indelible grace.

June 3

Who makes you differ from another? 1 CORINTHIANS 4:7

In an ethnic sense, the world's multitudes are alike in that all are descendants of our first parents, Adam and Eve. However, we are totally different in respect to nationality, color of skin, customs, religion, and personality. Among the billions of global inhabitants, no two persons can be found exactly alike. The God who makes sure that "one star differs from another star in glory" (1 Cor. 15:41) also makes possible the difference between the people of Egypt and the people of Israel and the difference between the unholy and the holy. Twins may exhibit a strong, physical resemblance, yet a close study reveals certain contrasts. What a dull, monotonous world ours would be if we were all exactly alike! John Wesley once said that when God fashioned him He broke the mold, and the world has never seen his like.

Paul was dealing with gifts and positions in the early church, and with those puffed up over their possessions, when he asked the Corinthians, "Who makes you differ from another?" (1 Cor. 4:7). The difference was in the nature of the gifts, not in their source. Gifts for service are not attained by personal excellence; all are the free gifts of God. There is, of course, a wide difference when it comes to one's relationship to God. In this age of grace there is no difference between Jews and Gentiles, for all are sinners and need the same Savior. Upon Israel of old, God said He was laying the necessity of separating the clean from the unclean, putting a difference between them and also between His redeemed people and surrounding nations. The call in this age is to come out from the godless and be separated to the Lord. Regretfully, in many cases the line is not as distinctly drawn as it should be. Little difference is observable between some who confess to be Christ's and those who make no profession. "This above all: to thine own self be true,/And it must follow, as the night the day,/Thou canst not then be false to any man."

June 4

This is the will of God in Christ Jesus for you. Do not quench the Spirit. 1 THESSALONIANS 5:18–19

In a previous reading (May 22), we considered Paul's reference to the Trinity as found in 2 Corinthians 13:14. In the passage above, he again emphasizes the same truth of the Godhead, expressing the will of God and of Christ and the absence of quenching the Holy Spirit. Although the term *Trinity* is not found in Scripture, the truth of God, the One in Three, is clearly evident from beginning to end. In many ways, three is associated with the Godhead. Three times the seraphim cried, *Holy* (God), *Holy* (Christ), *Holy* (the Spirit) (see Is. 6:3). Reginald Heber has this divine triad in his hymn of worship:

Holy, holy, holy! Lord God Almighty!
Early in the morning our song shall rise to thee;
Holy, holy, holy! merciful and mighty;
God in three persons, blessed Trinity!

The benediction given by Moses emphasizes the same Trinity: "The LORD [God] bless you and keep you;/The LORD [Christ] make His face shine upon you,/And be gracious to you;/The LORD [Holy Spirit] lift up His countenance upon you,/And give you peace" (Num. 6:24–26). In Ephesians each chapter refers in some way to the Trinity.

In the final chapter of the Bible, Revelation 22, John deals with the One-in-Three mystery of the Godhead united in the glorious task of redemption: God the Father *judging* (vv. 18–19); God the Son *witnessing* (v. 16); and God the Spirit *wooing* (v. 17). While the truth of the Trinity cannot be wholly comprehended by human reasoning, faith accepts such a revelation.

Holy Father, hear my cry;
Holy Savior, bend Thine ear;
Holy Spirit, come Thou nigh;
Father, Savior, Spirit, hear.

June 5

The precious blood of Christ. . . .
He is precious.

1 PETER 1:19; 2:7

Occurring over seventy times in Scripture, the term *precious* is applied to many things of value. Peter had a fondness for the adjective in his vocabulary, and he wrote of the preciousness of Christ (see 1 Pet. 2:7); of "your faith . . . more precious than gold" (1 Pet. 1:7); of "the precious blood" (1 Pet. 1:19); of the Son, "chosen by God and precious" (1 Pet. 2:4). Our Lord is most precious in Himself and the source of all that is precious to the believer. As Charles H. Gabriel expressed it:

> So precious is Jesus, my Savior, my King,
> His praise all the day long with rapture I sing;
> To Him in my weakness for strength I can cling,
> For He is so precious to me.

What is your personal estimation of His character and worth? Can you confess with the psalmist, "You are fairer than the sons of men;/Grace is poured upon Your lips;/Therefore God has blessed You forever" (Ps. 45:2)?

As we think of every name He wears, every virtue He bears, every relation He fills, every office He sustains, none can be compared with Him. Do we value Him above all others, love Him as we do no other, prefer Him above all things, and consider Him altogether lovely and beyond all human wealth and worth? The more we come to know, follow, and obey Him, the more we come to prize Him not only as our personal redeemer but also as the most wonderful figure to appear in human history.

June 6

"Abide with us, for it is toward evening." LUKE 24:29

In the closing chapter of his gospel, Luke records one of the distinct appearances of Jesus after His resurrection. This is one of the most moving chapters in the four Gospels. Two of the disciples had witnessed the bitter end of their Master at Calvary. Full of sorrow, they journeyed home to Emmaus, some seven miles from Jerusalem where He died. Companions in grief, they were doubtless rehearsing all they could remember of His life, teaching, suffering, and death. While thus communing, the two sad men were joined by a stranger. They did not recognize Him as the One they were mourning, because He appeared in another form. Asking them about the subject of their conversation, Jesus, although He knew what it was, heard from their lips the story of His last hours and how crushed their hopes were by His death.

Then came our Lord's matchless exposition concerning Himself. "He indicated that He would have gone farther" (24:28) and traveled on, but for the entreaty of the disciples to stay with them. "They constrained Him, saying, 'Abide with us.'" How the Lord loves to be entreated by His people! Gideon said to the illustrious angel: "Do not depart from here, I pray" (Judg. 6:18). The plea, "I pray," proves that the Lord, in love, often tries our faith as He appears to go on. When the heartfelt invitation, "Abide with us," came, Jesus responded, and a glorious revelation came to those willing to give Him shelter. Those two delighted disciples could not bring themselves to part with One who had done so much for them. While "Abide with Me" has become one of our most popular evening hymns, we do not have to entreat Jesus to remain, as the disciples did. We have His own gracious promise: "I will never leave you nor forsake you" (Heb. 13:5). As the darkness deepens and we draw near to His glorious appearing, our blessed hope is that, in heaven, ours will be the joy of abiding with Him forever.

June 7

"Is the Spirit of the LORD restricted?" MICAH 2:7

Lord Byron, in "Childe Harold's Pilgrimage," eloquently described creation as God's "glorious mirror," in which was seen His form, "boundless, endless, and sublime—The image of Eternity." Because the Holy Spirit played a vital part in the creation, He can never be restricted, or straightened, in His activities since He, too, is "boundless, endless, and sublime." His hand is never shortened that it cannot redeem or deliver, nor His ear heavy that it cannot hear the cry of sorrow for sin.

When we think of the unnumbered, unreclaimed multitudes in the world, the power of the Spirit may seem limited and feeble to us. If He is omnipotent, we wonder, then surely the knowledge of God's salvation should have transfigured this sinful world before now.

We are the ones who are blameworthy, not the Spirit of grace who is restricted in the manifestation of His power by *our* "unbelief" (Mark 6:6). The church has been restricted and negligent in her mission to reach earth's millions who cry, "Come and help us, or we die." There are no restraints with God's Spirit when it comes to the evangelization of a lost world.

Must we not confess that we have been living far below our privileges as those regenerated and indwelt by the omnipotent Spirit? If His mighty hand is withheld in blessing, the fault is ours, not His. We have been guilty of limiting His power by grieving Him, quenching His operations, and sowing to the flesh instead of sowing to Him, thereby causing Him to restrict His activities. Without the mighty Spirit, we can do nothing. But with His controlling every phase of life, there is no limit to what He is able to accomplish through us. This old world of ours has yet to see what He can do through those who give Him the unrestricted control of their lives. Are we among the number who are willing and ready for such an abandonment to heavenly resources?

Resolve this day to free the work of the Holy Spirit in your life and sphere of influence.

June 8

"Your Father knows the things you have need of before you ask Him." MATTHEW 6:8

How precious is Christ's assertion regarding the sweet omniscience of God's love! If this is true, and it certainly is, then why waste breath asking God for what He already knows we need? The simple answer is because Christ said, "Ask, and you will receive" (John 16:24). What consolation is in His Sermon on the Mount, especially in the prayer He taught His disciples to pray (see Matt. 6:9–13)!

Your Father. This privileged relationship is ours through the finished work of the Cross and the regenerating power of the Holy Spirit. Our Lord taught His own to look up into the face of God and address Him as their Father in heaven. God is not the Father of all. His fatherhood is based upon our acceptance of His Son.

Knows. In this word, Christ emphasized the foreknowledge and omniscience of His Father, attributes associated with Him throughout Scripture. No personal detail of your life—past, present, or future—is beyond His knowledge. Nothing escapes the eye of Him whose grace covers our life from start to finish.

The things you have need of. This phrase implies the Father's knowledge of what we need and not our own estimation of our needs. Whether the needs are physical, material, or spiritual, He has a register of them all; and because of His omnipotence, He can meet any need according to His riches in glory. How comforting and assuring it is to believe that before our lips can recite our need, our loving Father is on His way to meet it!

Before you ask Him. Before we enter His presence with our plea for help, God knows the burden upon our spirit. He has bottled our tears and recorded beforehand what His omniscient mind knows already. His knowledge is perfect, and our needs are real. When the two meet, relief is ours. Let us, then, rest in the joy of all He is in Himself, the One from whom nothing is hidden.

June 9

"The people are hungry and weary and thirsty in the wilderness." 2 SAMUEL 17:29

Probably the most heart-breaking experience David endured in his long and varied career was that of the rebellion of his handsome and much-loved son, Absalom. With all his physical attraction, Absalom had little difficulty stealing the hearts of the men of Israel. What a pathetic sight it must have been to see King David, who in earlier days defied Goliath, flee from his own impetuous son. Although some in David's household and ranks were traitors, others remained faithful to their honored leader and cared for him in his days of distress and defeat. Among them were those named in the narrative (see 2 Sam. 17:27–29), who took supplies to David and his loyal followers in the wilderness.

Their triple need is also descriptive of the child of God, to whom the world is a wilderness and heaven his final home. He is found coming up through the wilderness leaning on the arms of his Beloved. He is ever *hungry,* for there is nothing in the world to satisfy him. He is *thirsty,* always thirsting after righteousness and panting after God as one panting for a drink of water. "Blessed are those who hunger and thirst for righteousness, For they shall be filled" (Matt. 5:6).

The saint, like his Master, is often *weary* with his journey. Constant and conscientious service can produce weariness of body and mind. He is weary *in* his service for the Lord but never weary *of* it. When Paul wrote not to be weary in welldoing, he had in mind despair or disappointments in service. Our safeguard against such weariness is to wait upon the Lord and exchange such weariness for His strength, enabling us to run and not be weary as we labor for Him who is never weary.

June 10

"Where moth and rust destroy and where thieves break in and steal." MATTHEW 6:19

The Gospels reveal Jesus as the master teller of simple, easy-to-understand illustrations in His enforcement of truth. He could see "books in the running brooks,/sermons in stones." In dealing with the ways heavenly treasure can be lost, He suggests the moth, rust, and thieves as subtle, insidious, and secret perils, slowly and silently robbing us of our treasures.

The moth. Silky, beautiful, and innocent as it flits about in the twilight of the day, it may seem to be a little, harmless creature. Yet what destruction the larva can cause when it hides and burrows among costly garments, riddling them with holes until they are only fit to be burned. The moth, then, can stand for those little sins, or those seemingly harmless and innocent thoughts, imaginations, and desires heedlessly admitted into the inner life, gradually consuming one's moral and spiritual strength.

Rust. Rust stems from neglect. Tools and utensils never rust if kept clean and in constant use. Talents can be lost through negligence, which is just as destructive as rust and must be guarded against. To neglect God's great salvation is to be in peril of eternal woe.

Thieves. Robbers never give any warning of their attack upon the property and possessions of others. We may take every precaution to safeguard our homes and businesses, yet thieves break in and steal. These thieves can represent the world, the flesh, and the devil. Jesus warned us against these perils with the exclamation: "Beware!" The Lord enables us to be on our guard against such deadly perils and to beware of giving shelter to anything that would cause us to lose His benediction.

Pray for awareness and sensitivity to all negative forces that would seek to destroy your Christian influence and heavenly treasure.

June 11

Deliver me, O Lord, from my enemies;/
In You I take shelter. PSALM 143:9

We are prone to seek refuge from our sin, trials, disappointments, and conflicts in different ways. Many drink to hide their sins and sorrows. Others flee into suicide as the way out of their anguish. When forced from home as a result of his deceit, Jacob fled to his Uncle Laban in Haran. A murderer of old hastened to a city of refuge provided for the manslayer. Asa sought physicians for relief. Saul, whose refuge was once in God, hurried to a woman who was a medium. Ephraim in his peril found his way to King Jareb for shelter and help. But the child of God has no other refuge than God Himself who is his "refuge and his strength" and his "hiding place." The psalmist, harassed by foes, cried to God, "I flee unto thee to hide me" (Ps. 143:9 KJV).

Satan always outwits himself when he drives us to our God who presents Himself as our shelter in the time of storm. We are always in danger from sin, self, and Satan. Fear, painful though groundless, may be ours because we are unable to defend ourselves to overcome our oppressors. Yet wisdom is ours if we see the storm approaching and make for cover to hide for safety and comfort. May grace be ours to be found at all times fleeing to our heavenly Deliverer who is "a very present help in trouble" (Ps. 46:1). As we flee from the world, the flesh, and the devil, may we prove Jesus to be a wonderful shelter, for we have no other refuge. Praise Him, His ear is ever open to our cry. His heart always yearns to hide us. His hand is ever ready to deliver and protect. If we flee to Him by prayer and hope for His deliverance, then we can sing:

> Thou hidden source of calm repose,
> Thou all sufficient love divine,
> My help and refuge from my foes,
> Secure I am if thou art mine.

Recall the ways God has delivered you, and give thanks.

June 12

*My gospel, for which I suffer . . .
even to the point of chains;
but the word of God is not
chained.*

2 TIMOTHY 2:8–9

The apostle Paul found deep satisfaction in calling himself not a prisoner of any Roman emperor but "the prisoner of Jesus Christ" (Eph. 3:1), who had permitted his prison chains for the gospel's sake. As we can see from the verses above, he used his bondage as a striking contrast to the unfettered Word he loved and lived to preach. Roman authority might cast him into a dungeon and chain his hands and feet, but it could not prevent the gospel he preached from traveling on its free, unrestrained way. Paul's foes tried to circumscribe his influence and to retard the spread of the Christian truths he declared, but—and you can feel something of the glow in his heart—he exultantly testified, "The word of God is not chained."

Godless rulers may imprison those who love and preach the Word, but they cannot clamp chains upon it or silence its voice. Because it is God's infallible Word, it must have free course and be abundantly used as the Word that lives and abides forever.

During the reign of Charles II, the state sought to silence John Bunyan by throwing him into prison. But within his cell he wrote *Grace Abounding* and dreamed of *Pilgrim's Progress,* which, next to the Bible, has enjoyed the largest circulation of any Christian book. Communism may silence preachers in cruel ways and seek to expel the Word of God from those under the sway of an atheistic philosophy. But God's Word will continue to reveal itself as the charter of liberty, freeing those bound with the chains of their godless systems of government. Yes, praise God, His Word cannot be bound with chains. This truth is borne out by the fact that today more Bibles are being sold and read than ever before in the history of God's emancipating truth.

June 13

Suddenly a chariot of fire appeared. 2 KINGS 2:11

Everyone faces death. As the result of sin's entrance into the beautiful world God created, countless millions, from the time of Adam and Eve to the present hour, have passed into eternity through the tunnel of death. The exceptions are two godly men, Enoch and Elijah. All persons, whether Christian or unsaved, will continue to leave the world by the way of the grave until Jesus returns for His church. Then all the redeemed living at that glorious moment will escape death. They will be caught up to meet Him in the air and thus, like Enoch and Elijah, will not taste death.

What are some of the truths to be gleaned from Elijah's dramatic, sudden translation to glory? He had an inner conviction that he was about to meet the God he had so faithfully served. When persons live in close communion with God, as Elijah did, they become very sensitive to divine purposes. Somehow, they catch the whisperings of heaven. When Elijah's last day on earth came, he spent it quietly in his prophetic ministry. The companionship of Elijah and Elisha was most precious during those last days. Elijah knew that Elisha had a heart like his own, and he wanted him near when his unusual disappearance occurred.

When the hour did arrive, it seemed to Elisha that twenty thousand chariots surrounded Elijah, along with the angels doing God's bidding, as a flame of fire. As a prophet of fire, Elijah had defied Ahab: "The God who answers by fire, He is God" (1 Kin. 18:24). Elijah left the earth, not in quiet peacefulness like Enoch before him but in the whirlwind and the flame of his career.

Elisha received not only Elijah's mantle, a badge of his prophetic calling, but also a double portion of his master's loyal spirit. The only person who saw Elijah in the chariot of fire caught up to heaven in a whirlwind was Elisha. The first to see the risen Jesus was Mary. This is ever the sight love receives. Such love is not blind but has the keenest of all sight.

June 14

Be thankful. COLOSSIANS 3:15

That Shakespeare abhorred thanklessness is seen in his frequent condemnation of it. In addition to his comment in *King Lear,* "Ingratitude, thou marble-hearted fiend," we have the following song from *As You Like It:* "Blow, blow, thou winter wind!/Thou art not so unkind/As man's ingratitude." Paul declared that the ungodly did not glorify God "nor were thankful" (Rom. 1:21).

As those who are the Lord's, we have much to be grateful for, since we are surrounded by mercies—physical, material, temporal, and spiritual. As we think of our salvation, are we not thankful that God chose us in His beloved Son before the foundation of the world? The Father sent Him to be the propitiation for our sins, making us, thereby, heirs and joint-heirs. Surely, we should strive to live as glad, grateful, and loving children, rejoicing the heart of our heavenly Father who emptied heaven of the best for our redemption. Having His grace in our hearts, His infallible Word in our hands, His mercies in our homes, and His joy in our daily lives, may we be found giving thanks continually to His name.

We must constantly guard against harboring the marble-hearted fiend of ingratitude in our hearts. If thanklessness has been ours, let us confess it before the Lord, mourn over it, and ask Him to fill our souls with daily praise for His unmerited grace and goodness. May He enable us to live as thoughtful dependents upon His bounty.

Through all eternity to Thee,
A joyful song I'll raise;
For O, eternity's too short
To utter all Thy praise.

June 15

The race is not to the swift,/
Nor the battle to the strong. ECCLESIASTES 9:11

Among the wise sayings of Solomon, none is more eloquent in the praise of perseverance than the one before us. Far too many of us start well, but we never reach our goals. We lack what is known as stick-to-itiveness. Matthew Henry's comment on this passage is significant:

> One would think that the lightest of foot should, in running, win the prize; and yet *the race is not always to the swift;* some accident happens to retard them, or they are too secure and therefore remiss, and let those that are slower get the start of them. One would think that, in fighting, the most numerous and powerful army should be always victorious, and, in single combat, that the bold and mighty champion should win . . . but *the battle is not always to the strong.*

Young David, in his slaughter of Goliath, proved that the weak can carry the day against formidable powers. Prayer and perseverance count in the long run and keep honor bright.

Aesop's fable about the hare and the tortoise illustrates this truth. The proud hare laughed at the short feet and slow crawl of the tortoise. But the latter, in confidence, said, "Though you be swift as the wind, I will beat you in a race." The hare accepted the challenge, and they decided that a course should be chosen and a goal named. The day came for the race, and the hare and the tortoise left the starting line together. The hare was soon far ahead of the tortoise that lumbered on with a slow but steady pace. Confident that the race was in the bag, the hare fell fast asleep. Awaking, he ran on, thinking the tortoise was still far behind. But when he reached the goal, he found the tortoise whose perseverance won him the race.

How inspired we are as we read that Jesus set His face and feet steadfastly toward Jerusalem and never halted! He reached there to die upon a tree as the Savior of the world.

May He enable us to persevere in the race before us, never halting, until we finish our course with joy and with His reward!

June 16

I saw three unclean spirits like frogs. REVELATION 16:13

Some people find the book of Revelation so mysterious and impossible to understand that they do not attempt to study it. Although it is prophetic and symbolic in content, it contains no figure of speech that is not explained for us in some other part of Scripture. In the revelation granted him, John saw things both beautiful and bestial. Among the latter are the three froglike unclean spirits representing the trinity of hell, namely, the dragon, the beast, and the false prophet.

These three demon spirits will attempt to abolish God from the earth. They will be froglike in nature, not in shape, as they come forth from the quagmire of the universe to accomplish their dread mission amid the world's evening shadows. Creeping and croaking, slimy and filthy, this hellish trinity will defile the ears of the nations with their croak of destruction.

The dragon, who is "the Devil and Satan" (Rev. 20:2), is a fitting symbol of his role as God's chief adversary. He not only works actively to accomplish his diabolical plans but also to activate his two prime ministers to share in his grim task.

The beast. As Satan's masterpiece, this most awesome person ever to appear on earth will be the embodiment of all misrule and anarchy and the personification of iniquity (see Rev. 13:1–10.)

The false prophet. Through his lies this unclean spirit, like his companion the beast, presents himself more as a pretender lamb as he comes out of the earth. As a *religious* beast, he will be more feared than the previous *political* beast. Thus, the arrogant imitation of the divine Trinity is complete. But the heavenly Trinity of God the Father, Christ, and the Holy Spirit finally triumphs over the trinity of hell, which is cast into the lake of fire forever (Rev. 20:10).

June 17

Now abide faith, hope, love, these three; but the greatest of these is love. 1 CORINTHIANS 13:13

In the whole realm of literature, nothing is more appealing in beauty of language and sentiment than Paul's hymn of praise in honor of the Christian graces of faith, hope, and love. Paul gives us three closely bound virtues, another threefold cord that cannot be broken. Our spiritual activity is composed of faith, the dynamic; hope, the incentive; love, the expression of the heart's desire.

Faith. Our access to God is by faith in the supreme sacrifice of the Savior. By this grace we are enabled to attempt great things for God. Faith is placed first because it is where we begin our spiritual pilgrimage and continue exercising it until faith vanishes into the sight of Him in whom we have believed. Beginning as a mental surrender to the truths of the gospel, faith becomes implicit trust in and obedience to the Lord Jesus in all that He commands. Faith makes the uplook good, the outlook bright, the inlook favorable, and the farlook glorious.

Hope. As one of the dominant words of the Bible, hope implies the elements of desire, expectation, and patience. Paul wrote of the blessed hope, which represents not merely an event or advent but a person. Jesus Himself is the hope of our salvation. If faith appropriates, hope anticipates; faith believes and receives, hope desires and waits. Faith is the root. Hope is the fruit.

Love. This grace has the pre-eminence in Paul's triad of virtues. Love is the greatest of the three. It manifested the heart of God at Calvary, satisfies the demands of a loving God, is the badge of true discipleship, and secures a glorious eternity with the Trinity. The moment we see Jesus, faith will vanish into sight and hope will be fully realized, but love will abide as our never-failing treasury, filled with boundless stores of grace.

As we await the coming of our Lord, let us exercise the unceasing labor of love.

June 18

Jesus Christ is the same yesterday, today, and forever. HEBREWS 13:8

This gracious promise of the unchangeableness of our Lord offers constancy as well as consistency. It weans us away from our fitfulness, fickleness, and irresolution. To the Eternal One, past, present, and future are as one vast illustrious scroll bearing the inscription: "I am the LORD, I do not change" (Mal. 3:6). Divine utterances are unalterable, just as God in His being is invariable. Because of all He is in Himself, He is stable and permanent. All that He was in a past eternity, He is in time and will be throughout the endless future.

We are creatures of change. We live in a constantly changing world. Circumstances, friends, health, and desires change amid the changing seasons of each new year, and we are in dire need of the Friend who changes not. One who is ever the same and is such a friend is Jesus. "Change and decay is all around I see;/O thou who changest not, abide with me."

Because of His own inherent constancy and consistency, His love toward us never changes. Eternally stable, He never is fitful in His dealing with us. What our Lord was in the yesterday of His eternal past and of His life and labor while on earth, He is the same today in the age of grace.

Forever is a term covering not only our future here below, but the eternal ages beyond earth's life span. When we meet Him in glory, He will be the same unchanging and unchangeable Jesus. We confess the "Lord God Almighty, Who was and is and is to come!" (Rev. 4:8).

How expressive are the lines of S. Trevor Francis:

> My *yesterday* was Christ upon the tree,
> Who bore the condemnation due to me.
> *Today* I journey on and He shall lead,
> He knows my pathway, and He knows the need.
> *Tomorrow* is not; but His wisdom plans,
> I leave my future in His loving hands.

June 19

We should live soberly, righteously, and godly. TITUS 2:12

These virtues—soberly, righteously, godly—can help the struggling saint develop and maintain a Christian character. Paul's use of each term guides us closer to an understanding of how Christians should live.

Live soberly. Paul urged Titus to live in relation to the world within him. The word *soberly* implies self-control. W. E. Vine says that in its original form it suggests "the exercise of that self-restraint that governs all passions and desires, enabling the believer to be conformed to the mind of Christ." The similar word *sobriety* expresses the thought of a constant rein on all the passions and desires associated with temptation. In Romans 5–8 Paul takes up the necessity of mastering our inner, lower nature by allowing the high impulses of the Holy Spirit to dominate it.

Live righteously. We travel from our life within to our life without and around. We are to have a good report of all persons. This second aspect implies living right in all our relations with others. Our positional righteousness must be translated into practical righteousness. Our standing in the Righteous One must become our state before others. We must endeavor to be conspicuously right, as well as being substantially right.

Live godly. This aspect brings us to the Godward and upward aspirations that should be ours. The term *godly* indicates a devout manner of life, a reverence manifested in Godlike actions. Only as we are controlled by God can His virtues be manifested in our lives. Through the power of the indwelling Holy Spirit we become Godlike in our opinions, judgments, aims, and decisions. Just as God is righteous, kind, sympathetic, and forbearing, we become so, too. Paul wrote to the Ephesians that all Godlike virtues are ours as "the fruit of the Spirit" (Eph. 5:9).

Draw thou my soul, O Christ,
  Closer to thine;
Breathe into every wish
  Thy will divine!

June 20

"Give us . . . forgive us . . . lead us." MATTHEW 6:11–13

The Lord's Prayer is so simple that a child can use it, and multitudes of children are taught to do so. Yet it is so profound that the most experienced saint cannot exhaust it. Often thoughtless lips utter it but live in a way contradicting the spirit of this pearl of prayers. To live the prayer is a hard task even for the saintliest Christian. Only as we come to practice it do we discover how far-reaching it is and how it embraces all our needs.

Give us. In this petition, Jesus emphasized the providential care and provision of His Father for His own children. Daily we require food to maintain us physically. Knowing of our material needs, He has assured us that our bread and water will not fail.

Forgive us. More than daily food we need daily forgiveness. While the first need of the body may be bread, the first need of the soul is pardon. Yesterday's bread should be used in such a way as to make us more fit to live for God's glory today. Divine forgiveness is the first manifestation of grace in the one turning to God from sin. And when forgiven by God, we are to exhibit the same grace toward others, "As we forgive." Tennyson wrote of "little hearts that know not how to forgive." May our forgiveness of others be as Godlike as the pardon He provided us.

Deliver us. We need a daily victory over all our enemies, within and without. Because of His power, God is able to make us more than conquerors over all that is alien to His holy mind and will. God may permit temptation, but He never provides temptation. He permits it so that we may resist it and by faith appropriate the victory He has provided over the tempter, the devil. Each victory helps us to win another.

The bravest of all prayers is the one that asks to be free from evil at whatever cost.

June 21

"You shall love your neighbor as yourself." GALATIANS 5:14

Love is the moving principle of all the graces. John Bunyan has said: "Love is the very quintessence of the Gospel." Of love, joy, peace, Bishop Lightfoot wrote: "The fabric is built up, story upon story. Love is the foundation, joy the superstructure, peace the crown of all."

Love is the root of all Christian fruit, the life-sap giving form and substance to the rest of the cluster. Evidently the Galatians were in dire need of the initial grace of love. Paul rebuked the people for biting and devouring one another, "lest you be consumed by one another!" (5:15).

Dr. A. B. Simpson wrote of Galatians 5:22–23:

> It is all one fruit. We have not a great many things to do, but just one, and that one thing is love: for all these manifestations of the fruit are but various forms of love.
>
> Joy is love exulting;
> Peace is love reposing;
> Longsuffering is love enduring;
> Gentleness is love refined;
> Goodness is love in action;
> Faith is love confiding;
> Meekness is love with bowed head;
> Temperance is true self-love;
>
> so that the whole sum of Christian living is just loving.

The works of the flesh combine to destroy love—love for God, for home, for society, for self-respect. We must remain alert to destructive influences that seek to overwhelm us. We must maintain a strong foundation of love so that we may be able to carry out Jesus' instructions to us.

In his soul-stirring hymn, "Love Divine," Charles Wesley has taught us to sing: "Breathe, O breathe Thy loving Spirit/Into every troubled breast."

May such a prayer be answered for us all!

June 22

"That your joy may be full." JOHN 15:11

Joy is the flower of love, the very loveliness of love. A joyless Christian is a contradiction of terms. Fabre has reminded us that "God's will on earth is always you, always tranquility."

But sin and worldliness can rob a saint of joy. Like parasites, they suck out life's pure joy. David felt this as he cried: "Restore to me the joy of Your salvation" (Ps. 51:12).

Christ pledged Himself to impart joy, His own untainted joy. Anointed with the oil of gladness above His fellows, He bestows a joy unspeakable and full of glory. Such a divine joy springs from a realization of forgiveness; it comes as the result of abiding in Christ.

Further, this joy is of the Spirit. It is not something the believer has to work up. We are familiar with the line of Newton's hymn: "Joy is a fruit that will not grow." We cannot produce it. The fruit of the Spirit is joy. The Spirit made possible our Lord's joy.

The fruit of joy implies glad acquiescence in the promises of God. It is a joy that becomes our strength, leading to vigorous action. As the work of the Spirit, this joy makes the child of God genuinely happy, and how the sad world around needs the glow of such gladness!

The pleasures of the world are hollow, false, momentary. Only in God's presence do we have fullness of joy and pleasures forever more.

> There is a heritage of joy
> That yet I must not see,
> The Hand that bled to make it mine
> Is keeping it for me.

The acrostic *J–O–Y* has been used many times: *J* for Jesus; *O* for others; *Y* for you. Blessed joy is always ours as we place Jesus first, others second, and self last. Another way of using the word is to say that abiding joy always comes when *J*esus is first, *y*ou last, and nothing (*0*) in between.

May you accept this promise of joy for your life today and live in God's presence!

June 23

The unity of the Spirit
in the bond of peace. EPHESIANS 4:3

Dr. Griffith Thomas said, "Peace is the restfulness of our abiding attitude, and disposition of the soul in relation to God." Peace, built on love and joy, is not the absence of trouble but the promise of the presence of God in all circumstances, pleasant or painful.

Peace is a close relative of faith and joy, because there are joy and peace in believing. Peace is faith's first resting place.

Peace is of a threefold nature. There is peace *with* God, which was made by Christ who became our peace. There is the peace *of* God, the impartation of His own attribute, a peace passing all understanding. There is peace *in* God, a tranquil attitude of soul that He alone can make possible.

Peace such as the Spirit produces is not a state of spiritual coma, a condition of mental or spiritual insensibility, but a conscious resting in the will and Word of God. It is a deep, perfect, settled peace of heart and mind amid the turbulent experiences of life. We must learn to sing: "There's a deep, settled peace in my soul."

Peace is Christ's legacy to His own; He is the Prince of Peace. The question, however, for each of us is: Am I bearing this precious fruit of the Spirit? God knows too many of us are restless amid the restlessness of the world! Love, joy, and peace are so opposite to the hatred, dissatisfaction, and restlessness characterizing our world today.

Like a river glorious
  Is God's perfect peace,
Over all victorious,
  In its bright increase;
Perfect, yet it floweth
  Fuller every day;
Perfect, yet it groweth
  Deeper all the way.

God grant that the fruit of the Spirit may be evident in the peace we have in our lives.

June 24

I will speak of the glorious honor of thy majesty. PSALM 145:5 KJV

How right John Milton was in "joining converse with love, for it is out of the heart that conversation, whether sweet or sour, proceeds!" Therefore, we must keep our hearts with diligence and guard what comes from them through the means of our spoken words. Scripture instructs us about conversation. We are to be holy in all manner of conversation and serve as examples of chaste language. In many biblical references, the word *conversation* implies a manner of life rather than the actual words of our lips. David had no doubt as to the worthy content of his phrase "I will speak of the glorious honor of thy majesty."

In general, the habitual talk of the world is low, with buying and selling, gossiping, and trifling matters forming the staple subjects. Those of the earth are earthly, and their conversation reflects their earthly hopes, interests, and enjoyments. Where the treasure is, there will the heart be also. Where the heart is, there generally will the tongue be also. Out of the abundance of the heart, the mouth speaks. But as Christians we cannot shut out from our conversation all reference to the ordinary affairs of daily life and business. We have to earn our living by contact with people around us. What we have to watch is becoming worldly in our attitudes and conversations.

David would have us remember that we are not only to speak *to* God but *about* God, particularly of the glorious honor of His majesty. The word translated *speak* in the verse above does not imply an occasional reference to all God is in Himself. It calls for an entering into particulars, as though one took delight in speaking in detail of all that is involved in the majesty and mercy of our Lord. In this way sweet conversation and love are deeply combined.

May we ever be found among those who are not ashamed to "talk of Your deeds" (Ps 77:12).

June 25

Our soul has escaped as a bird from the snare. PSALM 124:7

The escape the Lord makes possible from the snares of the satanic trapper is complete. The dominant thought of the psalm before us is the perfect deliverance God provides for His people when they are confronted by circumstances that would destroy them. Often through our disobedience to the revealed Word of God, we involve ourselves in entanglements and are unable to extricate ourselves from perilous positions. Then we are brought to realize that only by divine action can we escape. We know that whatever temptation may face us, a way of escape is provided. Peter affirmed that only through the knowledge and power of Jesus can we escape "the corruption that is in the world" (2 Pet. 1:4).

Craftily and cleverly, Satan hides his snares, and we have to constantly pray that we may always be aware of his tricks. As F. B. Meyer expressed it: "Quite unexpectedly Satan begins to weave the meshes of some net around the soul, and seems about to hold his captive. And then, suddenly, the strong and deft hand of our heavenly Friend interposes, as we sometimes interpose on behalf of a struggling insect in a spider's web. The snare falls into a tangle heap, and the soul is free." "The snare is broken, and we have escaped" (Ps. 124:7).

May ours be the personal experience of having fully escaped from satanic snares and of being as free as a bird in the air! George Mathison, the blind Scottish poet, taught us to sing: "Make me a captive, Lord,/And then I shall be free;/Force me to render up my sword,/And I shall conqueror be."

For those who prefer captivity in sin and remain blind to their bondage, the solemn question may arise: How shall we escape? The only escape from perpetual bondage is through the liberating power of the shed blood of Jesus.

June 26

"Crop that sprang up, increased and produced: some thirtyfold, some sixty, and some a hundred." MARK 4:8

Let us examine this verse along with Mark 4:28 because the stages of growth are equivalent in both. Christian development is a gradual process. Although a crisis makes a sinner turn to Jesus, a redeemed one should progress from feeble beginnings to spiritual maturity. The divine Gardener expects a full harvest for His toil.

First the blade . . . some thirtyfold. Those truly regenerated by the Spirit begin fruit-bearing, although the cluster is not large. The days of the beginning of grace are not to be despised. God does not expect fully ripened fruit before its time. However, the problem with many people is that they are satisfied with remaining to the last as the mere blades they were at the beginning. They fail to grow in grace and in the knowledge of their Lord. The weeds of the old life linger and thus prevent the tender shoots of grace from developing.

Then the head . . . some sixty. In our garden, we do not look in early spring for the flowers that can only appear in summer. Just so God does not despair because He does not see in our growing Christian life all the wisdom, steadfastness, and fruit of spiritual maturity. He does expect, however, the blade to become the head and thereby to multiply, from thirty to sixty. Is ours the spiritual growth that is pleasing to the heart of the divine Gardener? Are we growing up into the full stature of Christ?

After that the full grain . . . some a hundred. Our passing years, spent in the service of our Lord, should register a maturity in spiritual things. Our fellowship with Christ should be more real and deep, our love for His Word more intense, our thirst for holiness more evident, and our fruitfulness more marked. How sad it is to see aging, professing Christians barren and unfruitful! At whatever stage in the Christian life we may be, may ours be the assurance that we have attained the spiritual growth, the "hundred" God expects of us.

May nothing hinder us from receiving a full reward from our heavenly Gardener when we meet at the judgment seat.

June 27

For we are His workmanship, created in Christ. EPHESIANS 2:10

The word Paul used for workmanship is *poiema,* "something made." Just as God made the universe a revelation of the deity and power of the Creator, so He makes Christians.

The original term for workmanship, *poiema,* is transliterated in our English word *poem.* In his verse to "Children," Longfellow reminds them:

> Ye are better than all the ballads
> That ever were sung or said;
> For ye are living poems,
> And all the rest are dead.

Living poems! This was the symbol Paul used. To him, the two great poetic masterpieces of God were the creation of the universe and the creation of born again believers. In both instances, *poiema* suggests something produced with effort, object, and design. As the meter varies in poems, so the course of one life differs from another.

We are His poem. How wonderful it is to know that all who are in Christ form the highest, finest, and most beautiful expression of God's thought and purpose! They are the masterpieces upon whom He bestowed His best, and therefore they surpass His first creation, which only cost Him His breath when "He spoke, and it was done" (Ps. 33:9). As His new creation, the church results from the shedding of the precious blood of His beloved Son.

As saints in service, we represent God's poetic creation. Poems, as well as poets, are born, not made. A sinner becomes God's poem by the new birth. Thereafter, his good works of God eloquently express the rhythm and music of a divine creation.

Are others inspired and blessed as they read the verse of your life in God's poem?

June 28

Jesus wept. JOHN 11:35

While the Gospels do not mention the laughter of Jesus, they have something to say about His tears. Cecil Frances Alexander in one of his hymns said: "He feeleth for our sadness, He shareth in our gladness." When Jesus was only twelve years of age, He declared His God-given mission to the world, only to find that His family did not understand that mission. Living in a home in which He was not understood must have cost Him many tears. Thus from early manhood, Jesus was the man of sorrows.

The shortest and sweetest text in the Bible is *Jesus wept.* These two words have been blessed by God to the hearts of countless numbers, for next to the assurance of knowing that He shed His blood for us is the fact that He shed His tears for friends and enemies alike. When He rode in lowly guise into Jerusalem amid the hosannas of the people, "He saw the city and wept" (Luke 19:41). Those tears of grief and compassion were for a lost city, rejecting His love and grace. A few days later in dark Gethsemane, He shed not only His tears but also great drops of blood as He "offered up prayers and supplications, with vehement cries and tears" (Heb. 5:7). Our finite minds cannot grasp the depth of agony our Lord endured.

In Bethany, His tears were for the man He loved and whom death had claimed. Learning that Lazarus had died, Jesus wept. On Olivet, He wept for His enemies, resolved and doomed to perish. In the garden, His liquid agony revealed what He was enduring for us. At the grave of Lazarus, He wept in sympathy with bereaved loved ones. On each occasion His tears were the result of heartfelt anguish for others. No one has ever suffered as much as Jesus did. He still offers prayers and supplications since He lives to make intercession for us, but without strong crying and tears. For Him all tears have been wiped away; yet He always remains the same sympathizing Jesus and would have us follow His example by weeping for those who weep. May we be kept from becoming too dry-eyed!

June 29

In vain the net is spread/
In the sight of any bird. PROVERBS 1:17

Some commentators have suggested that a double meaning may be attached to Solomon's assertion regarding the net and the bird. They believe that no bird is so foolish as to hop into a net visibly spread before it. Although a bird has a very little head and brain, it will not go into a trap. Other writers feel that Solomon meant to say that even if a bird sees you spread a net for it, it has not the wisdom to know what the net means and will hop into the trap.

While there may be some doubt as to what Solomon thought the birds might do, there is no uncertainty at all as to the lesson to be gathered from his saying. If souls are foolish enough to go into the net of sin, spread by the devil for their destruction, to gather a few crumbs of worldly pleasure, then they are easily gulled. The word *gull* is said to be derived from birds who come down from the Arctic regions to fish in flocks in our harbors and coasts and are thus easily caught. This may be an insult to the gulls who are not so readily tricked as some humans are who find their hearts tangled in amorous nets. Are we not warned of the strategies of the devil? Left to ourselves, we have no wisdom to detect his shrewdness as the archdeceiver. He is a "roaring lion" (1 Pet. 5:8). God gave lions their roar so that everybody would keep out of their way.

Satan may spread his net before us, but he cannot compel us to go into it. If our ears and eyes are open, he spreads his net in vain. Satan once spread his nets to entrap Jesus, but His anointed eyes could see them. Thus, He is well able to "preach deliverance to the captives...To set at liberty those who are oppressed" (Luke 4:18). Having escaped as birds out of the snare of the fowler, we should never cease to praise the Lord who rescued us. We must not cease to tell those who are still trapped of the glorious deliverance He can accomplish for them.

June 30

Blessed are the people who know the joyful sound! PSALM 89:15 NASB

How blessed are the people who know the blast of the trumpet and shout of joy! A similar exhortation is: "With trumpets and the sound of a horn;/Shout joyfully before the LORD, the King" (Ps. 98:6). The world abounds in sounds, many of which are delightful. We first observe the joyful nature of the sound referred to by the psalmist. How we love the sound of good, inspiring music and of the warbling birds! But a sound sweeter than all other sounds that reaches the inner ear of the soul is the voice singing to us out of Scripture of the love of God in Christ Jesus. Priscilla J. Owens's familiar hymn expresses it: "We have heard the joyful sound: Jesus saves!" Such a sound is joyful because it tells us how we can be emancipated from sin's power and made new creatures in Christ.

All who know the joyful sound of sins forgiven are indeed blessed. The word *know* used here implies more than a mere mental comprehension. It includes a deep personal experience. Some may not hear a joyful sound easily detected by others, either because they are deaf or because they cover their ears. The godless have ears but do not hear simply because they deliberately close their ears. If a treasure were left to us in a will, it would be joyful to hear about. If we did not claim it or failed to acquaint ourselves with such a heritage, then we would lose the possession of it and its blessing. If possessions are willed to us, we must learn about them, believe the provision of the will, and claim all that is ours. This applies to all the precious, spiritual legacies willed to us by the One who died for us. We have been blessed with all spiritual blessings in the heavenly places in Christ. Are we possessing our possessions and experiencing the blessedness and joy that come through the acceptance of all that is ours through matchless grace?

July 1

"Believe in the LORD your God, and . . . be established." 2 CHRONICLES 20:20

Emily Bronte's "Last Lines" proves that she herself was "surely anchor'd on the stedfast rock of immortality." How moving is the opening verse of her great poem:

> No coward soul is mine,
> No trembler in the world's stormtroubled sphere:
> I see Heaven's glories shine,
> And faith shines equal, arming me from fear.

In believers, faith and fear cannot exist together. Believing that the Lord is almighty, the Christian is armed against fear. "God is our refuge and strength. . . . Therefore we will not fear" (Ps. 46:1–2). When such "faith shines equal," then we can laugh at seeming impossibilities and shout, "It shall be done." The proper object of our active faith is not God as the God of nature but God in Christ. He is our covenant God, always ready to undertake for us. Believing in such a God produces peace of heart, humility, zeal, strength to accomplish His will, and deliverance out of every difficulty.

We receive faith from God; it is a gift He bestows upon sinners who accept His salvation. Faith, then, is an attribute He increases in those who are saved by His grace. If our Lord returned today, would He find such a faith in our hearts: faith in Himself as the sovereign One; faith in His Word as being true; faith in His abiding presence; faith in His power, since nothing is too hard for Him; and faith in His faithfulness, which is as steadfast as the mountains and abides forever? "This is the victory that has overcome the world—our faith" (1 John 5:4). The ancient writer continues in the text: "Believe His prophets, and you shall prosper" (2 Chr. 20:20). Is this not the other side of the shield of faith? Since God gave the revelation of Himself to the prophets, it is essential to believe that they were holy men led of the Spirit and the holy prophets of whom God is Lord.

July 2

Do not cast away your confidence, which has great reward. HEBREWS 10:35

Bible references to *confidence* and its cognates are numerous. Taken together they reveal much about the nature and necessity of this commendable quality. Ellicott's commentary gives us a reading of the verse for today:

> Cast not away therefore your *boldness,* seeing it hath a great recompense, . . . to *cast away boldness* is the opposite of holding fast the boldness of our hope (Heb. 3:6); the one belongs to the endurance of the faithful servant, the other to the cowardice of the man who draws back (Heb. 3:12, 16, 18). This verse and the next are closely connected. Hold fast your boldness, seeing that it belongs to great reward; hold it fast, for *he that endureth to the end shall be saved.*

Isaiah reminds us that "in quietness and confidence" is our strength (Is. 30:15). The writer to the Hebrews affirms that we have "boldness to enter the Holiest by the blood of Jesus" (Heb. 10:19). In these days of liberal approaches to fundamental truths of Scripture, doubt is being cast upon the effectiveness of the blood of Jesus to remove sin. But its never-failing power to cleanse from all sin is one aspect of confidence we must not throw away. Virgil had a saying: "Nowhere is confidence safe." It is certainly not safe in some theological centers today. Unfortunately, too many young people learn to doubt the beliefs they once held and enter the ministry believing their doubts. Arthur Hugh Clough gave us this verse of warning:

> In controversial foul impureness
> The Peace that is light to thee
> Quench not! In faith and inner sureness
> Possess thy soul and let it be.

Our confidence in the faith once delivered to the saints will often be sharply tried. We must seek grace to hold fast our confidence until the end, knowing that a great reward awaits.

Without being contentious, we must earnestly contend for the faith, casting none of it away.

July 3

Pray without ceasing. 1 THESSALONIANS 5:17

We often sing about the privilege of carrying everything to God in prayer. But we often take this blessed privilege for granted. Who are we, that we should be able to take God's name upon our lips and tell Him all that is upon our hearts? He is the Lord God almighty; yet we humans have authority to come before Him at any time and in any place. We do not have to wait upon any whim or movement of God. No matter where we are or who we are, by grace we have the right to enter immediately into the presence of Him who instructs His children to ask and receive. Many barriers keep us from conversing with important government leaders or celebrities in our land, but we may approach the King of kings at any time.

Our common tragedy is our failure to take advantage of such a priceless privilege. We are not victorious in life and fruitful in service because the communication line with heaven is not in constant use.

Old Testament saints understood something of the privilege of approaching God. But during those times, God localized His presence in the temple and the Jew had to go there to pray. Now we have the promise that we can draw near to Him anywhere. Such is our broad privilege that through Christ we can converse with Him in a barn or in a cathedral.

Even though He can be approached wherever we are at any moment, we must not treat God as our equal—One with whom we can barter and selfishly petition: "Let's make a deal, God. You do this for me and I'll live like this for you." Such an attitude is an abuse of our privilege; it is a modern manifestation of the primitive sacrifice, an offer to trade incense for luck.

Lord, teach us how to pray aright,
With reverence and with fear;
Though dust and ashes in Thy sight,
We may, we must draw near.

Prayer is heaven's toll-free telephone line. It is free to all; there are never any busy signals and it is never out of order. We must use this line with reverence and godly fear and realize that prayer is a very priceless privilege and promise.

July 4

"When you [Nathanael] were under the fig tree, I saw you." JOHN 1:48

Joseph Addison would have us remember that the eyes of the Lord are ever open upon us: "His Presence shall my wants supply,/And guard me with a watchful Eye." Nathanael, praying under the fig tree, did not know that the watchful eyes of Jesus saw him on his knees, and he was surprised when Jesus told him, "I saw you." Hagar called the name of the Lord who spoke to her, "You-Are-the-God-Who-Sees; for she said, 'Have I also here seen Him who sees me?'" (Gen. 16:13).

Adam and Eve sought to conceal themselves among the trees of Eden from God's all-seeing eyes. Elijah, thinking he was alone in a cave, was startled by the divine question: "What are you doing here, Elijah?" (1 Kin. 19:9). Zechariah affirms that the eyes of the Lord "scan to and fro throughout the whole earth" (4:10).

It is true; "Your eye sees me." As the omnipresent one, God is present everywhere. As the omniscient one, he sees the needs of His redeemed children no matter where they are. If His eye is on the sparrow and marks its fall, then surely, as those He died to save, we are of more value to Him than many sparrows. What pains Him as His eyes are upon us is the sight of that which is contrary to His holy character and will. The eyes of Jesus glowed with delight as they gazed upon Nathanael praying at his favorite, hallowed spot, and those same loving eyes are filled with joy as they watch us seeking to live in the realm of His will.

In Thy bright beams which on me fall,
Fade every evil thought:
That I am nothing, Thou art all,
I would be daily taught.

July 5

She [Rebekah] went to inquire of the LORD. GENESIS 25:22

Appearing over seventy times in Scripture, the terms *inquire* and *inquired* reveal the nature and necessity of our approach to God. In the case of Rebekah, after twenty years of marriage, she and Isaac were still childless. Prayer to God, however, prevailed and the great trial of faith ended. Realizing that there was more than one child struggling in her womb, she inquired of the Lord and learned she would give birth to two children, who in turn would be the progenitors of two nations or "two peoples." They would be the house of Jacob and the house of Esau. What an excellent example Rebekah left us to follow!

God commands us to inquire of Him at all times. "I will also let the house of Israel inquire of Me" (Ezek. 36:37). Joshua and his men greatly erred when they failed to ask counsel of the Lord in respect to the deceit of the Canaanites. When trouble overtook Job and his mind was perplexed over what God had permitted, he turned to God and prayed: "Show me why You contend with me" (Job 10:2).

Are you disturbed over trials and disappointments that have come your way? Go and inquire of the Lord. Ask Him for the design of your tears, and He will unfold the reason why the dark threads are as necessary as those of gold and silver. A proverb states, "For much inquiring is bad," but we often fail from too little inquiry of the Lord. Although heaven's inquiry office never closes, we are not persuaded as we ought to be that whatever our circumstances or trials may be, the ear of the Lord is ever open to hear our request and His hand ever ready to undertake for us.

If painful and distressing experiences overtake us, we should not be despondent or complain over God's providential dealings. We should go to the throne of grace and inquire of the Lord the reason for our chastisement. David is often described as inquiring of the Lord in the varied crises of his life and of receiving all necessary guidance and direction.

May we be faithful followers of his example!

July 6

Ananias, with Sapphira . . .
kept back part of the proceeds. ACTS 5:1–2

In *Don Juan,* Byron asks and answers a question as to the exact nature of a lie: "And, after all, what is a lie? 'Tis but/The truth in masquerade." The lie Ananias and Sapphira told was most odious and wicked because it was the truth in masquerade. They professed to have sold all their possessions for the Lord's cause and to have given Peter all they received in payment. The tragic story of these two disciples is that they withheld, for themselves, part of the full price received. For lying against the Holy Spirit in this way, both received sudden death. The doomed deceivers tried to imitate the complete surrender of Barnabas who sold all he had and gave all he received in payment to his Lord. Proudly and plausibly, Ananias and Sapphira presented to Peter a part of what their land had brought as if it had been the whole amount. But God revealed to Peter their hypocrisy, and a few minutes later they were corpses.

The same incomplete obedience and partial dedication was Saul's sin when he declared he had slain everything belonging to Amalek and he said to Samuel: "I have performed the commandment of the LORD" (1 Sam. 15:13). But Samuel, discerning the lie, replied: "What then is this bleating of the sheep in my ears?" (1 Sam. 15:14).

Are we not humbled as we reflect upon such triflings with God? We have professed to have placed our all on His altar; yet ours is but a partial surrender, only part of the price. May we be saved from acting a lie! May He, who is the truth, constantly cleanse us from all secret faults!

July 7

"We know that You are a teacher come from God." JOHN 3:2

In *Canterbury Tales,* Chaucer partially described a clerk of Oxenford by writing, "Gladly would he learn and gladly teach." Such an axiom is certainly true of the Lord Jesus who delighted to do His Father's will and who learned many things by obedience to that will. He came to make the glad tidings of the gospel possible, and He manifested great joy of heart as He fulfilled His ministry as a teacher and one sent from God.

The craft of teaching is recognized by the fact that all three persons of the Trinity are presented as teachers. *God*—"Who teaches like Him?" (Job 36:22); "I am the LORD your God,/Who teaches you to profit" (Is. 48:17). *Christ*—"Jesus began both to do and teach" (Acts 1:1); "He taught them as one having authority" (Matt. 7:29). *Holy Spirit*—"The Holy Spirit will teach you . . . what you ought to say" (Luke 12:12); "He will teach you all things" (John 14:26).

After the ascension of Jesus and the advent of the Spirit, the apostles became conspicuous as teachers and were found "in the temple and teaching the people!" (Acts 5:25). Paul gloried in his mission as "a teacher of the Gentiles" (1 Tim. 2:7). Among the gifts to the church are "teachers" (Eph. 4:11), with older women functioning as "teachers of good things" (Titus 2:3). All teachers of the Word, whether in the home or at church, must look upon their mission as being *from* God. It is essential, therefore, that they be undertaken *for* God.

What glorious victories the patient teaching of Jesus through some three years achieved in the lives of His disciples, as their noble ministry in the book of Acts proves! At times flesh and blood find the slow, painstaking, and persistent task of teaching hard and disappointing. In eternity the Great Teacher Himself will graciously reward those who were teachers after His example and for Him.

Of course, we must realize that we cannot teach others unless we are directly taught of God.

July 8

The fruit of the Spirit is in all goodness, righteousness, and truth. EPHESIANS 5:9

The apostle Paul possessed deep insight into, and understanding of, the ministry of the Holy Spirit. Permeating his writings is the philosophy that if we sow to the Spirit, a golden harvest will be ours. Three aspects of this harvest are mentioned in this verse.

Goodness. Often this virtue is lacking in an otherwise attractive, fruitful life. Goodness reveals itself in disposition, talk, and action, and in sympathy, generosity, and love. It forms the first fruit of the Spirit. Used by Paul, the word *goodness* speaks of grace embodied. All selfishness, envy, malice, and temper are burned out of the heart by the holy fire of divine love. By the Cross, warmth, tenderness, and generosity are created within us, and we become good. Several key words and phrases give us a more complete picture of the fruit of goodness: "abounding" (Ex. 34:6); "promised" (2 Sam. 7:28); "for saints to rejoice in" (2 Chr. 6:41); "great" (Ps. 31:19); universal (Ps. 33:5); "endures continually" (Ps. 52:1); reason to "give thanks" (Ps. 107:8, 15); leads "to repentance" (Rom. 2:4); for the believer's fullness (Rom. 15:14); and "fruit of the Spirit" (Eph. 5:9).

Righteousness. The Lord is the personification of this quality. Practical righteousness is the outworking of our positional righteousness, which we do not produce but only bear as fruit. It is the sanctification of conscience, the distinct aroma of a character contrary to all that is unworthy. High principle, scrupulous honor, a stern fidelity to duty, even in the smallest things, form part of this fruit of the Spirit.

Truth. Christ came as the personification of truth: "I am . . . the truth" (John 14:6). When we walk in the light as He is in the light, our lives are characterized by no sham, unreality, inconsistency, or falsehood but by a transparent blamelessness.

As those redeemed by the blood of Christ, we should reflect to a godless, unrighteous world all Christ is in Himself—good, righteous, and true.

July 9

> *[Moses] took some of its blood and put it on the tip of Aaron's right ear, on the thumb of his right hand, and on the big toe of his right foot.* LEVITICUS 8:23

The consecration of the ancient, holy priesthood is symbolic of the dedication of the believer who, through grace, is a priest to God. In the setting apart of his sacred task, Aaron was blood-marked in a special way. The priests first had to be cleansed by a threefold process from personal sin, then set apart for God's service in a threefold blood-mark.

The right ear. The sacrificial blood on the ear intimated that the ears had to be always open to heavenly voices but closed to earthly voices, which entice one away from truth and godliness. Today, when alluring voices of the world are more insistent than ever, we need ears sensitive to the quiet whispers of the Spirit. We need ears alert to the cry of a lost world, desperately in need of God. Blood-marked ears instinctively close to all gossip, slander, and questionable jokes.

> Open my ears, that I may hear
> Voices of truth thou sendest clear;
> And while the wave-notes fall on my ear,
> Everything false will disappear.

The right hand. Consecrated ears inevitably lead to consecrated hands. Listening to the voice of God calling us to service and hearing the cries of sinners and sufferers result in hands ready to help. Loving hands are held out to strugglers in the troubled sea. Consecrated hands willingly surrender consecrated money to God's work.

The right foot. Ear, hand, and foot marked by blood seem to say: "You have been redeemed and every organ, faculty, and power must be surrendered to the Redeemer." Our great High Priest, in the days of His flesh, was consecrated to God. His *ears* were ever open, listening for His Father's voice and for the cry of the needy. His *hands* were ever active in the gracious task of relieving all the distressed around him. His *feet* carried Him over rough and rocky roads and were often weary in His work but never weary of it.

July 10

[Look] diligently . . . lest any root of bitterness springing up cause trouble. HEBREWS 12:15

Such a solemn warning to believers is most necessary because bitterness poisons everyone and everything it is leveled against. Like a fever it can spread and impair human relations. The writer of Hebrews may have had in mind the message Moses delivered to Israel about the sin and terrible end of idolatry, "that there may not be among you a root bearing bitterness or wormwood" (Deut. 29:18). Wormwood is a poisonous herb. Its inclusion here implies that the root from which sin springs is not only bitter but poisonous. Peter, in his exposure of Simon Magus, referred to the warning of Moses when he declared that the sorcerer was "poisoned by bitterness" (Acts 8:23). Simon was a root of bitter poison in the early church.

A root is hidden in the ground, and we become aware of it only when fruit or flowers appear. When a person with the root of poisonous influences in the heart is among an assembly of believers, he brings disruption and bitterness into the church. An evil root may now lurk hidden in some heart, but when the fruit appears, it will be a harvest of misery to many. We should search our own soul to discover if there is any root of bitterness growing in the soil. If there is, then with all prayer and thoroughness we should root it out before it can spring up to cause trouble to ourselves and others. A root always grows as long as it is left living in the ground. By nature, it cannot remain inactive but is always spreading out beneath the surface before it reveals itself in branch and leaf. Similarly, the longer bitter feelings remain in the heart, the stronger they grow and become harder to kill.

On the way to Damascus, the bitter root in Saul of Tarsus was transformed in a moment by Christ's redeeming love and power. With the root of a renewed nature implanted, Saul became Paul, the greatest figure in the New Testament other than Jesus who Himself came as a root out of the dry ground to bear a glorious harvest.

July 11

"O Death, I will be your plagues!/ O Grave, I will be your destruction!" HOSEA 13:14

Among ancient Greek legends is the one about the city of Athens doomed each year to supply a tribute of young men and maidens to the monster of Crete. However, the hero Theseus embarked with a crew and accompanied the victims that he might confront the dreadful ogre in his den. Slaying him, Theseus would forever free his native city from the burden of death under which it had groaned.

Did not the prophet Hosea predict the victory of Jesus, our heavenly Theseus, when he affirmed that One would deliver from the power of the grave? "O Grave, I will be your destruction!" Did not the same song of victory come from Paul when he exclaimed: "O Death, where is your sting? O Hades, where is your victory?" (1 Cor. 15:55).

When Jesus left heaven and clothed Himself with the garment of our humanity, it was with the glorious purpose of becoming death's death. He destroyed death by dying at Calvary. Now the saint can sing, "The fear of death has gone forever." John depicted Jesus as having the keys of death hanging at His side, indicating that all power is the Lord's to shut so that none can open and to open so that none can shut. How blessed it is to know that the Lord is not far away when death, as the last enemy, is forever vanquished by Him who was once dead but is alive forevermore! "Up from the grave he arose, with a mighty triumph o'er his foes./He arose a victor from the dark domain,/ And he lives forever with his saints to reign."

Alive in Him when we come to the valley of the shadow of death, we will have no fear. The deathless One Himself is with us to lead us to His heavenly home where there is no death.

Until that time Evan Hopkins would have us sing:

Work on, then, Lord, till on my soul
Eternal light shall break,
And, in Thy likeness perfected,
I "satisfied" shall wake.

July 12

Their strength is to sit still. ISAIAH 30:7 KJV

Isaiah would have us experience the strength gained from a certain form of inactivity, namely, sitting still—a great trial for the person who must always be doing something. Ours would be a great achievement if only we could learn to sit and wait.

Isaiah recorded how the Jews desired to have a sense of security in the midst of their enemies and sought to secure it by forming an alliance with their ancient masters and oppressors on the banks of the Nile. Displeased at this effort, God told His people that the strength of Pharaoh would be their shame, and their trust in the shadow of Egypt, their confusion. The security they sought would not profit them. Their strength could only be found by sitting still under God's protection and providence.

To sit still does not imply an idle bodily composure but a humble dependence upon God. It is a contrast to dashing about, seeking help from various sources. Those who place their confidence in anything or anyone other than in the Creator will sooner or later find it a reproach to them. Martha was "distracted" about many things, but her sister Mary chose "that good part," sitting still at the feet of Jesus (Luke 10:40, 42). Moses assured Israel of divine deliverance when escape from the Egyptians seemed hopeless. "Do not be afraid. Stand still, and see the salvation of the LORD, which He will accomplish for you today" (Ex. 14:13). All the people had to do was "stand still," facing, as it were, graves in the sea. Standing still did not mean physical inactivity, for God commanded the people to "go forward." He expected trust in the divine promise: "The LORD will fight for you, and you shall hold your peace" (Ex. 14:14).

What spiritual strength is ours as we wait before the Lord and wait for Him to work in His own wonderful way!

July 13

Endure hardship as a good soldier of Jesus Christ. 2 TIMOTHY 2:3

Sometimes uncommitted people come to us asking what the Christian life is like. If we imply it is a bed of roses, we err. We should look to God's Word for the answer. Recall what that intrepid missionary Paul said about the Christian life: "You therefore must endure hardship as a good soldier of Jesus Christ. No one engaged in warfare entangles himself with the affairs of this life, that he may please him who enlisted him as a soldier" (2 Tim. 2:3–4).

1. *A good soldier endures hardships.* The first activity of an enlisted person is to go through weeks of basic training. The orientation period consists of drilling and running obstacle courses. Enlisted persons do not expect to have their breakfast served in bed. Rather, they know they will have to perform calisthenics before the morning meal and do KP duty afterwards. Before an inspection of the barracks, they will spend time shining, scrubbing, and polishing. A good soldier is willing to sustain injury, even to risk death.

2. *A good soldier avoids civilian entanglements.* The person on combat duty is ready to move out when needed on a mission. That person cannot get involved financially or emotionally with civilian goals.

3. *A good soldier tries to please the one who enlisted him.* The soldier is loyal to the commander. He also fears punishment if he disobeys.

Every one of these points applies to the Christian life. This message is so different from the worldly themes of ease and affluence that we must heed Paul's word to be a good soldier.

Must I be carried to the skies on flow'ry beds of ease,
While others fought to win the prize and sailed thro' bloody seas?
Sure I must fight if I would reign; Increase my courage, Lord;
I'll bear the toil, endure the pain, supported by Thy word.

Reaffirm your commitment to your Savior, and endure hardships with His help.

July 14

You shine as lights in the world, holding fast the word of life. PHILIPPIANS 2:15–16

In *Pilgrim's Progress,* John Bunyan described Christian and Hopeful drawing near to the deep river of death where they met two shining ones whose raiment shone like gold and whose faces shone as the light. Being thus illuminated, they were able to lead the two pilgrims into the city as they emerged from the river. Bunyan was not portraying angels in his figure of shining ones, but the saints shining as lights in the world—a world lost in the darkness of sin. As Jesus was about to leave His disciples, He prayed not that they should be taken out of the world but left in it to shine in the dark places.

Absence of light means not only darkness but also *danger,* as can be our experience when a blackout occurs because of electrical failure. The question is: Are we helping to banish the spiritual darkness in the little piece of the world we represent? We must think of the place where light is needed as well as what the light is in itself. The word Paul used for lights means "luminaries," and it is the same term found in the account of creation: "Let there be lights in the firmament of the heavens" (Gen. 1:14). We are to shine as the stars in the azure sky, scattering beams of grace to all around us. The sacred light we manifest is not self-created but comes from Him who declared Himself to be "the light of the world" (John 8:12). Our light then is reflected and shines more and more until the perfect day.

Paul makes it clear that the manner of our shining is associated with the Word of life. We are to hold it forth as a lamp to our feet and a light to our path. God made the sun, moon, and stars to shine for the benefit of the world. As His new creation, we are to display the illuminating Word so that it can be seen by those who are perishing in sin and who are in danger of eternal darkness. May the Lord enable us to shine constantly as lights!

July 15

"They all with one accord began to make excuses." LUKE 14:18

An old proverb has it: "Do it and make excuses." This is exactly what the ones Jesus described were guilty of; they indulged in an act of disobedience and then, when exposed, excused themselves. Excuse making was originated by Adam. Forbidden by God to touch the tree of knowledge, both Adam and Eve tasted of its fruit; then struck with conviction, they foolishly tried to hide from God. Called from his hiding place, Adam crept out and heard the divine question: "Have you eaten from the tree?" (Gen. 3:11). His excuse was ready: Eve gave me the fruit; it was not my fault. Then God confronted Eve, and her excuse was, "The serpent deceived me, and I ate" (Gen. 3:13). From those first excuses we have had a succession of their kind, accusing or else excusing one another.

No matter how good an excuse, it is impossible to persuade oneself, and very rarely anyone else, that the excuse is truth. An unknown poet left us the lines:

> Oftentimes the excusing of a fault
> Doth make the fault worse by the excuse;
> As patches set upon a little breach
> Discredit more a hiding of the fault
> Than did the fault before was so patched.

A person good at making excuses is seldom good for anything else. This is certainly true of those Jesus described as being invited to a great supper but who, with "one accord," came up with excuses that were disguised lies. For instance, the farmer bought some ground, without seeing it before the purchase. What good farmer would be guilty of such folly? As those who profess to be the Lord's, we should not have the word *excuses* in our vocabulary. If we err, it is a fault to excuse ourselves.

Instead of making excuses, it is better to confess the fault and claim anew the blood of Jesus that is able to cleanse us from all sin.

July 16

"You give them something to eat." MATTHEW 14:16

The Anglican Church observes a Sunday in Lent known as Refreshment Sunday. It is so called because in the gospel reading for the day is an account of people resting in the fields, eating divinely provided food they found refreshing and nourishing. It is the record of Christ's miracle in the feeding of the five thousand. Miracles are shadows revealing something spiritual behind them, and the miracle Jesus performed at the close of a busy day was a lesson that He is the Bread of Life.

There was the *recognition of need,* for Jesus said, "[They] have nothing to eat" (Mark 8:2). He knew that the people who followed Him would starve if food were not forthcoming. He is always concerned about our daily food, as He taught us to pray: "Give us this day our daily bread" (Matt. 6:11).

There was also the *recognition of order,* for Jesus commanded the people to "sit down in groups of fifty" (Luke 9:14). It would have been a hard task to feed thousands if they were all walking around. That day Jesus revealed that order is one of heaven's laws.

Then there was the *recognition of that which we have.* The village was too far away to purchase the large amount of food required. The disciples produced the five loaves and two fishes they collected, and with these, Jesus satisfied the hunger of a vast crowd. Little is much if God is in it. God the Son multiplied what a boy surrendered.

Further, there was the *recognition of waste,* for the fragments of food were gathered into twelve baskets for later use. How careful Jesus was concerning those leftovers! As His followers, we should avoid any willful waste. Our axiom should be: "Waste not, want not."

Finally, there is *the recognition of Himself* as the One who is able to feed our souls as well as our stomachs. Does He not daily feed us with Himself and with His promises?

Thank God for His refreshing care.

July 17

"Friend, go up higher." LUKE 14:10

In "In Memoriam" Tennyson gave us the lines:

I held it truth, with him who sings
  To one clear harp in divers tones,
  That men may rise on stepping-stones
Of their dead selves to higher things.

Sir Philip Sidney expressed his aspiration in the words: "And thou, my mind, aspire to higher things." Spiritual elevation should be our constant aim as indicated in Sarah Adam's great hymn: "Nearer my God to Thee,/Nearer to Thee." We are like mountain climbers. The higher we climb, the purer the air and more widespread the view.

We fail, however, to remember that humiliation is the ladder to elevation, that the only way up is down. Jesus took upon Himself the form of a servant and humbled Himself to the brutal death of the cross. Afterwards, He was highly exalted and given a name above every name. If we are to rise higher, we must die to self and become more conscious of our spiritual poverty. Further, ours must be a total separation from the world insofar as its godless pleasures and practices are concerned. We cannot rise higher if the things of earth are not growing dim in the light of His glory and grace. Contamination prevents elevation. Commented Matthew Henry: "The way to *rise high* is to *begin low.* Thou shalt have honor and respect before those who sit with thee. . . . Honor appears the brighter for *shining out of obscurity.*"

God always delights in exalting those of low degree. May He always find us kneeling at His feet, recognizing that without Him we are nothing, have nothing, and can do nothing! Before the humblest individual there are inconceivable possibilities, endless discoveries, and undreamed-of blessings.

Before long, the sweet voice from heaven will say, "Come up higher," and we will rise from the dusty lanes of earth to the golden streets above.

July 18

"The LORD is God of the hills, but He is not God of the valleys." 1 KINGS 20:28

How entirely wrong the Syrians were, when they limited the jurisdiction of God! Both hill and valley are within reach of His hand, and over both His heart beats graciously. Oliver Cromwell, in a letter to the general assembly of the Church of Scotland in 1650, wrote: "I beseech you, in the bowels of Christ, think it possible you may be mistaken."

The best of persons makes mistakes. In a speech at the Mansion House in London, E. John Phelps said: "The man who makes no mistakes does not usually make anything." The only person in the world I have ever known who never made a mistake is Jesus.

King Ben-Hadad, ruler of the Syrians, made a colossal mistake, as he discovered to his loss, when he declared that the God of the hills was not the God of the valleys. The king went against a small handful of God's people, and they defeated him, causing him to flee. Ignorantly, Ben-Hadad put his reserves in battle, counting on the fact that it would be fought in the hills. Returning with a larger army and staying away from the hills, he kept to the valleys, doubtless with the idea that he would be out of the way of Israel's God. But again he was routed and made to escape for his life. Thus two defeats forced the king to believe that God is God of the valleys as well as of the hills.

This mistake of thinking God is in one place and not in another is a common one today. Some people seem to think that God is in the church but not in their business, and they often act as if He were not omnipresent and omniscient. But there is no place where God does not exist, whether it be in the hills or valleys. When David asked, "Where can I flee from your presence?" (Ps. 139:7), he answered his own question by saying that if he took the wings of the morning to fly to the uttermost parts of the sea, he would find God waiting for him there.

In the desert with only a stone as a pillow, Jacob had a dream that God was in all places. When he awoke, he confirmed: "Surely the LORD is in this place, and I did not know it" (Gen. 28:16). What a comfort it is to know that whether we are on the mountaintop sparkling with light or in the valley of shadows, God is always surrounding us!

July 19

Thus Noah did; according to all that God commanded him. GENESIS 6:22

Noah will always be a sterling example of obedience to God. In accordance to the divine command, this man, who walked with God, crossed every *t* and dotted every *i*. Although he was not a shipbuilder living in a seaport town, Noah was commissioned to build a large ship, the likes of which had never been heard of before. How easy it would have been for him to make excuses and to reply truthfully to God: "I know nothing about building ships, nor do my sons, and there are no ship carpenters around I can engage to help me." But Noah did not raise the slightest objection and went to work at once. Implicitly, he obeyed God and fashioned the ship, or ark, to divine specifications.

To Noah's godless contemporaries, the story of a coming flood seemed an idle tale. They must have thought godly Noah a bit of a nut, but he fearlessly forged ahead with his task, and as did Paul, he proved that he could do all things through God who strengthened him.

Have we learned that God's commands are His enablings, that what He asks of us He always imparts strength to obey? "He who calls you is faithful, who also will do it" (1 Thess. 5:24). One day Charles Wesley said to his famous brother, "If I had a pair of wings I would fly away!" John Wesley replied, "If God told thee to fly, he would give thee a pair of wings."

Never say, "I can't," to anything God tells you to do. At the marriage in Cana, Mary, the mother of our Lord, said to the servants of the house: "Whatever He says to you, do it" (John 2:5). And they did obey, helping thereby in the miracle of turning water into wine. With Shakespeare in *Henry VIII*, may we learn to say: "The will of heaven be done, and the King's pleasure/By me obeyed."

July 20

"Little by little I will drive them out." EXODUS 23:30

Both Scripture and human experience agree with Sir Arthur Conan Doyle who wrote: "It has long been an axiom of mine that the *little things* are infinitely the most important." Little by little, the Canaanites were driven out of their land by the Israelites. Our hearts and lives are what Canaan was when the Israelites succeeded—full of wild beasts, or lusts, evil thoughts, and desires. But little by little as God's sanctifying grace works in us, more of the territory of our lives becomes His. How we must guard against those little sins and faults that spoil Christian character—the little foxes that spoil the grapes!

The whole record of great scientific discoveries and inventions suffices to show that the apparently trivial may be of vast importance. The falling of an apple led to the discovery of the law of gravitation. The steam issuing from a kettle was the starting point of the steam engine. Greatness of little things can also be seen in nature, as Julia A. Fletcher Carney wrote: "Little drops of water,/Little grains of sand,/Make the mighty ocean/And the pleasant land."

Tennyson tells us how he came "to be grateful at last for a little thing." Is such gratitude ours? We read that Bethlehem Ephrathah was "little among the thousands of Judah" (Mic. 5:2); yet out of it came the mighty ruler. That little things count in human life is suggested by Hannah More in her lines:

> The sober comfort, all the peace which springs
> From the large aggregate of little things;
> On these small cares of daughter, wife, and friend,
> The almost sacred joys of home depend.

May we remember the words of Wordsworth: "That best portion of a good man's life,/His little, nameless, unremembered acts/Of kindness and of love." Jesus reminded His disciples that the gift of a small cup of water to a needy one would merit a reward.

July 21

Empty pitchers, and torches inside the pitchers. JUDGES 7:16

In Israel's sad days, God raised up Gideon, and thousands flocked to follow his brave leadership. Out of thirty thousand soldiers, he chose three hundred. Dividing them into three companies, he gave each man a ram's horn and an earthen pitcher with a torch, or lamp, hidden within it. One midnight Gideon grouped his valiant three hundred around the tents of Midian and Amalek, then silently moved them closer and closer to the sleeping foes. When Gideon blew a great blast on his own horn, every man did the same, and they all cried: "The sword of the LORD and of Gideon!" (Judg. 7:18). The soldiers broke their pitchers, and the lights within flashed forth.

The robber army was startled from sleep by the sound of the horns and shouting. Seeing the flashing lights through the darkness, the enemies were overtaken by panic and fled, only to be pursued by Gideon's band and killed. Thus the gallant judge achieved a great victory for Israel.

One wonders whether Paul had this incident in mind and applied it when he wrote: "God who commanded light to shine out of darkness who has shone in our hearts to give the light of the knowledge of the glory of God in the face of Jesus Christ. But we have this treasure [of light] in earthen vessels, that the excellence of the power may be of God and not of us" (2 Cor. 4:6–7). The pitchers, the outflashing of the lights at night, and the excellent power that gained the victory hold a precious lesson for our hearts. Poor, weak, and fragile though we may be as vessels, we carry a divine light and life which cannot be destroyed and which can shine forth and win glorious victories for God who is able to fill the weakest with strength for His service. In ourselves we are vessels of neither gold nor silver but of clay—earthen and empty vessels.

When the brilliant light and power of God are revealed through us, what marvelous things are accomplished as we shine as lights for Him.

July 22

"Glistening stones of various colors, all kinds of precious stones." 1 CHRONICLES 29:2

Among the most valuable items David collected for the building of the temple he was not permitted to build were precious stones. The exact nature of these costly gems is not easy to determine. For "glistening stones," the New American Standard Bible gives us "stones of antimony." The Revised Standard Version in Isaiah 54:11 has the same description, "stones in antimony" instead of "colorful gems." Antimony is a bright, silvery white, metallic substance used in many ways. Applied to the stones David stores up to adorn the temple, antimony can suggest their sparkling beauty and splendor.

Smooth and brilliant stones can be made more beautiful by being polished with their dust. Roughly cut and coarse at first, a diamond is rubbed and rubbed again with diamond dust and thus made to sparkle. A proverb has it: "Experience teaches fools." But this is only partially true, for experience also teaches those who are wise. As living stones, we take on a better polish as we rub against our old sins and mistakes and learn to leave them behind. When we learn from our failures, they become like the dust of our old selves to make our lives glistening for Him who is the brilliant chief cornerstone.

The heavenly lapidary, the Holy Spirit, is unceasingly active in removing all that is coarse and rough in God's jewels, or redeemed children, polishing them to adorn His palace with its gates of pearl. Among the precious stones of Scripture, from which Bible students can gather many insights, is the white stone, the symbol of heavenly glory. According to ancient custom, a white stone was given to an acquitted person after being tried; a black one to the guilty and condemned. Through grace, ours is a divine acquittal. The writing of "a new name" in the "white stone" denotes not only a freedom from condemnation but also an adorning of victory with heavenly glory (Rev. 2:17).

Some of David's people presented their precious stones for the Lord's treasury. As the giver of the best, He should receive our best.

July 23

But He gives more grace. JAMES 4:6

James, a pillar in the early church, described himself as "a servant," or slave, of God and of the Lord Jesus Christ. His mission was to minister "to the twelve tribes which are scattered abroad" (James 1:1). Without a doubt, he was a preacher of the generosity of God. James 1:5 proclaims that God "gives to all liberally." Evidently James remembered the words of the Lord Jesus: "Whoever has, to him more will be given, and he will have abundance" (Matt. 13:12). So James came to write of the generosity of God in giving.

God never limits the supply nor is He ever weary of giving while we are asking and receiving His ever-expanding grace. The range of God's sympathy is seen in that He gives to all. Whosoever will may beg at His footstool. God always gives with an open hand, never meagerly, partially, or grudgingly. He loves a cheerful giver, since His grace is unmeasured and unmerited. God gives joy, and it is always unspeakable. The magnanimity of God's liberal heart comes out in the words, "without reproach" (James 1:5). He blesses in the gentlest way all who seek His abundance. Said an unknown writer: "God mingles no acids with His honeycomb . . . He is too eager for my temporal and spiritual wealth to mar the welcome gift with a harsh word."

Further, James affirms the certainty of God's response to our request for wisdom or other virtues to make us more effective witnesses. It will be given to us. From experience, James himself knew how liberally God answered prayer.

How encouraging it is to know that we cannot carry to our generous God a petition that dismays or overwhelms Him. The more we desire, the more He will grant. Philip P. Bliss, inspired by James 4:6, gave us the lines:

Have you on the Lord believed?
Still there's more to follow.
Of His grace have you received?
Still there's more to follow.

July 24

"He does not give an accounting of any of His words." JOB 33:13

Elihu claimed that God does not give an account of all His doings. As God does according to His will, which is perfect, why should He give an account to mankind of what He does? The call is, "Be silent, all flesh, before the LORD" (Zech. 2:13). Because He is the omnipotent God, He is not responsible to puny human beings who often complain about divine providence. He is not accountable to any and will not be questioned by the curious or called to account by the proud.

Our finite minds cannot grasp the infinity of God nor fully understand His purpose behind many of the perplexing experiences of life. "With whom did He take counsel, and who instructed Him?" (Is. 40:14). Not until we see Him will all be fully revealed, and then we shall bless the hand that guided and the heart that planned. Because of the perfection of His character, He demands that we trust Him where we cannot trace Him. To strive against Him or to resist Him is actually rebellion and treason, for His designs, although mysterious to us, are always gracious and beneficial.

In his "Ode to Napoleon Bonaparte," Lord Byron has the verse:

> 'Tis done—but yesterday a King!
> And armed with Kings to strive—
> And now thou art a nameless thing,
> So abject—yet alive!

Those who continually strive against the King of kings, against His Word, His commands, and the dispensations of His providence, become as abject, nameless things. God's wisdom is infinite; His love, unchangeable; His power, unlimited. Therefore, may we cease to strive against Him and, instead, lovingly and willingly submit ourselves to His perfect will and trust Him completely.

July 25

God said, "Ask! What shall I give you?"

1 KINGS 3:5

It would seem as if God presented Solomon with a blank check to draw what he liked from heaven's plentiful treasury. But the young king took no undue advantage of God's bounty that knows no winter of scarcity. All Solomon desired was "an understanding heart to judge Your people, that I may discern between good and evil" (1 Kin. 3:9). God liberally supplied Solomon with such unusual wisdom that "there has not been anyone like you before you, nor shall any like you arise after you" (1 Kin. 3:12). We may link God's request, "Ask! What shall I give you," to Christ's word to His own, "Ask, and you will receive" (John 16:24), but heaven does not respond indiscriminately and give us anything we ask for. We have to remember, too, the words of James: "You ask and do not receive, because you ask amiss" (James 4:3).

Had Solomon asked selfishly for long life, riches, or the death of his enemies, he would have asked amiss and not received. Scripture must be balanced by Scripture. John said, "We know that we have the petitions that we have asked of Him" (1 John 5:15). But he was careful to affirm that God only responds to those requests in harmony with His will: "If we ask anything according to His will, He hears us" (1 John 5:14). Thus, in all things we ask, we must observe this proviso: *according to His will.* God always gives freely and plentifully when there is harmony between His will and our wishes. Having endless resources, He is never restricted in Himself and constantly asks us to avail ourselves of all we have in Him, in whom dwells all the treasures of wisdom and knowledge. Like Solomon, we can pray for wisdom. Our understandings need to be enlightened, our wills brought into perfect agreement with the will of God, and our affections fixed on Him and on holy, heavenly things.

'Tis so sweet to trust in Jesus,
  And to take him at his word;
Just to rest upon his promise,
  And to know, "Thus saith the Lord."

July 26

She fastened it with the pin. JUDGES 16:14 KJV

The Bible is the most fascinating book in the world to those who love and study under the inspiration of its divine Author. For instance, have you noticed what it says about the value of small things we lose more than use? The pin Delilah used to entangle Samson's long hair was not the same as the little, metal, straight pins we buy today. A pin in Scripture refers to a small piece of wood fashioned like a peg. The New King James Version has it: "She wove it tightly with the batten of the loom."

Scripture warns us against despising small things (Zech. 4:10). What lessons a slim, sharp-pointed pin can teach us! When we say, "You could have heard a pin drop," we imply that it is silent and noiseless in action. Is this not how the Holy Spirit works in heart and mind? Another old expression is, "bright as a new pin," often used of a child who is clever. Jesus, we are told, "grew in wisdom," and He will ever remain a shining example to the young. Further, pins are of little use if they are blunt. To fulfill their function they must be sharp. When Paul wrote, "Not lagging in diligence . . . serving the lord" (Rom. 12:11), he implied that we must not be dull or blunted in any way. The smallest pin has both a point and a head—the former is necessary to pierce its way into a garment, and the latter to prevent its going too far. Its head seems to say, "I stop here." Do we not need grace to guide us when to start and when to stop? Anyone who works with pins knows only too well that a crooked pin cannot fulfill its purpose. Jesus died and rose again that crooked lives might be made straight and fit for His use.

In *Richard II,* Shakespeare comments on small things:

> As if this flesh that walk about life
> Were brass impregnable, and humour'd thus
> Comes at the last, and with a little pin
> Bores through his castle wall, and farewell king!

Dedicate the little things of life to God's greatness.

July 27

"I have the keys of Hades and of Death." REVELATION 1:18

The symbol of keys in Scripture offers a most profitable meditation. If we lose our metal keys, a clever locksmith can duplicate them. But Bible keys are irreplaceable. They are symbolic of authority, of sovereignty, and of commanding regal and legal power. Keys in Christ's hands signify His ruling power in forbidding, punishing, binding and loosing, condemning and saving. As the head and heir of all things, He possesses absolute power and authority. As the "only Potentate, the King of kings and Lord of lords" (1 Tim. 6:15), He rules supremely and universally. He has "the key of the house of David" (Is. 22:22), and as the One who came as the Son of David, He has the prerogative to open shut doors and to close open ones (Rev. 3:7–8).

Christ declared Himself to be the possessor of "the keys of Hades and of Death," the sphere of departed spirits, whether they are in heaven or hell. As the One who died but is now alive forevermore, He has regal power over the devil, demons, and hell, and thereby provides eternal security for those redeemed by His precious blood. To the apostles, Christ gave the keys of the kingdom of heaven, a ministry and office they, and all saints, exercise. The nature of these particular keys is revealed in the context, namely, His deity, His sufferings, His death and resurrection. These facts constitute the gospel. We must accept them before we can enter the kingdom. Along with Peter, every child of God can use these keys to open the door of salvation for the lost.

How we rejoice to have the key of Scripture in our hands and the Holy Spirit within our hearts to open for us the inner understanding of all truth! So we sing:

> Open my eyes that I may see
> Glimpses of truth thou hast for me;
> Place in my hands the wonderful key
> That shall unclasp and set me free.

July 28

That in all things He may have the preeminence. COLOSSIANS 1:18

Our Father is pleased to cause all fullness to reside in His beloved Son. Christ is pre-eminent in Scripture. Martin Luther said: "There is one Book and one Person. The Book is the Bible: And the Person is Jesus Christ." Every part of the sacred volume reflects His blessed person: "In the scroll of the Book it is written of me" (Ps. 40:7).

Christ is also pre-eminent in creation. He is the creator and sustainer of all creation. It is His child. He upholds all things by the word of His power.

Christ is also pre-eminent in grace. In this realm, He is supreme, peerless, and incomparable. His grace is sufficient at all times and under all circumstances. He is the source of every precious blessing.

The truth of our Lord's pre-eminence has been realized and revered by the greatest minds in every age and sphere. If He is not Lord *of* all, He is not Lord *at* all. He claims the recognition and admiration of the highest and the lowest. He is the magnetic attraction to which the point of the human needle flies.

Christless eyes see no beauty in Jesus that they should desire Him, but true faith acknowledges Him to be the center and sum of all things.

We thank Thee, Lord, for this fair earth,
  The glittering sky, the silver sea;
For all their beauty, all their worth,
  Their light and glory, come from Thee.
Thine are the flowers that clothe the ground,
  The trees that wave their arms above,
The hills that gird our dwellings round,
  As Thou dost gird thine own with love.

July 29

Hadassah, that is, Esther. ESTHER 2:7

Although no divine name is found in the book of Esther, divine providence is most conspicuous. God is shown overruling in the affairs of His people in a foreign land. Secretly He works until His purpose is achieved. As James R. Lowell expressed it: "Standeth God within the shadow, keeping watch above his own."

The record unfolds the story of Esther, an orphan girl cared for by her uncle Mordecai who treated her as his own daughter. The sacred historian gave the young Jewess a double name—Hadassah and Esther. The significance or virtue of a name depends upon the character of the person or object bearing the name. Shakespeare asks, "What's in a name? That which we call a rose/By any other name would smell as sweet."

Hadassah means "myrtle," a plant that remains green and beautiful even through winter months. Mordecai took this precious plant into his home (long before the Persian king took her into his palace) and nurtured her until she became a plant of renown. Her physical beauty was matched by an inner loveliness of soul.

Esther means "star." Mordecai is most likely the one who changed her name to Esther. When she became a great queen, her humble fear of God shone like a brilliant star. Through God's overruling providence, Esther grew up like a myrtle and came to glow like a star, and her character illustrated the significance of the two names she bore. A myrtle with its sweet fragrance remains ever green. A star sparkles because God clothed it; it shines "up above the world so high, like a diamond in the sky." Esther remains in sacred history because of her brilliant action in saving the whole Jewish nation from slaughter.

The desire of God is to fashion all His human myrtles into stars.

July 30

Josiah was eight years old when he became king. 2 KINGS 22:1

At the early age of eight, Josiah assumed the kingship of the Jews. He reigned for thirty-one years. This youngest king in Israel's history has a parallel in English history in Edward VI, who was sometimes called the "Josiah of England" because he became king at nine years of age. Like Josiah, Edward had a reverence for God and His Word. As a boy he saw somebody secure a large Bible to stand on, in order to reach something on a shelf, and the young king said, "You must not stand on the Bible, it is God's Book." What a joy it would be if only we could see more children loving and honoring the Bible and treating it with the reverence it deserves!

Both Josiah and Edward VI turned out to be good kings. Josiah had a wicked father, Amon, but a very good mother, Jedidah, who doubtless had a large share in influencing her noble son. No doubt she trained him to do what was right in the sight of the Lord. For those who are surrounded by the young, they should remember that children can be guided in life by Christ Jesus.

In the eighth year of his reign, Josiah began to seek after God. From early childhood he had loved everything about God. Loving God's house, then in a bad state, he set about repairing it. When the Book of the Law was found and read, Josiah tore his clothes and joined in the repentance of his people. God was pleased with the youthful king because his "heart was tender" (2 Kin. 22:19). At sixteen years of age Josiah began thirsting after God in a more intense way, and he gained a rich reward in his godly reign. If you are a parent or have care of the young, may grace and patience be yours to teach the young at your side to do what is right in the sight of the Lord. When we lead a boy or a girl to Jesus, we do not know what great things that one may accomplish for Him in later years.

July 31

A certain man drew a bow at random, and struck the king of Israel. 1 KINGS 22:34

Chance can mean "the unpredictable way events occur," "leaving things to risk," "probability." Alexander Pope reminds us that a chance can be a direction we cannot see. John Milton would have us think of "That power/Which erring men call Chance."

What the captains, with their special commission to kill the king of Israel, failed to do, a Syrian soldier accomplished. Taking aim at the enemy, the soldier drew a bow by chance, and away the arrow sped, piercing not another ordinary soldier but the king of Israel himself.

Our words and deeds are often like those randomly shot arrows striking an unexpected target. God gives them a direction we could not see. Doubtless, if the soldier who drew a bow at random had been told that he would shoot the king and win a battle, he would have laughed and said: "Not I!" Is not this same principle also seen in the things we do?

Some of the greatest consequences come out of the smallest chance actions. Invading Scotland, the Danes prepared for a night attack on the sleeping garrison. All of them crept forward, barefooted, but one of the Danes stepped on a large thistle that made him cry out. That cry aroused the sleeping Scottish soldiers, and springing to arms, they drove the Danes back.

The lesson we must learn from the Syrian soldier is that no words or deeds are really unimportant. An unkind word may escape our lips without any purpose on our part to hurt anybody, but out it goes like a poisoned arrow into another heart. The arrow hits a mark we did not expect. Of this we can be certain: If all the arrows we shoot are kind, helpful, Christlike words and actions, direction from heaven will guide them to beneficial ends.

August 1

I am the rose of Sharon. SONG OF SOLOMON 2:1

In today's meditation, we consider the rose of Sharon. Sharon, an area near Joppa and perhaps notable for flowers, is used figuratively of excellence. Fragrant and beautiful, the rose is the fitting emblem of the Lord Jesus, whose grace and merits are sweet and refreshing to the spiritual senses. His very name is as precious "ointment poured forth" (Song 1:3).

Roses are my favorite flowers. How beautiful, pleasant, and delightful are their colors to the eye! Added to their perfect beauty is their fragrant, most excellent scent. The parallel to Christ is not difficult to see. He came as an "aroma of life" (2 Cor. 2:16) and as the One "white and ruddy" (Song 5:10). Benjamin Keach believes that these colors may suggest our Lord's two natures while among men: the *white,* His deity, natural purity and innocence; the *ruddy,* His humanity, bloody agony and suffering for our sakes. Truly, no object is so heartbreakingly beautiful to the eye as Jesus in His humiliation and sacrifice for our sins and in His exaltation. As the rose, complete beauty and fragrance are His.

The roses that grew in Sharon were the best and most singular in their loveliness as the queen of flowers. Is this not true of the Lord Jesus who is the glory of things in heaven and things on earth? In every way He is fairer than the children of men. As the rose of the heavenly Sharon, Jesus never fades but remains "the same yesterday, today, and forever" (Heb. 13:8). His beauty and glory remain the same in summer and winter.

Let each soul make haste our Sharon's Rose to get.
In Him is life, we perish if we taste not.
In Him are joys, eternal joys that waste not.

August 2

The lily of the valleys. SONG OF SOLOMON 2:1

In yesterday's reading we compared Jesus to the lovely beauty and fragrance of a rose. Today we will think of Him as having the attractive qualities of a lily. First of all, this lovely flower is a fitting symbol of Jesus since it is always pure white and has a whiteness exceeding all flowers. Within it are seven grains, or seeds, of a golden color. Calling those around Him to "consider the lilies," Jesus said that "Solomon in all his glory was not arrayed like one of these" (Matt. 6:28–29). Because whiteness implies holiness, this virtue is absolutely inherent in Christ in whom is no sin. His holiness is the perfection of beauty. His bride is clothed in white and will "walk with [Him] in white" (Rev. 3:4).

Another similarity is seen in that the lily, although a very tall flower, hangs its head, directing its beautiful little bells toward the ground. This characteristic is also symbolic of Jesus who, although superior to any on earth, was meek and lowly in heart. Such humility should also be the glorious ornament of a Christian. A universal flower, with an unusual sweetness all its own, the lily resembles Him who came as the Savior of the world with a beauty all His own. The lily grows in the earth which is dark and black, yet it grows up white, illustrating the transforming power of Christ. When He was on earth, He was despised and rejected; He was as "a lily among thorns" (Song 2:2).

Jesus beautifies and cares for His children, and in turn, they manifest a loveliness and a fragrance that bring joy to His heart. Notice that the plural *valleys* is used in today's verse. Believers experience many valleys between the cradle and the grave. When they reach the last valley, the valley of death, the precious and beautiful Lily will be with them: "I will fear no evil;/For You are with me" (Ps. 23:4).

August 3

Owe no one anything
except to love one another. ROMANS 13:8

Some people push the interpretation of this verse to its limits and claim that it means the Christian should never borrow money. They have a point, but this verse does not say that. It says, in effect, that the debt of love is the only debt saints should owe. Remember that the apostle Paul closed his precepts of civil order with the universal command of love. Our world would be a better place to live in if all of us shared the expressed hatred of C. H. Spurgeon, who once said that he hated three things—dirt, debt, and the devil.

As those forgiven for our spiritual debts, we must avoid absolutely the social disloyalty of debts and, with watchful eye, pay every creditor in full. Great truth is expressed in Emerson's phrase, "Pay every debt, as if God wrote the bill." All of us who have been redeemed by the blood of Jesus should be prompt and punctual in payments; we should not be guilty of rash speculations resulting in heavy debt, which is a breach of the divine precept. We should live within our means and not bring disgrace upon our Christian witness by contracting debts we are unable to pay. Too often, in order to keep up with the Joneses, we incur debts that become a burden.

As the children of God whose debt of sin was paid at Calvary, we should be more concerned about adorning the doctrine of God our Savior than about spending beyond our means in order to keep up appearances. To quote Bishop Handley Moule: "Love is to be a perpetual and inexhaustible debt, not as if repudiated or neglected, but as always due and always paying." An unknown writer has said: "Let all who bear the Christian name their loving vows fulfill;/The saints—the followers of the Lamb—are men of honor still."

August 4

Heap coals of fire on his head,/
And the LORD will reward you. PROVERBS 25:22

When Paul repeated Solomon's gospel of magnanimity, he added a proverb of his own: "Do not be overcome by evil, but overcome evil with good" (Rom. 12:20–21). Overcoming evil with good illustrates the heaping of coals of fire upon an enemy's head. Longfellow's description of Hiawatha is appropriate: "For his heart was hot within him,/Like a living coal his heart was."

Coals of fire suggest warmth. In ancient times the process of melting and purifying metal was crude. Rough nuggets of gold were hard to soften, but heaping coals of fire on the head of the crucible greatly helped to melt and refine the metal. The hearts of scribes and Pharisees were not hot with love, but when Jesus came, He gave the old commandment new life by loving His enemies. Great patience was His, but He knew that the gold of hard hearts melts slowly. Burying them in the warmth of His love, He heaped coals of fire upon them until enemies were made friends. The kindness Jesus manifests will either bring about contrition and friendship or harden His foes.

The divine way to treat those in need of kindness and friendliness is to mollify them as the refiner melts his metal in the crucible, not only by putting it over the fire but by heaping coals upon it. We can transform enemies into friends only by acting toward them in a loving, friendly manner. Nothing can nourish those in need like the milk of human kindness. The psalmist's heart was strangely warmed by the marvelous kindness God showered upon him in a strange city. When we love our enemies, bless those who curse us, do good to those who hate us, and pray for those who despitefully treat us and persecute us, we heap coals of Calvary's heart-warming fire upon their hearts and heads. We earn, thereby, our loving Father's reward.

August 5

Joshua the high priest standing before the Angel of the LORD, *and Satan standing at his right hand to oppose him.* ZECHARIAH 3:1

In his valuable commentary on the book of Zechariah, Dr. F. B. Meyer says that hope is the one thought pervading Zechariah's prophecy. Like Peter, the prophet is a messenger of hope. This feature is clearly evident in the chapter before us with its divine rebuke of Satan. In the opening verses we have the conflict between the adversary and the advocate, with the latter victorious over the former. Some writers suggest that "the Angel of the LORD" is a person of high dignity in the angelic realm—perhaps Jesus in one of His preincarnation appearances. This, however, could hardly be the case in light of Zechariah 1:12–14, where the personality of this special angel of the Lord is distinct from the Lord Himself.

Satan, whose name means "adversary," has acted in this capacity since man's creation and was justly rebuked by the question: "Who shall bring a charge against God's elect?" (Rom. 8:33). The saints of God are persistently accused by Satan who ever stands by to resist them as they seek to live and witness for their Lord. Their unfailing source of relief and victory is the knowledge that Jesus, the advocate and mediator, is at hand. Jesus enables them to resist all the fury of the fiery darts sent by the satanic adversary. By His power, believers are more than conquerors over hellish tricks. We should be encouraged and assured that Jesus is at our side to preserve us against all who would condemn us.

Although heavily assailed by hellish influences with no one standing by to help him, Paul could say: "But the Lord stood with me and strengthened me, so that the message might be preached fully through me. . . . I was delivered out of the mouth of the lion" (2 Tim. 4:17). Anne Steele, of the eighteenth century, left us these lines: "Look up, my soul, with cheerful eye,/See where the great Redeemer stands/The glorious Advocate on high."

August 6

No chastening seems to be joyful
for the present, but grievous;
nevertheless, afterward it yields
the peaceable fruit of righteousness. HEBREWS 12:11

The writer of the wonderful epistle to the Hebrews knew how to deal with God's chastening of His redeemed children and also with the results of any adversity He permits. The writer would have us know that the ripest benefits are sorrow-borne. There is clear shining after rain. In his *Epistle to a Protestant Lady* William Cowper wrote: "The path of sorrow, and that path alone/Leads to the land where sorrow is unknown."

Divine searching and scourging are never joyous. Nevertheless, afterward we come to bless the hand that guided our way and the heart that planned it, although part of the plan included tears and sorrow. How full of significance is the term *afterward*! What despairing would be ours if there were no afterward to explain the meaning of our tears! Scripture is replete with the records of saints like Joseph, Hannah, and Job who, severely tried and tested, came to experience a blessed afterward. God's discipline of His redeemed children is never misguided but always wisely administered for their profit. Those who allow themselves to be corrected by it come to prove its beneficial and blessed results. Harsh plowing yields joyful and bountiful harvests.

The believer grows rich by his losses, rises by his falls, lives by dying, and becomes full by being emptied. Grievous afflictions result in the peacable fruits of righteousness in this life and the full vintage of joy in the afterward of heaven. Sometimes the heart is perplexed over what God may permit in life, but patience must be allowed to do her perfect work. The cross may be our lot today, but tomorrow, the crown. As an unknown hymnist reminds us:

> We may not fully understand
> How underneath God's chastening hand
> Pain is fulfilling love's command
> But afterward!

August 7

"A stronger than he . . . overcomes him." LUKE 11:22

In our Lord's discourse about casting out demons, His illustration symbolizes His victory over Satan (see Luke 11:14–23). As the stronger, Jesus came upon the boastful strong man and overcame him. Through His life, death, and resurrection, He conquered the satanic foe. We sing about marching *on* to victory, but actually, since Calvary, we march *from* victory. Triumph over all hellish enemies, as well as the security of our redemption, was in Christ's final cry of conquest: "It is finished!" (John 19:30). Now, by faith, we make His victory our own. Satan still displays his strength as the enemy of all righteousness and is the unwearied foe of all saints. Only too well, we know that he excites to sin, accusing us before God, and strives to overcome our faith in God and His Word.

Calvary's victory over Satan enables us to steadfastly and successfully resist him through all that Christ, his opponent, is to us. Satan is still a deadly serpent, but Jesus is the brazen serpent who heals. Satan is still a roaring lion whose roars warn us of his attacks, but Jesus is the prevailing "Lion of Judah." Satan is still a wolf assaulting the little flock, but Jesus is the good and great shepherd protecting His sheep. Satan is still our foe, but Jesus is our abiding friend. Satan is still a liar and the father of lies, but Jesus is ever the truth. Satan is still branded as the accuser, but Jesus is the advocate. Satan is still the prince of darkness, but Jesus is the light of the world. Satan is still a murderer, but Jesus is the resurrection and the life.

Satan may continue to boast his power and position as the god of this world, but our triumphant Lord is ever stronger than the world's hellish deity. As A. C. Dixon expressed it:

Jesus is stronger than Satan and sin,
Satan to Jesus must bow;
Therefore I triumph without and within,
Jesus saves me now.

August 8

I will run in the way of Your commandments, / For You shall enlarge my heart. PSALM 119:32

Benjamin Disraeli gave us the dictum, "Experience is the child of Thought, and Thought is the child of Action," which is the sentiment of our text. Running implies vigorous action, but, as David reminds, we must run on the track of the divine Book. To run and not be weary is dependent upon the enlargement of one's heart. The strong action of the heart in all holy things comes as the result of the Spirit's operation upon it. Only those who wait upon the Lord can run without weariness. Our Great Physician knows that all spiritual disease is heart disease, which must be remedied before effective action in service can occur. Athletes know that running is a strong, healthy movement of the whole body, requiring energy and a sound heart. We cannot run in the way of God's commands except in the strength and vigor He calls "enlargement of heart," which implies a love for and cheerfulness in doing the will of God.

Alas, sitting Christians are more numerous than running Christians. Paul decided that the Christian life is a race we have to run and run well if we would win a prize. Enlargement of the heart by God implies an outgoing beyond all the limits that self-interest would impose. Heartiness as an action for God depends upon the heart cleansed and kept clean by Him. Our hearts must be daily enlarged to take in ever-increasing thoughts of God. When He fills our hearts to the limit, He enlarges this capacity to receive more, and so the faster we run.

The word *walk* is often used to denote the habitual obedience to Christ, but the term *run* signifies the energy of such a life. Scripture also has a great deal to say about rest, and some commentators assert that this and not action is the rule and privilege of our life in Christ. But it is neither, for our privilege is rest for the soul and our rule must be action.

Action then becomes ours through the power and anointing of the Holy Spirit.

August 9

I . . . tell you even weeping, that they are the enemies of the cross. PHILIPPIANS 3:18

The apostle Paul always lived under the impact of the record of his master weeping over the sins of Jerusalem. His warm, Christlike tears were shed not only over those who were utterly godless and positively hostile to the idea of a man dying for their sins but also over those who professed Christ and sought to shelter beneath His cross. Paul's tears, his liquid agony, over those in the Philippian church indicate at once the tenderness of a mourner and the awful certainty of the coming ruin of those who were enemies of the Cross because they did not see in it the evil of sin. They had the distorted belief that although under grace, they could give the reins to sin instead of being strangers to its attractions. They would not submit to the authority or conform themselves to the example of Christ who died upon a cross.

To such enemies, the *Christian liberty* Paul preached meant license. Continuing in sin that grace may abound, those Philippians made themselves the foes Paul described them to be. Thus they turned "the grace of our God into licentiousness" (Jude 4) and earned for themselves the severe judgment of destruction. If the Cross is all our glory, then we must never by conduct or conversation bring disgrace upon it. We must endeavor in every possible way to advance its victory, spread its glory, and bring sinners to trust Him who was crucified upon it for their salvation.

Because that wondrous Cross is the foundation of our hope, the key opening the gates of paradise, the object of angelic wonder and the cause of Satan's everlasting destruction, it should give us pain to be considered its enemy in any way. May grace be ours never to be ashamed of, or a shame to, the Cross! May He who died in our place enable us to glory in His cross, declare its triumphs, and hold it up in the face of a godless world as its only hope for life, here and hereafter!

August 10

"How often I wanted to gather your children together, as a hen gathers her chicks under her wings, but you were not willing!" MATTHEW 23:37

In this heart-rending cry of Jesus, so full of compassion and affection not only for Jews but for all who spurn His love and provision, three aspects can be discerned: (1) His infinite grace and patient endeavor—"How often I wanted to gather your children together"; (2) His way of accomplishing His gracious design—"As a hen gathers her chicks under her wings"; and (3) His wail of disappointment—"But you were not willing!" In this sad utterance our Lord's use of the image of a hen is indicative of His lowliness and brooding love, so tenderly pouring itself out, not only in tears but also in blood.

It is said that no creature is so moved with compassion toward her young ones as the hen. When Jesus wept over Jerusalem and cried with mournful voice, "O Jerusalem, Jerusalem," He revealed His great compassion. He had an eagerness to seek and save as He made Himself a beggar pleading to be taken in. Naturalists have also observed that the hen will attack any ravenous birds seeking to destroy her chicks and will defend them at the risk of her own life. No matter what enemy strives to devour His own, Christ is always at hand to shield and preserve them. The hen provides nourishment as well as shelter for her brood and scratches all around, gathering any good thing for them but often wanting food for herself. Does not our sacrificial Lord provide us with spiritual sustenance as well as safety? He offers Himself as the Bread of Life, even His body: "My flesh is food indeed, and My blood is drink indeed. He who eats My flesh and drinks My blood abides in Me, and I in him" (John 6:55–56). Another characteristic of the hen is that she soon forgets her chicks, which she has bred and brought up. But Jesus is different from the hen, for He will never forget His saints.

May we never be guilty of disappointing the seeking love of Jesus!

August 11

"I bore you on eagles' wings and brought you to Myself." EXODUS 19:4

Among the numerous symbols illustrating all the Lord Jesus is in Himself, none is more forceful than that of the eagle, a royal bird. It spreads its strong, large wings for swift flight and for succor and help of its young. Jesus, with His great affection like two great wings, is ever ready for the help and succor of His own. Swifter than an eagle, He is at hand to protect His church against her enemies.

The eagle tends to rest on the highest rocks (Job 39:27–28). After our Lord's resurrection came His ascension, when He mounted up exceedingly high, far out of human sight into the heavens. At the Rapture, swifter than an eagle He will snatch His own, in a moment, in the twinkling of an eye, from a godless world. The "flying eagle," prophesied by John, portrays God's swiftness in the execution of His power in creation and judicial government (Rev. 4:7).

An eagle trains her young to mount up on high, even as she flies. Isaiah's prophecy is that the Lord is able, if only we wait upon Him, to grant us strength to "mount up with wings like eagles" (Is. 40:31). The question is: Have we a yearning for the spiritual heights to which the Lord, high and lifted up, calls us?

How our hearts praise the Lord for all He sacrificed for us when His heart, hands, and feet were pierced for our salvation! May we ever be found hiding under His wings for gracious protection and provision! Said David: "In the shadow of Your wings I will make my refuge,/Until these calamities have passed by" (Ps. 57:1).

August 12

"The hope of the hypocrite shall perish . . . whose trust is a spider's web." JOB 8:13–14

Although only three references to spiders appear in the Bible, precious truths can be gathered from the description given of them. We are fascinated as we watch spiders weave their beautiful webs. Nevertheless, we think them horrid creatures and mistakenly seek to destroy them. In spite of our aversion to spiders, we must not forget that they only fulfill the instinct an all-wise Creator implanted within them and that they are of much value in diminishing the swarms of insects assaulting us. Deprived of these crafty hunters, we would be plagued like the Egyptians of old with flies. Public prejudice may be against the spider, but we can all imitate its prowess in seeking to destroy that which is evil. While hiding in his cave from foes, King Robert the Bruce of Scotland learned a lesson as he watched a spider trying again and again to weave its web.

As a weaver, the spider shows remarkable skill. Its web, although so frail, is a marvelous production distinguished by beauty of design, fineness of construction, and sensitivity to touch. By its frailty, the web illustrates the trust of the hypocrite. The weaving of the web by the wicked will not supply them with a garment (Is. 59:5–6). How fruitless is the effort to provide refuge from the wrath of God!

The spider is no respecter of persons or places. Whether in a hovel or a king's palace, it displays the same skillful weaving of its web. But in spite of its wonder and charm of design, its sole purpose is that of destruction, as Mary Howitt suggests in "The Spider and the Fly": "Will you walk into my parlor?" said the spider to the fly;/"'Tis the prettiest little parlor that ever you did spy." Insects learn too late that the web is a murder chamber, not a cozy parlor.

The satanic spider seeks to entrap the unwary souls of men. That the spider's web can be easily destroyed reminds us that the hypocrite's hope, so cleverly conceived, will perish like a fragile web; the Christian's hope is the enduring Rock of Ages.

August 13

This honor have all His saints. PSALM 149:9

The emphasis in David's affirmation is on the small word *all.* All God's redeemed children form a spiritual republic in which the highest places are within the reach of even the poorest ones. The most unworthy can be a prince in His realm. Wordsworth, in "The Prelude," reminds us we are "Brothers all/In honor, as in one community,/Scholars and gentlemen."

All persons by divine grace are one in Christ Jesus and thus share equality in the honor of being a people close to the Lord. The particular honor the psalmist associates with saints includes "high praises" and joyfulness, "a two-edged sword in their hand" and God-given authority to execute "judgment" (Ps. 149:6, 9). Honor becomes an empty bubble if we do not realize how wonderfully we have been blessed by God.

When asked to cover up the stars on his uniform, Lord Nelson replied, "In honour I gained them, and in honour I will die with them." All we have through grace was gained for us by the honor of our heavenly substitute, and that has become our eternal honor.

The only recipients of the honor mentioned by David are the saints. All redeemed by the blood of God's holy Son are saints. Scripture seldom uses the singular word but nearly always the plural, *saints.* The multitudes on earth are divided into two sections: "The Saints and the Ain'ts." Among all the titles by which Scripture describes believers, *saint* is the most expressive one of the life they must live as followers of their holy Lord. Called to be saints, we are born again of incorruptible seed by the Holy Spirit through the Word and acknowledged by God as His children and as His heirs and joint-heirs with His beloved Son, who is our advocate on high. Such honor includes our glorification and participation in Christ's future universal reign. May we always be mindful of the honor that is ours to be His saints!

August 14

*"Spring up, O well!/
All of you sing to it."* NUMBERS 21:17

This sole Bible reference to the well of Beer is important because it was the subject and object of a divine promise. God commanded Moses to gather his thirst-stricken people there, and He would give them water for themselves and their cattle. As the people quenched their thirst, filled their vessels, and watered their cattle, they burst forth in the song of joy of which we have only a fragment: "Spring up, O well! . . . sing to it!"

In times of revival when there is the marvelous manifestation of the Holy Spirit's power in the salvation of the lost and the quickening of the saints, holy joy exists. Today an acute spiritual thirst exists. Multitudes are dying in sin because of the lack of the water of life.

May the Spirit so possess all preachers of the Word that out of them may flow those living waters to enliven those smitten with thirst! We must keep in mind that what God has promised to give, we must earnestly inquire after and prepare for.

The well of Beer was the object of effort, for we read that it was "dug by the nation's nobles . . . with their staves" (Num. 21:18). As C. H. Spurgeon put it:

> The Lord would have us active in obtaining grace. Our staves are ill adapted for digging in the sand, but we must use them to the utmost of our ability. Prayer must not be neglected, the assembling of ourselves together must not be forsaken: ordinances must not be slighted. The Lord will give His grace most plentiously, but not in the way of idleness. Let us, then, bestir ourselves to seek Him in Whom are all our fresh springs.

For each of us, may there spring up that marvelous grace of God in fountains over our souls, causing the dry places to blossom as the rose and to be as beautiful as the garden of the Lord. Let our personal prayer be: May the living waters rise within me forever.

August 15

The commandment is a lamp,/
And the law is light.

PROVERBS 6:23

Solomon seems to have had in mind his honored father's image of the lighted lamp that appears in Psalm 119: "Your word is a lamp to my feet/And a light to my path" (v. 105). God has hung up in the heavens the lamps of sun, moon, and stars to give a flood of light upon the darkness of earth. But the light of truth in God's most holy Word is brighter than the heavenly luminaries, and it never goes out and never sets. It never requires trimming or relighting as will a lamp of our own making. This perpetual, infallible lamp gives more light than we can use, shines brighter when trials and sorrows make life darkest, and sheds its light through the valley of the shadow of death to the gate of heaven.

A lamp is of no use if there is no light within it. We can think of the lamp as the written Word itself—the Bible, printed, bound, and ready to be read and studied. The light is the Holy Spirit within it who inspired holy persons of old to fashion the lamp and who ever waits to shed light upon its precepts and promises and enlighten our minds to receive and understand them.

It is comforting to know that we can take this divine lamp and make it our very own to throw light upon our way as we journey through life. When the Spirit shines through the lamp, He brings the truth to sight, causing the commandments and counsels to shed a searching light upon our hearts and lives. William Cowper wrote these truths:

A glory gilds the sacred page,
  Majestic, like the sun.
It gives its light to every age;
  It gives, but borrows none.

Let the lamp of His Word lighten your life through diligent, Spirit-led study.

August 16

"The LORD *is my portion,"*
says my soul. LAMENTATIONS 3:24

God is frequently referred to as the portion or inheritance of His people. The term itself implies a part of the whole, a share received by gift or inheritance. God's people are His heritage, indicating His great love and His providential care. How privileged the saints are to have a share of and in God! Shelley termed it, "A portion of the Eternal." The surprising aspect is that God condescends to consider His people His portion. The difference is that He does not have a share in them, He owns them. They are His redemption right.

As the recipients of the Lord as our portion, we are ever with Him. All He has is ours. What a suitable, sufficient, and satisfying portion He is! We have His power to support us, His wisdom to guide us, His love to comfort us, His mercy to relieve us, His goodness to supply us, His justice to defend us, His covenant to assure us, His person to accompany us, and His heaven to receive us. We should recognize that having God as our portion means that we are to draw upon His resources, rejoice always in Him, trust Him for all we need, daily walk with Him, renounce worldly portions, and glorify Him in all our life.

We should be constantly assured of the security we have in Him; no one can deprive us of that. He is our heavenly portion, and nothing can destroy it. Those around us may fail or deceive us, but God is our impregnable fortress.

> A mighty fortress is our God,
> A bulwark never failing;
> Our helper He, amid the flood
> Of mortal ills prevailing.

August 17

Who is he who will harm you
if you become followers
of what is good? 1 PETER 3:13

Notice the little word *if*. As we consider Peter's assurance of preservation from danger, we need to bear in mind that he has given us one of those conditional promises of Scripture. Immunity from harm can only be ours *if*—this *if* is the door of the condition—if we "become followers of what is good." In the next few verses Peter tells us what constitutes the good—the sanctification of "the Lord God," "good conduct in Christ," and obeying "the will of God" (1 Pet. 3:15–17).

Chrysostom, the courageous church father of the fourth century, was not afraid to tell the Roman emperor that he could do nothing to harm him since God was his portion. The pagan monarch replied: "I will take your riches." The fearless saint answered: "My treasure is in heaven." The ruler threatened: "I will banish you from your friends." Chrysostom replied: "My best Friend will never leave me." The emperor continued: "I will exile you from your country." The church leader readily answered: "Heaven is my fatherland; heaven is my home." Somewhat exasperated by this time, the godless emperor said: "I will take away your life." The dauntless warrior, however, boldly met the threat in his final reply: "My life is hid with Christ in God. There is nothing you can do to hurt me."

In Christ, we are not only saved but also safe and secure. The people of Malta, when a viper out of the fire fastened itself on Paul's hand, thought the apostle was a murderer. They were truly amazed when he shook the viper off into the fire, but Paul himself "suffered no harm" (Acts 28:5). The command of old was: "Do not touch My anointed ones,/And do My prophets no harm" (1 Chr. 16:22). Nothing can harm us if we truly believe, "As the mountains surround Jerusalem,/So the LORD surrounds His people/From this time forth and forever" (Ps. 125:2).

August 18

"I will search Jerusalem with lamps." ZEPHANIAH 1:12

The wax candles with which we are familiar were unknown in biblical times; hence, the term *lamps* for "candles" appears in all recent translations. The language the prophet recorded suggests the meticulous care of God in His thorough searching out of hidden things He must expose. No corner is missed in which sin could escape its just punishment. All must be brought to light. The unexamined life is not only fruitless but fatal, which is why the Bible recommends both divine and human examinations of the heart (see 1 Cor. 11:28; Ps. 26:2). As it is sadly possible for a person to work *for* the faith and yet not be *in* the faith, the double search is imperative for the soul's eternal welfare.

The thoroughness of the heavenly Searcher's effort is emphasized most fully in the wonderful Psalm 139 (compare "searched" in v. 1 to "search me" in v. 23). When we work with God to minutely search our hearts, we discover those forbidden things we did not seek. Are we prepared to examine ourselves carefully, deliberately, and prayerfully, taking God's Word as our rule and guide? Is our daily prayer to be searched to discover whether there is any wicked way within us? James Morris, in "Poems," expresses it:

> Searcher of hearts! Oh, search me still:
> The secrets of my soul reveal;
> My fears remove: let me appear
> To God and my own conscience clear.

Whenever I think of the kind but searching glance of God, who with lamp in hand throws light into the darkened cells within the heart, the hymn of F. Bottome comes to mind:

> Search me, O God! My actions try,
> And let my life appear
> As seen by Thine all-searching eye,
> To mine, my ways make clear.

August 19

Be content with such things as you have. HEBREWS 13:5

How appropriate are the lines on the virtue of sweet contentment that John Bunyan gives us in *Pilgrim's Progress*:

I am content with what I have,
Little be it or much;
And, Lord, contentment still I crave,
Because Thou savest such.

The Bedford tinker goes on to describe how it is best for those on a pilgrimage to have "Here little, and hereafter bliss."

Looking out on life, Paul observed, "Having food and clothing, with these we shall be content" (1 Tim. 6:8). Baron Houghton, a nineteenth-century poet, wrote of the "land of lost content." Do we not live in such a land? Is not discontent the most conspicuous feature of multitudes around us who are bent on seeking out some new thing? In our industrial world we forget the biblical declaration: "Be content with your wages" (Luke 3:14). We may not have what we wish, but if we are the Lord's, we certainly have what He thinks best for us. Such godliness is the source and secret of true contentment. As a solitary virtue, contentment has no beneficial end.

We may find it hard to learn Paul's lesson: "I have learned in whatever state I am, to be content" (Phil. 4:11). In "Sweet Content," Thomas Dekker, of the seventeenth century, has written the verse:

Art thou poor, yet hast thou golden slumbers?
Oh sweet content!
Art thou rich, yet is thy mind perplexed?
Oh punishment!

The inspiration of all true and satisfying contentment is the abiding companionship and provision of Christ: "Be content. . . . For He Himself has said, 'I will never leave you nor forsake you.' So we may boldly say: 'The LORD is my helper' " (Heb. 13:5–6). It is said that "grass grows content through the heat and the cold." We should develop such a peaceful contentment in our hearts.

Gratefully revel in the contentment your Savior provides.

August 20

We do not have a High Priest who cannot sympathize. HEBREWS 4:15

Jesus was always touched with the feeling of our infirmities. One of our gospel hymns speaks of Him as "The Sympathizing Jesus." Sir Walter Scott, in *The Lay of the Last Minstrel,* embodies this virtue that makes us kind:

> It is the secret sympathy,
> The silver link, the silken tie,
> Which heart to heart and mind to mind
> In body and in soul can bind.

One of the wonders of our Lord's incarnation is that when He became man, He forged a silver link with humanity and came to experience its sorrows, temptations, and needs. Too often, we confuse sympathy with sorrow. But one can have genuine sorrow for a person afflicted in some way or another without personally experiencing the anguish he or she may be bearing. You cannot, however, have sympathy for the person if you have never known in your life what that person is enduring. Jesus was the sympathizing friend as well as the sorrowing one. In his prophetic portrayal of the Savior, Isaiah wrote: "In all their affliction He was afflicted" (Is. 63:9). Because He became acquainted with our grief, He is able to console and help us in our sorrows. "'Man of sorrows!' what a name/For the Son of God who came/Ruined sinners to reclaim!"

Ezekiel became a scholar in the school of sympathy when, finding himself sharing the captivity of those around him, he confessed: "I sat where they sat" (Ezek. 3:15). *Sympathy,* then, means an "affinity or relationship," "a correlation," "the capacity of entering into and sharing the feelings, interests, and trials of others." Jesus enables us to learn life's secrets in the school of experience so that in turn He can use us in a world of tears to weep with those who weep.

There would be fewer broken hearts around us if only the virtue of a God-inspired sympathy were more manifest.

August 21

"I know your . . . poverty (but you are rich)." REVELATION 2:9

In Scripture, riches represent the wealth of heavenly things, spiritual gifts received through Christ who, although rich, became poor that we through His poverty might be made rich. The spiritual wealth of the believer is different from the wealth of the wretch Sir Walter Scott described who, although "Boundless his wealth," was "concentered all in self" and died "Unwept, unhonor'd, and unsung."

The saints at Smyrna were materially poor, yet Jesus could say of them: "But you are rich." Broadly speaking, the majority of saints today are poor in respect to what the world counts as wealth, but as James reminds us: "Has God not chosen the poor of this world to be rich in faith and heirs of the kingdom?" (James 2:5). Graciously, He has bestowed upon His own as much spiritual wealth as they wish to claim. As a hymnist expressed it:

Call'd by grace, the sinner see,
Rich though sunk in poverty,
Rich in faith that God has given,
He's a legal heir of Heaven.

Paul highly commended the churches of Macedonia who "in a great trial of affliction the abundance of their joy and their deep poverty abounded in the riches of their liberality" (2 Cor. 8:2). This is the gold refined in the fire, making us rich. As poor sinners enriched by grace, we have received donated wealth, since Jesus has bequeathed us unsearchable riches. We have the wealth of all the good things He has promised us. We are rich in relationship, having God as our Father, Jesus as our Savior and advocate, and the Holy Spirit as our invisible companion. Because all who believe inherit all things, they should be rich in good works and in expectation of the eternal city God has prepared for them. Our true wealth, then, is beyond compare. His righteousness justifies us. His blood cleanses us. The Spirit sanctifies us. The angels minister to us. Heaven is to be our everlasting habitation.

May grace be ours to claim our boundless wealth and not live as spiritual paupers!

August 22

"I will bless you . . .
you shall be a blessing." GENESIS 12:2

Frequently occurring in the Bible are the related terms *bless, blessed, blesses,* and *blessing*. These words emphasize the favor, goodness, kindness, and all the good things God bestows upon His people and also are the means of conveying a beneficial gift or ministry to those in need. From God, we have material blessings and those of a spiritual nature.

When Abraham answered the call of God to journey into the unknown, he received a double blessing, "I will bless you . . . you shall be a blessing." Unless ours is the continual dew of heaven's blessing, we cannot be a blessing to earth's needy. God cannot bless and use us above the level of our own spiritual experience. God's grace saves us, forms our characters, and fits us for His service. By His wisdom He charts our course, imparts strength to accomplish His will, and supplies all that is necessary to complete His design and ultimately crown our efforts. "I will bless you." How richly He has kept this promise! We must be careful, however, to be more concerned about the Blesser than His blessings, about the Giver than the gifts.

Blessed of God, the source of all blessings, we are to function as a channel of blessing to others by a meek and quiet spirit, by the imitation of the Savior's example, by our intercession and service for the lost, by our efforts to spread abroad by lips and literature the knowledge of the Lord to save. Is our desire to be made a blessing since God has abundantly blessed us? If so, eternity alone will reveal all who have been blessed as the result of our life and consecrated service. We are to abound with blessings. As Johnson Oatman, Jr. would have us sing:

> When upon life's billows you are tempest tossed,
> When you are discouraged, thinking all is lost,
> Count your many blessings—name them one by one,
> And it will surprise you what the Lord hath done.

August 23

"Come with me, and see my zeal for the LORD." 2 KINGS 10:16

Scripture clearly distinguishes between true and false zeal. *Zeal* is "an ardor or fervor in the pursuit of anything." A *zealot* is "an uncompromising partisan." True zeal is a divine quality (Is. 9:7). Epaphras had a "great zeal" for the spiritual welfare of the Colossians (Col. 4:13). Saul exhibited false zeal in the slaying of the Gibeonites (see 2 Sam. 21:2). Paul's persecution of the church proved his false "zeal" (Phil. 3:6).

Alexander Pope depicted those who fight for "modes of faith" as "graceless zealots." Jehu was certainly a graceless zealot. He had zeal but lacked grace. Consumed by ardent passion, he acted with speed and thoroughness as an instrument of divine judgment upon Ahab and the followers of Baal when his own life was corrupt. There was no spiritual life at the core of his diligence. Indulging in the sins of Jeroboam, he "took no heed to walk in the law of the LORD God" (2 Kin. 10:31). He offered strange fire upon the altar. Jehu's zeal was not according to God's will, and his invitation to Jehonadab to accompany him on his ruthless mission revealed in a flash the central pride of his spirit. We cannot have too much of the holy fire or too little of the strange and forbidden fire.

Jehu had zeal, but he was destitute of the passion to act only for the glory of God. He was proud of his ardor, and such pride is always perilous, wherever it exists, since it leads to other personal evils. How perilous is self-glorification in the fulfillment of a divine mission! We manifest a perverted zeal when we strive to promote the cause of God by lack of tenderness toward others or when we exhibit a fervor to build up a righteousness of our own while neglecting and spurning the true righteousness of divine provision. We may find it hard to forego confidence in our own merit and ability and to accept the fact that only Jesus is our hope and glory. God might have to ask of us the questions Isaiah posed to Him: "Where are Your zeal and Your strength,/The yearning of Your heart/and Your mercies toward me?" (Is. 63:15).

August 24

"The eternal God is your refuge." DEUTERONOMY 33:27

Several times in Scripture God is portrayed as the strong and safe refuge of His people. The term *refuge* means "a safe habitation in a person or place to which we hasten to be secure from danger." When human help fails, our only hiding place is in Him who offers Himself to keep us safe. "He is known as her refuge" (Ps. 48:3). To provide necessary shelter and protection, a refuge must be a monument of strength and provision, having no fear of approach and attack by foes. As the omnipotent one, God is a glorious refuge, infinite in strength, and He will be able to protect us against all satanic assailants. He carries us on His shoulders, and we "dwell in safety by Him" (Deut. 33:12).

Further, it is important that a refuge is not too distant, so that when trouble or danger is near we can run quickly into it and be safe. Is it not wonderful to realize that our heavenly Refuge is always near to all that call upon Him? God is not only a God afar off but also "a God near at hand" (Jer. 23:23). In a refuge, quietness and confidence are our strength, no matter what adversity may be ours. Our minds are fortified against all fear, even against the chastening of God. When the powers of heaven are shaken, the hearts of the ungodly are smitten with terror But our security is assured for, with David, we can say: "In the shadow of Your wings/I will make my refuge,/Until these calamities have passed by" (Ps. 57:1).

The Old Testament cities of refuge were provided against the avenger of blood by divine appointment for the retreat and safety of the manslayer. Through Christ, God appointed an all-sufficient refuge from all who accuse and pursue poor sinners. By His blood and mediation, Christ protects them against wrath and vengeance and graciously delivers them from eternal condemnation.

August 25

"There was a certain landowner who planted a vineyard and set a hedge around it, dug a winepress in it and built a tower." MATTHEW 21:33

Without doubt, this parable of Jesus depicts God as the landowner. He planted the vineyard (a symbol of the Jews settled in Canaan), set a hedge around them, dug a winepress for them, and built a tower. The vinedressers mentioned later in today's verse are responsible for farming the vineyard. They are God's priests, prophets, judges, kings, and apostles who help make the vineyard fruitful. Ultimately, God sent His Son to take care of the vineyard, but the Jews killed Him.

The term *landowner* suggests three aspects of such a profession, namely, "a person possessing an estate or portion of land"; "a person active in the oversight of such holdings"; and "a person with servants to assist him." Typically, these three aspects are applicable to God who is, first of all, possessed of a vast estate, for the earth with its fullness is His; He "formed the earth and the world" with all its inhabitants (Ps. 90:2). He is "the LORD of all the earth" (Zech. 6:5). Second, God never ceases to further His oversight of His own creations, accomplishing His will on earth as well as in heaven. Third, God has a vast company of angels and servants to assist Him. They receive a divine reward for being good and faithful servants.

A good landowner equips the family and household for the furtherance of their service. All are assigned to tasks they are capable of fulfilling. As Benjamin Keach expressed it:

> God as the great and good Householder hath made nothing in vain, but has fitted each creature with natures to do work, suitable to their proper station; the angels to dwell in Heaven, to praise God there, to fly to earth and do service for the sons of man; men are fitted to look up to Heaven, to pray, to reverence God, and to propagate and replenish the earth; beasts are fitted for labor and service, with all other creatures who know where their prey is, and who fulfil their assigned use.

August 26

"Underneath are the everlasting arms." DEUTERONOMY 33:27

Attributed to God, the arms suggest many qualities. As the strength of a man is manifested by his arms, whether it is by work or war, so such a quality denotes divine power. In *Oliver Twist,* Charles Dickens described Mr. Podsnap's habit of putting things behind him he wanted out of his existence: "Mr. Podsnap had even acquired a peculiar flourish of his right arm in often clearing the world of its most difficult problems, by sweeping them behind him." But God uses His right arm in a totally different way. Shakespeare said of Antony, "His rear'd arm/Crested the world," which is also true of God with His glorious, almighty, stretched-out arm.

What can a human body do for itself or for others if it has no arms to guard, protect, defend, and assist it? As the use of the arm is to the body, so God is to believers. He guards, protects, and provides for His mystical body, the church, exposed as she is to satanic assaults in a godless world. "Who . . . With His glorious arm,/Dividing the water before them" (Is. 63:12). Our assurance is that "underneath are the everlasting arms." We have the arm of God's mercy and the arm of His power, His body, the church, cannot spare either of these divine arms.

God's arms of grace and mercy embrace all who turn to Him. Christ is said to embrace His bride; "His left hand is under my head,/And his right hand embraces me" (Song 2:6).

Arms reveal care and compassion when they carry the young and the weak. God manifests these two qualities toward His weak children: "He will gather the lambs with His arm,/And carry them in His bosom" (Is. 40:11).

> What have I to dread, what have I to fear,
> Leaning on the ever-lasting arms?
> I have blessed peace with my Lord so near,
> Leaning on the ever-lasting arms.

Pray to learn from His everlasting arms how to embrace those who need affection and to minister to those who need help.

August 27

Jesus has become a surety of a better covenant. HEBREWS 7:22

At the outset, let us determine the primary meaning of a *surety*—a term that appears twelve times in Scripture. It denotes "one who pledges to undertake to pay another's debts or to provide necessary help or relief to a friend in need." It was an ancient custom in a suretyship for the surety to give his hand to, or to strike hands with, the debtor. Many suffered by being a surety for another and had to bear the loss involved. To become "surety for a stranger" will cause suffering, and the practice is condemned (Prov. 11:15).

God is our surety for good. Christ is presented as the surety of "a better covenant" than the one made to Israel (Heb. 7:22). Since a surety is one who becomes the warranty of a mutual contract, Christ is our spiritual surety undertaking on God's part. "All the promises of God in Him are Yes, and in Him Amen, to the glory of God" (2 Cor. 1:20). In every way He acts on God's part for us and prays for us that we may fulfill our obligation. A surety sometimes undertakes for another whose credit is not good or whose ability to repay a debt is suspected. When Christ became our mediator, He knew how impotent we were to provide solvency. He took our curse and debt and blotted out the handwriting against us.

At times, a surety offers to undertake not only for sincere debtors but also for criminals. Christ as surety undertook to act not only for spiritual debtors. Sins are called "debts" in the Lord's Prayer (Matt. 6:12). He acts for criminals, as His response to the cry of the dying thief proves. He acts also for all who are spiritually dead. Suretyship is a voluntary action, and all Christ assumed as our surety was voluntary, as implied by His assertion: "I lay down My life. . . . No one takes it from Me" (John 10:17–18). Rich, for our sakes He became poor. What grace and unspeakable favor He provides through the great mystery of redemption! Our debts are paid, for "the LORD has laid on Him the iniquity of us all" (Is. 53:6). Hallelujah! What a Savior!

August 28

"LORD, I pray, open his eyes that he may see." 2 KINGS 6:17

What an invisible world Scripture presents! God's "invisible attributes" can be clearly seen (Rom. 1:20). "Things . . . visible and invisible" are of God's creation (Col. 1:16). Christ came as "the image of the invisible God" (Col. 1:15). Moses endured much affliction through "seeing Him who is invisible" (Heb. 11:27).

Francis Thompson, in his poem "The Kingdom of God," affirmed the Christian ability to see the invisible: "O world invisible, we view thee,/O world intangible, we touch thee,/ O world unknowable, we know thee,"

Elisha's prayer for his young servant, when he was distressed by the visible hosts encompassing the city of Dothan, was, "Do not fear, for those who are with us are more than those who are with them. . . . open his eyes that he may see" (2 Kin. 6:16–17). Graciously, the Lord answered the prayer. He opened the eyes of the young man, who saw the world invisible—a mountain full of horses and chariots of fire.

Jacob was another who endured manifold trials, through seeing Him who is invisible to the naked eye. Jacob said: "I have seen God face to face, and my life is preserved" (Gen. 32:30).

How we need to constantly pray: "O Lord, open our eyes that we may see"! Living in a visible world, we are in fear and bondage because of all our eyes can see. Invisible satanic foes surround us, often causing us to feel that we have no way of escape from evil powers. The consciousness, however, that God's chariots are surrounding us delivers us from panic and despair and maintains our hearts in courage and in confidence. We, too, come to endure by seeing Him who is invisible. Such a faith is the assurance that invisible things are clearly seen by those who constantly pray: "Open my eyes that I may see!"

Silently now I wait for thee,
Ready, my God, thy will to see.
Open my eyes, illumine me,
Spirit divine!

August 29

"Lo, I am with you always,
even to the end of the age." MATTHEW 28:20

People want to know what is ahead. They want to see into the future. The number and nature of our days ahead are unknown, in spite of horoscope forecasters and fortune tellers. The God of our days is the only one who knows how many are left to us and what events will characterize them. Of this we are certain: the path in front of us will be strewn with flowers or thorns, probably the mingling of both. The days awaiting us will contain darkness and light, loss and gain, sunshine and shadow. But with the Lord Christ as our abiding companion, we have the confidence that He can and will always meet our every need.

There will be days of the pruning knife, the cleansing fire, the rod of discipline. But because the rod is in the hand of love, the necessary correction will be a benediction, not a blight.

There will be days of drudgery and monotony—the common round of little things such as household chores, daily anxieties, and constant toil. We long for an experience more exciting and romantic; yet drudgery can be our daily companion. Jesus' life was lived among carpenters' tools, village streets, and peasant people.

There will be days of trial and tribulation, in the home, in business, or in school. But the promise is, "As your days, so shall your strength be" (Deut. 33:25). The Lord will be with us during the press of the storm, imparting deeper faith, more courage, trust, and patience.

Finally will come the day to end all the days—the day of death, with its separation from all below. But we will not moan when we put out to sea, if He who was dead but is alive forevermore is our pilot. His everlasting arms will be around us as we cross the flood and reach the celestial city in which there are no days, since there is no element of time in eternity.

We do not need anyone to predict the future for us. It will be glorious for the redeemed sinner.

Make each day count because your tomorrows will be spent with Him.

August 30

*"Even the stork in the heavens/
Knows her appointed times."* JEREMIAH 8:7

From Scripture we learn several things about the stork:

1. It makes its nest in the fir trees (see Ps. 104:17). A large bird, it selects a tree that is high and will be able to support its nest; the height also protects it from harm.
2. It is represented as being in the heavens (see Jer. 8:7). It flies very high, especially when migrating.
3. It possesses very powerful wings (see Zech. 5:9).
4. Its name is in harmony with its nature. The word *stork* can be translated "merciful." This bird is remarkable for its tender care not only of its young but also of the aged of its kind.
5. It is classed among the unclean birds, because it feeds upon mice, snakes, and other reptiles (see Lev. 11:19). In some areas, it is valued because of its attacks upon serpents.

The stork knows its time of migration and exhibits this mystery, which is a remarkable evidence of the unsearchable greatness of God. We believe that on the fifth day of creation when He fashioned fowl that "fly above the earth across the face of the firmament of the heavens" (Gen. 1:20), He created birds with a built-in instinct enabling them to fly thousands of uncharted miles over land and water to warmer climates. Naturalists are still seeking to discover how birds are directed in their long flights.

When God created people, He gave them a built-in instinct. As Augustine wrote, "Thou hast made us for Thyself, O Lord, and our hearts are restless until they rest in Thee." By His indwelling Spirit, the same creative God guides and directs us in the days and years of our earthly pilgrimage to "a land of pure delight,/Where saints immortal reign." Does not our spiritual instinct tell us that our flight from this earth is not far distant? Are we ready for our heavenly migration, when the heavenly voice will say, "Arise, My loved one, and come away"?

August 31

"Make a fiery serpent, . . .
that everyone who is bitten,
when he looks at it, shall live." NUMBERS 21:8

In *Romeo and Juliet,* Shakespeare has the phrase: "Men's eyes were made to look, and let them gaze." The serpent-bitten Israelites of old put their eyes to good use when they looked and gazed upon the brazen serpent lifted up on a pole. Actually, no healing virtue was in the metal serpent Moses was commanded to make and exhibit. Physical relief came through the look, which indicated obedience to the divine decree. All who looked, lived. But all who refused to look and live perished from the poisonous bite of the serpents sent by God as a punishment for their sin. Bitten by death-dealing serpents, the people had to gaze at the brazen serpent if they wanted to live. In looking, they bowed to the divine will, thereby making it possible for God to heal and restore them.

The look required, however, was not to be a mere glance. The intense look of the dying Israelite indicated repentance for sin and a longing to be free from anguish. Faith was in the strange remedy God had provided. Jesus used the serpent lifted up on a pole as an illustration of His crucifixion (see John 3:14). Made in the likeness of sinful man but without his sin, Jesus was lifted up on a tree for the sinner's restoration. The divine command is ever the same: "Look on Me, and be saved." Bless God, there is always life when we look at the Crucified One!

How grateful we are for the deliverance from the disease of sin we experienced before we surveyed the wondrous cross on which He died! As C. H. Spurgeon put it: "I looked at Him—He looked at me,/And we were one forever." Our appeal to the godless is always the wondrous story: "There is life for a look at the crucified One,/There is life at this moment for thee."

September 1

"Behold, the bridegroom is coming; go out to meet him!" MATTHEW 25:6

John used the same metaphor of the bridegroom for Jesus: "He who has the bride is the bridegroom" (John 3:29). The Lord Jesus acts as a lover or suitor to engage the love and affection of sinners to Himself, and upon their repentance and faith, He joins Himself to them in a glorious marriage relationship.

When a lover makes offers of marriage to the person attracting him, he then persuades the loved one to marry him. Jesus reveals how willing He is to embrace sinners in His arms of mercy and make them His own.

He commended His favor to sinners by taking their nature upon Himself and coming into their world. His love is proved in all He willingly endured for them, even to the shedding of His life's blood. The continual pleadings of the Holy Spirit upon the hearts of sinners and also the offers of grace by Jesus Himself denote His desire to have all who are lost in sin transformed as His bride.

Often a suitor exercises much patience in his endeavor to make the woman he loves his wife. Jacob served seven years for Rachel; yet "they seemed but a few days to him because of the love he had for her" (Gen. 29:20). What infinite patience God manifests in striving to prevent sinners from dying in their iniquity! Let us examine other Scriptures: "How can I give you up, Ephraim?... My heart churns within Me; My sympathy is stirred" (Hos. 11:8); "I have stretched out My hands/all day long to a rebellious people" (Is. 65:2); and "Behold, I stand at the door and knock" (Rev. 3:20).

Patiently, as the One desiring to be the bridegroom, He waits at the door until his head is "covered with dew" and his locks "with the drops of the night" (Song 5:2). For those who are His bride, the glorious news is that He is on His way to claim her, and before long the blissful union will be consummated in the marriage supper of the Lamb.

September 2

The express image of His person. HEBREWS 1:3

Among the many references to the word *image* in Scripture, the majority of them are associated with idolatrous graven and molten images, which the Israelites were forbidden to make. The term, however, has divine associations, the first being the creation of man in the image and likeness of God. Paul affirmed that man "is the image and glory of God" (1 Cor. 11:7). James also confirmed that man was "made in the similitude of God" (James 3:9).

The word *image* itself is from a Greek root signifying "to engrave," and it implies that Adam was a representation of God in some of his attributes. When Jesus was shown a coin. He asked His disciples whose image was engraved upon it. They said, "Caesar's," indicating that it was a representation of the emperor and of no one else. Man, alas, has battered and soiled the image of his Creator, but through Christ this lost image is restored.

The divine image is perfection and is seen in Christ, the Second Adam. By His resurrection, He superseded the first Adam, who was a type of Christ. As man, He was "the image of God" (2 Cor. 4:4). The Father indelibly engraved His whole essence and majesty upon His eternal Son. In the days of His flesh Christ was His Father's substantial image and exact likeness or representation, so much so that Jesus was led to say, "He who has seen Me has seen the Father" (John 14:9). Partaking of the nature of His Father, He came manifesting the goodness, power, holiness, grace, and all other glorious properties of His invisible Father. Jesus became God-man in one person: "God was manifested in the flesh" (1 Tim. 3:16). As the word *express* used in Hebrews 1:3 implies something engraved or impressed or corresponding exactly with the original, so Jesus always remains a perfect and complete correspondence to His Father's character, attributes, excellencies, and perfections. Paul would have us remember that "the light of the knowledge of the glory of God" is "in the face of Jesus Christ" (2 Cor. 4:6).

As Christ is God's and you are Christ's, is your life a constant reflection of His indwelling?

September 3

"Those who are well do not need a physician." LUKE 5:31

As the beloved physician, Luke must have had a deep feeling of heart as he came to write of Jesus as a physician. Outlining the eleven references to physicians in Scripture, *Cruden's Concordance* has this introduction: "These were not like our physicians, as science had not progressed far. But they were healers, according to their ability. The word is also used of healers of the mind, comforters as having to do with the human body."

An ancient sacred writing has this advice: "Honour a physician with the honour due unto him for the uses which ye may have of him: for the Lord hath created him." Without a doubt, Jesus was a physician whom many honored, for when the sick were taken to Him, He healed them. Isaiah prophesied that Jesus would be the Spirit-anointed healer of the brokenhearted (see 61:1). To those He met on earth He gave spiritual healing in soul-diseases and physical healing in bodily infirmities. Ultimately, all healing is divine. Although physicians can provide relief from pain, healing itself is of Him who said, "I am the LORD who heals you" (Ex. 15:26). The heavenly Physician never fails to cure those who receive His prescriptions. Job wrote of "worthless physicians" (Job 13:4). God, however, is the perfect physician and is of great value; He never fails to provide healing for sufferers, if He believes that healing is best.

To practice today, a physician must be able to produce his license stating that he is qualified to function as a doctor. When Jesus was asked about His power to heal, especially on the Sabbath, His reply was, "I do not receive testimony from man. . . . the works which the Father has given Me to finish—the very works that I do—bear witness of Me, that the Father has sent Me" (John 5:34, 36).

Thine arm, O Lord, in days of old
Was strong to heal and save;
It triumphed o'er disease and death,
O'er darkness and the grave.

Thank God you have a Physician who makes house calls.

September 4

My beloved is like...a young stag. SONG OF SOLOMON 2:9

Here the stag symbolizes the Lord Jesus Christ. Biblical writers refer to the stag, or deer, as a very stately creature, lovely and pleasant. Our Lord is altogether lovely. What loveliness and amiableness are His! The tragedy is that so many do not see beauty in Him and desire Him. To them, He has "no form or comeliness" (Is. 53:2). Naturalists tell us that the stag bears no ill will toward other creatures. Is not Jesus like it in this respect? He never manifested rancor of spirit in all the sufferings He received from men. For those who hung Him on a tree, He could pray: "Father, forgive them, for they do not know what they do" (Luke 23:34).

The stag is the most gentle and mild beast in the world and very loving to those of its kind. Did not the gentleness of Jesus make Him great? Did He not say of Himself, "Learn from Me, for I am gentle and lowly in heart" (Matt. 11:29)? That He loves His own people is evident by the promises given them as they pass through water and fire. If it is true that the stag is sociable and delights in the company of other similar animals, can we not apply this feature to Jesus whom the common people loved to hear and also to His delight with the children of men?

Isaiah wrote that "the lame shall leap like a deer" (Is. 35:6). David referred to the stag's swiftness when he wrote that the Lord made "my feet like the feet of deer" (Ps. 18:33). Are not agility and swiftness characteristic of Him who leaps over mountains and skips over hills to relieve His own? No impediments hinder Him in His speedy effort to assist His own: "You shall call, and I will answer you" (Job 14:15). A weak creature, the stag is often at the mercy of more powerful creatures. Jesus, however, excells all the prowess of the monarchs of earth and the powers of hell.

September 5

"Enter the sheepfold by the door. . . .
I am the door." JOHN 10:1, 9

Christ is the door into the kingdom of God. He must have had in mind this truth when He compared Himself to the common object of the door, which is vital to a house. A door is of the same substance of much of the house, for which it provides an entrance. As the spiritual door, Jesus was of the same substance of those He came to save, except He did not sin. A door is necessary to those dwelling in a house; Jesus is an absolute necessity if sinners are to be saved, as He Himself declared. Ordinarily, a door is the only legal entrance into a house, as Jesus implied when He said that anyone trying to enter a house in any other way is a thief and a robber. In this aspect He is the only way into the church and ultimately into heaven.

The sorrow is that so many keep the door of their heart closed, as William W. How described it in his hymn:

O, Jesus, thou art standing
Outside the fast-closed door,
In lowly patience waiting
To pass the threshold o'er.

We are all familiar with Holman Hunt's masterpiece, *The Stranger at the Door,* in which he depicts Jesus standing at an ivy-covered door and knocking upon it with His right hand that bears the mark of the nails. In His other hand is a lighted lantern, symbolic of the Word. On His head rests a crown of thorns. It is through Christ and Christ alone that God stretches forth His loving hand to welcome those entering by His Son, the door.

An ancient rhyme asks:

One Door, and only one,
  And its sides are two;
Inside and outside,
  Which side are you?

September 6

Casting all your care upon Him,
for He cares for you. 1 PETER 5:7

We know that we can make ourselves physically ill by worrying. The Scripture today offers us the wonderful promise of being able to cast our worries and doubts upon the listening ears and loving arms of our Lord. Another translation of Peter's exhortation has been stated, "Casting all your care upon Him, for it matters to Him about you." Dr. Weymouth interprets this passsage: "Throw the whole of your anxiety upon Him because He, Himself, cares for you." If we trust some of our care to Him, why not let Him have it all?

Sometimes we find ourselves saying that we are happy, "under the circumstances." But as Christians we should be on top of our circumstances, reigning over them with Christ.

We ought to be happy and free from worry because the Lord surrounds His own. He promises to protect our hearts and minds. We have a threefold protection against worry: (1) Be anxious for nothing, which really means *no thing*; (2) Be prayerful for everything. Our lives would be different if only we could adopt a prayerful attitude as we come up against the difficult experiences of life; and (3) Be grateful in all things. We are told that the Lord will supply all our needs according to His own time and plan for our lives. His goodness extends from the time we first meet Him until we go home to meet Him in heaven.

I hope you will be able to live today and each day until that time on "Thanksgiving Avenue." The houses there are no more expensive than those many persons reside in on "Worry Street." Pack up and leave such gloomy residence where the sun seldom shines.

The next time you are tempted to sit and worry, take a pencil and paper and list all the wonderful mercies you receive from the One who "cares for you."

September 7

"To him who overcomes I will give some of the hidden manna to eat." REVELATION 2:17

Many Bible miracles are related to food, both material and spiritual. A prominent food in these miracles was manna, which was supplied from heaven for the Israelites during their forty years of wandering. The term *manna* is from a Hebrew root meaning "prepare." It was food prepared from heaven for the people who, when they saw it like congealed dew, or snow, lying about the camp, asked, "What's that?" They did not know what it was at first; they had to learn about it. The divine principle of equality is seen in the people's gathering, every man according to his needs, so that nothing was wasted. The abundance of some contributed to the needs of others. Ultimately, the people came to loathe such "white bread," and they demanded flesh to eat, which God gave them in the disastrous plague of quails (see Num. 11:31).

That manna is typical of Christ is evident from His own description of His substance and service as the living bread sent by God from heaven to give life to the world. Matthew Green of the eighteenth century wrote of the news heard in a copper-bar as "the manna of the day." The glorious news of all Jesus is in Himself, and what He makes us able to receive, forms part of our daily manna. The manna of old was freely given to Israel, and Jesus is God's choicest gift bestowed upon the world for its salvation.

In His letter to Pergamos, Jesus promised to give hidden manna to the overcomer. *Hidden* means "secret" and suggests the sweet, secret communion His followers experience with Him. We need to bear in mind the qualification, namely, "to him who overcomes" (Rev. 2:17). Only as we are victorious over all that is similar to God's holy mind and will can we receive the spiritual nourishment Jesus imparts as the secret manna.

May He ever remain manna to our hungry souls and our eternal rest.

September 8

"The arrows of the Almighty are within me." JOB 6:4

Arrows of wood and iron, used for sport and war, are often used figuratively in Scripture. For instance, they indicate the terrible judgments God sent upon the people because of their idolatry and disobedience: "I will spend My arrows upon them" (Deut. 32:23). The bow and arrow also represent the power, wisdom, and love of God in discovering a successful way of delivering His people from their enemies. Joash brought deliverance with his bow and arrows, which Elisha advised him to use against the enemies of Israel (see 2 Kin. 13:14–19).

When Job came to misfortunes permitted by God, he spoke of them as being dipped in poison. The allusion is to the custom of evil men who pursued their enemies with deadly hatred and immersed their arrows in deadly poison. Is it not thus with the rebukes and judgments of God against all that is evil?

The psalms have several references to arrows. "For look! The wicked bend their bow,/They make ready their arrow" (Ps. 11:2); the weapon implies the wicked devices and evil words the depraved use against the righteous. David spoke of God's shooting at His enemies "with an arrow" (Ps. 64:7), the symbol of sudden and swift calamity. Children of the godly are compared to "arrows in the hand of a warrior" (Ps. 127:4). Through divine and parental care, the children became alert, skillful, and abundantly blessed in the service of God. How many godly parents today pray that their children might prosper in this way!

To Jeremiah, the tongue speaking deceitfully is like a sharp arrow that wounds and hurts: "Like their bow/They have bent their tongues for lies. . . . Their tongue is an arrow shot out;/It speaks deceit" (Jer. 9:3, 8). Famine and pestilence are used as arrows of the Almighty (Ezek. 5:16).

How blessed we are if we have God's arms underneath and around us, and not His arrows of deserved judgment directed at us!

September 9

"Consider what great things He has done for you." 1 SAMUEL 12:24

John Fletcher of the sixteenth century would have us don our "considering cap." So would Samuel. In his message at Saul's coronation, the prophet called the people to stop and consider the great things God had accomplished. Rehearsing the deliverance of Jehovah, Samuel emphasized how such consideration influences conduct. Lewis Carroll advised us to "consider anything, only don't cry!" But what else can we do when we consider how far short we fall from the purpose and glory of God? A glance at the over eighty occurrences of the word *consider* in Scripture reveals the many things worth considering. "God is God of gods" and is therefore the source of many great things for which we must greatly praise Him (Deut. 10:17). The phrase *great things* appears over thirty times, and we also have *great power, great works, great peace, great goodness, great faithfulness, great faith, great love,* and *great mystery.*

Too often we consider our miseries and fail to count our mercies. What else can we do but magnify God for the love that prompted Him to surrender His Beloved Son for our salvation? Let us consider, or "look attentively at," how Christ Himself never fails nor forsakes His own. He remains with them until He perfects that which concerns them. Let us also consider how He daily supplies us with all we need, corrects our mistakes, conquers our enemies, and withholds no good thing from us as we plead His promises. Consider the innumerable proofs of His faithfulness and, above all, the unmeasured marvel of His best treasure—Himself! We must echo the words of the hymn, "Then sings my soul, my Savior God to thee;/How great thou art!"

When we consider His greatness and the great things He has done for us, we must praise Him for the past and pledge ourselves to trust Him more confidently in the future. Is our considering cap well fixed upon our heads? May the Lord never have to say of us, "My people do not consider" (Is. 1:3)!

September 10

"As the LORD God of Israel lives,
before whom I stand." 1 KINGS 17:1

One of the meanings of the word *stand* implies "to remain unchallenged," "to hold one's ground in spite of opposition," "to be steadfast and immovable." In Elijah's first message, he declared his God-given authority and affirmed that Jehovah, Israel's God, lived. He said the message he was about to deliver was direct from His throne before which he stood unchallenged. The prophet knew that the Lord would stand up for him, protecting and providing for him in wonderful ways. Challenging all earthly authority and sweeping aside all human protection, Elijah remained God's "Mr. Standfast."

The sentries John Dryden described in *Don Sebastian* stand "in starless nights, and wait the appointed hour." When the appointed hour arrived for Elijah the Tishbite, he came not only as one standing before the Lord but also as one daring to stand up for Him until his chariot ride to heaven. Like a bolt from the blue, the prophet broke in on the national life of Israel and initiated a new method of divine rule, namely, prophetic ministry. On this point, the prophet was superior to the king.

Martin Luther, in an hour of challenge, asserted his defiance when he said: "Here I stand, I cannot do otherwise." In *Othello,* Shakespeare wrote, "He is a soldier fit to stand by Caesar." All soldiers of the Cross are fit to stand before Him who was crucified upon it. Heartily we sing, "Stand up, stand up for Jesus." Are we not blessed to know that Jesus is ever standing up for us? A character in Robert Browning's *Saul* cried: "See the Christ stand!" When Stephen came to die as a martyr, gazing up into heaven he saw Jesus standing at the right hand of God. Standing fast in the liberty by which the Cross has made us free, we need to stand before the Lord and the world as God's messengers, unafraid of our adversary the devil! "Therefore take up the whole armor of God, that you may be able to withstand in the evil day, and having done all, to stand. Stand therefore" (Eph. 6:13–14).

September 11

The LORD *will be your confidence.* PROVERBS 3:26

The word *confidence* has a threefold significance, namely, that of "boldness" (Acts 28:31), "reverent trust" (Job 4:6), and the "object trusted" (Jer. 48:13). When Solomon wrote of God's being our confidence, he implied that He would be our confidant, that is, one to whom secrets are told. As a friend sticking closer than a brother, God always keeps His ear open to hear the secrets of His children. All secret things about His children belong to Him and are never repeated but remain forever locked in His loving heart. What we tell Him about ourselves in the secret place never travels beyond Him. Because of who He is, He cannot betray His children.

A note in the New American Standard Bible reads: "The Lord will be *at your side.*" It is encouraging to know that He is ever at hand to help and to keep our feet from being caught in Satan's trap. The word *confide* is from a Latin root meaning "to trust," and we confide in the Lord because we trust Him. Our assurance is that God always listens sympathetically to all we have to tell Him about ourselves.

> What a friend we have in Jesus,
> All our sins and griefs to bear!
> What a privilege to carry
> Everything to God in prayer!

Solomon presents the Lord as being honorable. The Lord is one to whom we can confess all that concerns us. He is one from whom we can receive wisdom, guidance, and peace. The promise is that if we trust Him as our confidential friend, we shall be as unmovable as Mount Zion.

Such is the marvel of divine grace that our heavenly Confidant reciprocates by confiding in us. Has He not said that He will share His secret with us and reveal His covenant to us? "The secret of the LORD is with those who fear Him" (Ps. 25:14).

September 12

"He who believes in Me, . . . out of his heart will flow rivers of living water." JOHN 7:38

The symbol of the Holy Spirit as "rivers of living water" was initiated by Jesus. John confirms this in the next verse, "But this He spoke concerning the Holy Spirit . . . not yet given" (7:39). Notice that this water is living. The water we drink daily has no life-giving quality. It can ease our thirst, refresh us, and nourish our life, but it cannot impart life. The Holy Spirit, however, is "living water"; as the Spirit of life, He can impart and maintain life. Out of Christ, we were spiritually dead; but by His regenerating power, He quickened us into the newness of life in Christ. He is the Spirit of the living God.

Another aspect of the Spirit's person and ministry is seen in the plural *rivers*, indicating His plenitude, abundance, and the variety of His operations.

Ezekiel, in chapter 47, provides an image of the Spirit in the water flowing out of the temple door. Christ is the door, and the Holy Spirit was His ascension gift to His church. Where the water flowed, there was abundance, for it covered the ankles (our walk), the knees (our prayer life), and then the waist (our service). Finally, the waters were deep enough to swim in, the whole body being enveloped (v. 5), which illustrates the complete control of all that we are and have by the Spirit. Many fruitful trees were found by this river, and the believer is "like a tree/Planted by the rivers of water,/That brings forth its fruit in its season" (Ps. 1:3). The river also produced a "very great multitude of fish" (Ezek. 47:9). Only as we are fully possessed by the Spirit can we be used as "fishers of men" (Matt. 4:19). Just as the salty seas were "healed" (Ezek. 47:8), so the Holy Spirit makes sweet and blessed the life of the believer. He is the river gladdening the hearts of those He indwells. John reminds us that the Lamb leads us to "living fountains of waters," until there is "no more sea" (Rev. 7:17; 21:1). The sorrow is that so many people are ignorant of or forsake "the fountain of living waters,/And [hew] themselves cisterns—broken/cisterns that can hold no water" (Jer. 2:13).

September 13

The Spirit of God descending like a dove and alighting upon Him. MATTHEW 3:16

Because a symbol represents or illustrates an object and is not the object itself, John did not see the Holy Spirit descending upon Jesus in the actual shape of a dove. None of the persons of the Godhead is shaped like an animal or a bird with which Scripture compares and contrasts them. "Like a dove" means that He exhibited the qualities of the bird. The Holy Spirit descended upon Jesus in a great, sweeping spiral as a dove descends and rests upon the ground.

Although the dove is used in various ways in Scripture, it is as the symbol of the Spirit's association with Jesus that we are presently concerned. Jesus is pictured as our rock, and after that Rock had been split at Calvary, the dove came forth at Pentecost. What are some of the characteristic features of the dove? It is a meek, harmless, and innocent bird. Jesus urges us to be as "harmless as doves" (Matt. 10:16). The Holy Spirit is of a most dovelike disposition and is the perfection of all excellent qualities. Jesus "by the Spirit" was meek in heart.

The dove is the emblem of peace, because it lacks the destructive qualities of some other birds. Born of the Spirit, Jesus came to bring peace on earth and good will to all persons. Doves are also noted for their love and gentleness. Shakespeare referred to one who was as "patient as a female dove" and to "the gentleness of the sucking dove." Paul reminds us that "the love of God has been poured out in our hearts by the Holy Spirit who was given to us" (Rom. 5:5). In addition, the apostle wrote that "the fruit of the Spirit is love" (Gal. 5:22). David exalted the manifest swiftness of the dove in his cry: "Oh, that I had wings like a dove!/For then I would fly away/and be at rest" (Ps. 55:6). How quickly the gracious Spirit comes to the aid of believers when we experience sorrow, trouble, or temptation!

The dove Noah sent out of the ark "found no resting place for the sole of her foot" (Gen 8:9) on the earth destroyed by the flood. The Spirit-filled believer will find rest not in the beggarly elements of the world but in the ark of salvation.

September 14

"There should be time no longer." REVELATION 10:6 KJV

Time is not recognized in eternity. With us, time covers years, months, weeks, and days, but in heaven is one eternal *now.* "Time no longer" is a welcome angelic oath as well as a cheering divine promise. Time represents change. Our bodies, feelings, and circumstances change, but in eternity, changes will not be necessary to cultivate fear of the Lord. Time is also identical with conflict and loss, for we are as sheep among wolves and we are far from being perfect. Eternity will be good; it will bring us a life in full harmony with God who inhabits it, the presence and fellowship of our Savior, and likeness to Himself. The Revised Standard Version of this text reads, "There should be no more delay," and suggests that although our Lord's chariot seems to linger, it moves steadily forward to its eternal triumph.

Joseph Addison, seventeenth-century English essayist and poet, wrote, "Eternity! thou pleasing, dreadful thought!" Whether we are to find eternity pleasing or dreadful depends upon our relationship to Jesus Christ. Through Him alone we can enter the eternal mansions above. Tennyson could describe his fellow poet as the "God-gifted organ-voice of England" and as one "skilled to sing of Time and Eternity." Truly, we have many things to say about time, but what praises are ours as we meditate upon all that awaits us in the never-ending, glorious future! "Time, like an ever-rolling stream,/Bears all its sons away," but when time is no more, in heaven where there is no more death, everlasting life will be ours.

William Blake has reminded us that "He who kisses the joy as it flies/Lives in eternity's sunrise." Is the joy of the Lord enabling us as pilgrims to eternity to live in this sunrise? The moment Christ calls us home, "there should be time no longer" for all redeemed by His precious blood. We will have nothing to dread as we forsake time and pass into eternity for reunion with the glorified saints of all ages already there.

May we be found ready for the end when time shall be no more!

September 15

"I will cause you to ride on the high hills of the earth." ISAIAH 58:14

Persons in flight training say that one of the first rules they have to learn is to turn the plane toward the wind and fly against it. Then the wind lifts it up to higher heights. Was such an action learned from the birds who, when flying for pleasure, go with the wind? However, if the bird meets danger, it turns around and faces the wind in order to rise higher, even toward the sun in the heavens.

Is there not a spiritual lesson to be gathered from this innate action of birds? We read of the contrary winds Jesus encountered (see Matt. 14:24). God permits His children to battle against many contrary winds so that they may be lifted to higher levels of fellowship with Him. Just as storms clear an oppressive atmosphere, so life corresponds to the same principle. Sufferings, adversities, and obstacles set us singing. They become the means of our riding on higher hills. Disappointments, it has been said, should be spelled with a capital *H*—HIS appointments, for "All is most right that seems most wrong,/If it be His blessed will."

Often we find it hard to believe that God can cause us to ride on higher hills when so much seems to interfere with our flight. Yet things that are against us turn out to be the very things bringing us nearer God, even though it is a cross that He permits to raise us to higher heights. How familiar are the lines of Longfellow in "The Ladder of St. Augustine":

> The heights by great men reached and kept
> Were not attained by sudden flight,
> But they, while their companions slept,
> Were toiling upward in the night.

Welcome contrary winds that will lift you to spiritual heights, and dedicate all your strength to serving Jesus.

September 16

Let him kiss me
with the kisses of his mouth. SONG OF SOLOMON 1:2

Alexander Cruden, in his introduction to the list of Scripture references to kisses, says that in biblical times and countries, they were treated as signs of (1) reverence and subjection to a superior, (2) love and affection, and (3) idolatrous worship and adoration.

In our society, a kiss is an evident token of love or affection between two persons. Symbolically, it expresses the manifestation of the love God has for His children. Catullus, the Roman poet who lived before Christ, said: "Give me a thousand kisses." The spiritual mind can see in "the kisses of his mouth" the varied evidences of His boundless love for His beloved children.

One of the divine kisses we receive is God's kiss of reconciliation received in the moment of our surrender to His claims. The kiss of the father for his prodigal son meant a warm reconciliation in the home he had forsaken. The kiss of communion represents our daily enjoyment of God's unfailing love as the lips of His blessing meet the lips of our asking. Through the death of His beloved Son, "righteousness and peace have kissed each other" (Ps. 85:10). Thus He became our salvation: "Kiss the Son, lest . . . you perish in the way" (Ps. 2:12). An author of the fifteenth century wrote, "My kisses are his daily feast." May the kisses of our heavenly Lover be our daily feast! All previous kisses of His mouth, however, will be lost in His kiss of consummation, when we finally meet Him whom our hearts have loved. The following lines from the English poet, Frederick W. H. Myers, convey something of this idea: "Moses on the mountain/Died by the kisses of the lips of God."

Ask the heavenly Father to accept every evidence of your reverence and love.

September 17

"Sir, I perceive that You are a prophet." JOHN 4:19

While Jesus was among men, His prophetical office was fully recognized. In the country where He lived, He was a prophet "without honor" (Matt. 13:57). When He raised the widow's son, those witnessing the miracle glorified God and said, "A great prophet has risen up among us" (Luke 7:16). When Luke came to write the book of Acts, he quoted the prophecy of Moses that God would raise up "a Prophet like me from your brethren" (Acts 3:21–23).

How did Jesus function as a God-anointed prophet? A prophet is one who proclaims a revelation, one who speaks for God and declares future events. Jesus was a perfect prophet in these respects. Aaron was made a prophet to acquaint Pharaoh with the mind of God. Jesus came as the mouth of God, declaring His mind and will to the sons of men: "God . . . has in these last days spoken to us by His Son" (Heb. 1:1–2).

In ancient times the prophet also anointed others and installed them in a God-directed office, as Samuel did Saul and as Nathan did Solomon. As the prophet of God, Jesus anointed others for service. John could confess, we "have an anointing from the Holy One" (1 John 2:20). Paul could thank Jesus Christ for putting him into the ministry. The prophet of old prayed for others, as Samuel did for Saul. Similarly, Jesus was a good prophet in that He prayed for His friends as well as for His enemies.

The basic qualification of a true prophet was his ordination of God for a specific task. Before Jeremiah was born, God purposed that he should be a prophet to the nations. It was so with Jesus who was born to the service of a prophet: "I can of Myself do nothing . . . but the will of the Father who sent Me" (John 5:30). Paul would have us know that the church of God is "built on the foundation of the apostles and prophets" (Eph. 2:20). Jesus, however, excells all others in this way. That prophets had to be prepared to die as martyrs for the office they represented is declared in the lament of Jesus as He condemned Jerusalem for killing the prophets (see Matt. 23:37). The most perfect Prophet the world has ever known suffered the same fate.

Bless God for making clear His will through the perfect Prophet.

September 18

"In that day a fountain shall be opened . . . for sin and for uncleanness." ZECHARIAH 13:1

As a figure of speech, the fountain exalts the transcendent excellence and power of the Lord Jesus. A fountain represents the spring or head from which rivers of living waters issue. In connection with the Flood, we read, "All the fountains of the great deep were broken up" (Gen. 7:11). A twofold parallel can be noted. From God, the original fountain, the glorious river of the Holy Spirit proceeds. Christ also is the head of the waters of life, the spring of salvation, spiritual joy, and consolation. He is the fountain or well of life.

A fountain represents abundance, fullness, a constant supply of living water. To our Lord, the Holy Spirit was given without measure. Paul emphasized the redundancy of grace, peace, goodness, and spiritual refreshment to be found in Jesus. What a never-failing source He is! Further, God is depicted as sending "the springs into the valleys" (Ps. 104:10), and fountains always flow into low places. From Jesus our spiritual fountain, water pure and clear as crystal flows.

The precious ministry of the fountain that the prophet Zechariah stressed is that it is opened for "sin and uncleanness." Jesus is the only source of cleansing. Nothing but His blood can wash away the stain of iniquity and cleanse us from all sin. We can sing with gratitude:

> There is a fountain filled with blood.
> Drawn from Emmanuel's veins;
> And sinners, plunged beneath that flood,
> Lose all their guilty stains.

September 19

I call to remembrance my song in the night. PSALM 77:6

Although it was midnight, Paul and Silas were found "praying and singing hymns to God" (Acts 16:25). No wonder their fellow prisoners listened to them and God answered with a great earthquake. Another midnight hour the church will hear the cry: "Behold the bridegroom comes; go out to meet Him!"

Profitable though they may be, songs in the night do not come easily. In one of his letters, James Creedman, a worldwide traveler, described a trip through the Balkan states:

> In that memorable journey I learned for the first time that the world's supply of altar roses comes from the Balkan Mountains. And the thing that interested me most is that the roses must be gathered in the darkest hours. The pickers started out at one o'clock and finished picking them at two. At first it seemed to me a relic of superstition, and then I learned that actual scientific tests had proven that fully forty percent of the fragrance of roses disappeared in the light of day.

David affirms that God "made darkness His secret place" (Ps. 18:11). So when our sky is dark, it is comforting to know that He is with us bringing fragrance out of the night and light out of the darkness. He "gives songs in the night" (Job 35:10). There are songs and treasures darkness alone can produce.

Jacob and his stone pillow are the theme Sarah F. Adams uses to teach us the phrase that should always be on our lips: "Nearer, My God, to Thee."

> Though like the wanderer, The sun gone down,
> Darkness be over me, My rest a stone;
> Yet in my dreams I'd be
> Nearer, my God, to thee.

September 20

The LORD *shut him in.* GENESIS 7:16

As the heavenly porter, God has the asserted prerogative of shutting open doors and opening closed doors: "He shall open,/ and no one shall shut;/And he shall shut,/and no one shall open" (Is. 22:22). In his Rubáiyát, Omar Khayyám affirmed: "There was the Door to which I found no Key;/Here was the Veil through which I might not see."

The door that shut in Noah and his family for safety had no key, for God shut them in. When the hour came for those who were to be saved from the deluge, God did not say, "Go in," but "Come in." His words implied that He was already inside the ark and would remain with the eight persons through the flood until they rested again on dry soil and heard the divine voice say, "Go out of the ark" (Gen. 8:16).

During his loyal witness for God, Noah had many doors shut in his face, but those refusals mattered little after God had opened a door of escape from the death overtaking all who had despised his testimony. Are we not grateful that we, too, responded to the divine call, "Come into the ark, you and all your household" (Gen. 7:1), and that the door of electing purpose interposed between us and an evil world? We are assured that we are shut in *with God.* Outside Noah's ark was ruin for all, but the same disastrous flood only bore the family in the ark, experiencing rest and peace, nearer heaven. Out of Christ who is the ark of salvation, persons perish, but for those redeemed by His blood is salvation from the coming flood of judgment.

God alone has the key of several doors, and Scripture is one of them. So we read that Jesus "opened the Scriptures" (Luke 24:32). Prayer, too, is a key opening many closed doors: "When you have shut your door, pray to your Father who is in the secret place" (Matt. 6:6). Angels were also active opening doors. Paul looked upon opportunities for service as doors God opened for him.

Pray this prayer: Show me an open door of service, O Lord, and help me enter with Your power.

September 21

"I have tested you in the furnace of affliction." ISAIAH 48:10

The figure of a furnace is used in various ways in Scripture. It was an oven for the cooking of food. Furnaces were also associated with the smelting and refining of gold and other metals. The brick kilns had an opening in the top into which the metals were cast and a door at the bottom to emit them. The Babylonians used the furnace to inflict their cruel capital punishment. Both our Lord and John saw in a furnace a symbol of eternal anguish. However, for our discussion here, a furnace is a symbol of the believer's affliction and testing.

Since some furnaces were used to refine gold, the saints who are compared to gold are purified, refined, and made more Godlike: "When He has tested me,/I shall come forth as gold" (Job 23:10). Then the heat of the furnace must be intense, for a weak fire will not function as quickly in the softening of the metal. At times the trials of the believer are heavy and grievous; yet they are designed to make the heart soft: "I will leave you there [in the furnace] and melt you" (Ezek. 22:20). Such a purifying process removes all the impurities from the metals. The Spirit, as fire, burns up all that is alien to the holy will and purpose of God.

When used in ancient times as a means of torture and punishment, the furnace meant extreme pain and torment: "His fury is poured out like fire" (Nah. 1:6). Final judgments will register God's indignation and wrath against the devil and all who died without God. From the furnace of hell there is no escape.

Julius Stern gave us this poem:

> Pain's furnace heat within me quivers,
> God's breath upon the flame doth blow;
> And all my heart in anguish shivers
> And trembles at the fiery glow;
> And yet I whisper, *As God's will*!
> And in the hottest fire hold still.

Pray: From the furnace, let me come forth as gold.

September 22

We will remember your love more than wine. SONG OF SOLOMON 1:4

The word *remember* is often used for "will" and "desire." When Solomon wrote of the Beloved's love, he referred to true faith and sincere love as being more precious than anything else in the world. Samuel Rutherford, the seventeenth-century theologian and author, would often sigh: "Oh, for as much love as would go round about the earth, and over heaven—yea, the heaven of heavens, and ten thousand worlds—that I might let all out upon fair, fair, and only fair Christ!" If only we could give all the love in all pure hearts in one great mass, a gathering together of all loves to Him who is love and altogether lovely, what a perpetual benediction would be ours!

Let us take Shakespeare's lines in *Hamlet* and link them to Solomon's affirmation: "While memory holds a seat/In this distracted globe. Remember/thee!" Our constant remembrance of God's undying love for us saved us from being engulfed in our distracted globe. Wordsworth wrote "that nature yet remembers" as a "perpetual benediction." Surely no theme is as sweet and precious to God's children as that of the love of His heart immutably and eternally fixed on us. The Son of His love instituted His supper that we might remember the matchless history of divine love. Truly, such love will never let us go. May grace be ours always to remember God's eternal love that we may console our hearts amid changing friendships and encourage our minds amid the gathering darkness in the world. May we be inspired with fortitude in times of testing, beget patience when we find ourselves burdened and oppressed, reconcile our troubled minds under bereaving afflictions, and produce and maintain zeal and devotion in the Master's service. Whatever else we may forget, let us remember His love and daily rest in it.

September 23

"My days . . . pass by like swift ships." JOB 9:25–26

In comparison with the fast, fuel-powered vessels of today, ancient ships made of wood and dependent upon the wind and oars could not have been very swift. But Job compared the swift passing of his dismal life to those things noted for speed—on land, the runner; on sea, the ships; in the air, the eagle. The ships of old were used for war, commerce, and passenger traffic. One of the things wonderful for Solomon was "the way of a ship in the midst of the sea" (Prov. 30:19). This reference is to the ability of a ship to battle against storms. Spiritually, this can indicate the remarkable guidance of God in directing His own through the troubled waters of life. Longfellow's application of ships to life appears in this poetic form:

> Ships that pass in the night, and speak each other in passing,
> Only a signal shown and a distant voice in the darkness;
> So on the ocean of life we pass and speak one another,
> Only a look and a voice; then darkness again and a silence.

Isaiah predicted the destruction of the wonderful navy the king of Tarshish had created. Elijah pronounced judgment on the ships of Jehoshaphat that were "wrecked at Ezion Geber" (1 Kin. 22:48). What was the sin of this king of Judah that deserved the destruction of his proud navy? He had joined himself with Ahaziah, the ungodly king of Israel, and together they had built the ships. God could not approve such an alliance, hence His destruction of the ships. Does this tragedy not illustrate the Pauline principle about being unequally yoked with unbelievers?

If we are on an uncharted sea, the storms of sorrow and disappointment will wreck our ship. Our only safety is to have the divine Pilot, who has never lost a vessel and is in full control of our own. "Jesus, Savior, pilot me/Over life's tempestuous sea."

September 24

As newborn babes, desire the pure milk of the word. 1 PETER 2:2

The Bible employs various metaphors to illustrate its own nature and value. For example, wine, milk, and honey are symbols of sustenance God bestows through His Word without money and without price. Milk is especially likened to the spiritual, nutritious quality of God's Word for those who are young in Christ, the "newborn babes." Paul compared the simpler truths of Scripture to milk, whereas he compared the deeper truths to solid food, or meat (1 Cor. 3:1–2). "Everyone who partakes only of milk is unskilled in the word of righteousness, for he is a babe" (Heb. 5:13). Milk, however, is nutritious for adults as well as for children.

Newborn babies are eager for milk, and it is most encouraging to see those newly saved by grace desiring the sincere, or unadulterated, Word of God. Babies, of course, feed and grow on nothing else but milk. Those newly born of the Spirit thrive spiritually as they feed on the precepts and promises of God. Persons may quickly discern if they are truly regenerated by the Spirit, namely, by their desire for the simple truths the Bible presents: "Every word that proceeds from the mouth of God" (Matt. 4:4).

Among the warnings given to the people of Israel was, "You shall not boil a young goat in its mother's milk" (Ex. 23:19). Since milk may symbolize the Word of God, we can see in this prohibition a command not to use the Word to injure and destroy that which it should nourish and strengthen. The milk should have been used for the growth of the young goat into a strong, healthy animal. Instead it would halt the growth of the animal. God would have us use the milk of His Word in the way given for its constructive purpose.

September 25

"You meant evil against me;
but God meant it for good." GENESIS 50:20

What a testimony to God's overruling providence! Here we have an evidence of God's thoughtfulness, resulting in the fulfillment of His will and purpose. "I have purposed and will not relent,/Nor will I turn back from it" (Jer. 4:28). How gracious was Joseph in his treatment of his brothers! With kind and tender words he consoled them, because they feared the punishment he would give them for their past, cruel treatment of him. Instead, they were assured of his love and favor. He declared that God had made use of their wicked action, when they sold him as a slave, in order to preserve many from death and to fulfill His plans for Hebrews and Egyptians alike.

Both Scripture and personal experience confirm Shakespeare's dictum that: "There's a divinity that shapes our ends/Rough-hew them how we will." What a consolation to realize that there are never any mistakes in divine government, that our personal blunders and failures are overruled and resolved into the perfect wisdom, might, and purpose of God. When Jesus was on earth, the religious leaders were bent on evil against Him and ultimately succeeded in crucifying Him. But a divinity was shaping His end. Out of His anguish and death has come a vast, unnumbered multitude rejoicing in His shed blood.

God is superb in making crooked things come out straight, causing even the most unwelcome events of life to work together for our good. Truly "all things come from You" (1 Chr. 29:14). The sentiment expressed by T. W. Taber applies to Joseph and to the saints of every age:

> Ill that He blesses is our good,
> And unblest good is ill:
> And all is right that seems most wrong,
> If it be His sweet will.

Have you learned that all things have worked together for good in your life?

September 26

"Rabbi . . . where are you staying?"
He said to them, "Come and see." JOHN 1:38–39

John describes the enraptured feeling of the young disciple, Andrew, as he looked upon Jesus as He began His ministry and so humbly asked Him: "Where are you staying?" Jesus replied: "Come and see." He did not rebuke Andrew by answering, "That's no business of yours," but gave him the gracious invitation, "Come and see." Andrew and Peter went home with Jesus, and we can imagine the wonderful afternoon they spent, listening in growing wonder and deepening joy to Jesus as He talked with them through the hours they never forgot. Is it not the craving of every regenerated soul to meet Jesus privately in the home for fellowship with Him?

What impresses us most is the courteous way Jesus dealt with the two men desiring to follow Him after hearing John the Baptist describe Him. Julian, Anchoress of Norwich, a saint of ages past, loved to refer to Jesus as "our courteous Lord." Speaking of prodigals returning to Him, she said of His welcome: "Then showeth our courteous Lord Himself to the soul, with friendly welcoming, saying, 'My darling, I am glad thou art come to Me; in all thy love I have been ever with thee.'" Ever gentle, kind, and polite, Jesus was the mirror of true courtesy. Jesus showed kindness in the way He dealt with all who crossed His pathway. Hilaire Belloc wrote in his poem "Courtesy":

Of courtesy, it is much less
Than courage of heart or holiness,
Yet in my walks it seems to me
That the Grace of God is in courtesy.

Jesus never, because of His courtesy, thrusts Himself upon us. So delicate is this courteous One that never does He intrude in a life where His company is not desired. Thomas Dekker could write of Him:

The best of men
That e'er wore earth about him, was a sufferer,
A soft, meek, patient, humble, tranquil spirit.
The first true gentleman that ever breathed.

September 27

Some on boards and some on broken pieces of the ship. . . . they all escaped safely to land. ACTS 27:44

What a gruesome sight that must have been! What an opportunity for a unique picture that shipwreck could have produced, if only a photographer had been at hand! Evidently, those Luke describes were not among those who could jump overboard and swim to land. The soldiers had decided to kill all the prisoners, but through the centurion, God intervened. They were set loose on the sea, and all were finally saved.

God always knows how to frustrate the trickery of the devil. God did not send a convoy of angels to carry those in the sea to land, nor did He provide in some miraculous way another ship to take them to Rome. The lesson for our hearts is that although God has the power, we are responsible to obey His Word and manifest our faith by works. All those in the sea had trials and difficulties, but all 276 of them were saved.

During the entire episode, the apostle Paul exhibited faith and confidence in God. His dauntless courage generated consolation and hope in the hearts of his fellow prisoners at the mercy of the sea. What sufferings he endured for Christ's sake! Here we see him, not crushed or fearful of the future as he stands guard over the treacherous seamen and as he comes to swim with the others to the shore. There was no heavenly vessel to carry the noble prisoner, no supernatural provision for his safety. He was left to reach Rome in his own way. In this, the apostle is a pattern for all who believe in God and who have to live in a world with its real and ordinary environment, with so many conditions that have to be met in a thoroughly practical way. One writer has said:

> God's promises and God's providences do not lift us out of the plane of common sense and commonplace trial, but it is through these very things that faith is perfected, and that God loves to interweave the golden threads of His love along with the warp and woof of every day experience.

May our faith be perfected as we confront our everyday trials and tribulations, trusting in Him who loves us.

September 28

The spirit of man is the lamp/of the LORD,/Searching all the inner depths of his heart. PROVERBS 20:27

Scripture uses the lamp ("candle" in older versions) for any light, either real or symbolic. Solomon wrote, "The lamp of the wicked/will be put out" (Prov. 24:20). But of the wise woman, Solomon said, "Her lamp does not go out by night" (Prov. 31:18). God declared that He would "search Jerusalem with lamps" (Zeph. 1:12). The lamp is also typical of the testimony of God, manifested in those receiving it, and should not be hidden. In heaven there will be no need of the lamp of earthly light, for the Lord God will be our light. Lamps are a symbol of human, manmade religions and cults. But in heaven, human ideas and notions are not to be found; only God's truth and His light are there.

Lamps were made to give light in the night, and the spirit of man was formed by the Lord to provide light while he lives in the night of this world. A lamp will give light to no one unless it receives light from some other light. We use electricity to light lamps. The Lord is called Light, and He lights every man coming into the world. Said Job: "There is a spirit in man,/And the breath of the Almighty gives/him understanding" (32:8). A useless lamp is not left burning but is put out (see Prov. 24:20). Those who abuse the light and knowledge given them are given over to darkness.

Solomon tells us that the lamp of the Lord searches all inward parts of men, making known the thoughts and intentions of the heart. Man should live up to the light God has granted him. But what is the light of man's natural conscience in comparison with Him who came as the Light of the world and by whom we also shine as lights?

> Lead, kindly Light, amid the encircling gloom,
> Lead thou me on!
> The night is dark, and I am far from home;
> Lead thou me on!
> Keep thou my feet; I do not ask to see
> The distant scene; one step enough for me.

Let us walk in the light of His guidance.

September 29

Redeeming the time,
because the days are evil. EPHESIANS 5:16

As those redeemed by the precious blood of Jesus, we are under the obligation to redeem our time. This expression has been translated: "Making the most of your time"; "Making the most of every opportunity"; and "Buying up every opportunity." Time is not to be wasted; it is a commodity to buy and use to the best advantage. Benjamin Franklin asked, "Dost thou love Life? Then do not squander Time; for that's the stuff Life is made of." What we so often forget is that the way we use our time shapes our character and determines our future. When Christians are exhorted to redeem the time, it does not mean "to make up for lost time," but to seize every favorable opportunity of using it for the best purpose.

How significant are the lines of Tennyson in "Locksley Hall": "Love took up the glass of Time, and turned it in his glowing hands;/Every moment, lightly shaken, ran itself in golden sands." Much wisdom can be gained from the great instructor, time. We sometimes speak of killing time, but let us not be guilty of such murder. Let us realize that time comes each new day, hand in hand, with its companion, opportunity. Because the days are evil, we should seize every opportunity of glorifying God. Only thus can we leave behind us footprints on the sands of time.

A plaque hanging in our home reads:

TIME IS
Too slow for those who wait,
Too swift for those who fear,
Too long for those who grieve,
Too short for those who rejoice,
But for those who love,
TIME IS ETERNITY.

September 30

When the cloud continued long . . . the children of Israel . . . did not journey. NUMBERS 9:19

Filling an important place in the Word, the cloud was the celestial veil of the presence of God and the hiding place of His power. Wordsworth wrote of "trailing clouds of glory," and it pleased God to manifest His presence and guidance through them. The provision of the cloud was familiar to Israel. Before the tabernacle was erected, the movement of the cloud represented divine nearness and guidance. With the construction of the tabernacle came the promise of the pillar of cloud to direct Israel through the wilderness. The response of the people to the guidance given was an evidence of their obedience to God's commands.

On some special occasions God came down in a cloud to speak with Moses. At the dedication of the temple, the cloud filled the house, so much so that the priests could not minister. This visible symbol of God's glory is called the *Shekinah.*

In the New Testament, we find the cloud overshadowing those gathered at the Transfiguration and God's voice speaking out of the cloud. Then at Christ's ascension, a cloud "received Him," like a chariot taking Him to heaven (Acts 1:9). Paul affirms that at the Rapture the saints will be caught up in a cloud to meet the Lord in the air. When He returns to earth, He will come with clouds. John saw Christ, sitting on "a white cloud," executing judgments on the earth (Rev. 14:14).

The Israelites probably found the waiting period tiresome when the cloud "continued long," or tarried. The urge to strike tents and go forward may have been strong. But the tarrying was a supreme test of obedience. The omniscient God knew the exact moment when the people should go forward. Often it appears to us that God keeps us waiting, but He only keeps us at our post until He deems it the opportune moment to proceed.

May grace be ours to wait on our Lord's good pleasure, assured of His presence!

October 1

Set your mind on things above,
not on things on the earth. COLOSSIANS 3:2

Paul reminds us that because our citizenship is in heaven, we should not set our minds on earthly things. Our affection must be permanently fixed on the proper objects of love and desire to be found above. What are the things above?

The Father is there, dwelling in unapproachable light, and His truth never fails. His love is untiring. His wisdom is perfect. His promises are certain of fulfillment.

The Son of God's love is there, our adorable Savior exalted and glorified at the right hand of His Father. Surely, we cannot remember Him too often nor love Him too dearly.

The Holy Spirit is there, our divine and gracious comforter. He is the divine One indwelling us and the instructor leading us into all truth. Our affection for Him who loves us should be more evident.

The perfected saints are there. Having finished the course and kept the faith, they have the crown of righteousness. Should we not set our minds more yearningly on these glorified saints who have crossed the bar and wait to clasp our hands?

The many mansions are there. Our heavenly homeland with its eternal rest, peace, and happiness is there with its throne of glory and the promised rivers of pleasure. Above is this sure dwelling place where we shall be so very near to God. We must set our affection on our homeland where we never say good-bye.

In heaven above, where God our Father dwells,
   How boundless there the blessedness!
No tongue its greatness tells;
   There face to face, and full and free,
Forever, evermore we see Our God, the Lord of hosts!

October 2

You will guide me with Your counsel,/
And afterward receive me to glory. PSALM 73:24

God is often referred to as our infallible guide, and He has promised to be our guide even to death. *The Book of Common Prayer* reads: "Where Thou art Guide no ill can come." *The American Heritage Dictionary* explains a *guide* as being "one who shows the way by leading, directing, or advising; an example or model to be followed." God functions in all these aspects.

The term *counsel* implies "advice," "to deliberate with another." Because our human mind has been warped by sin and is not capable of perfect decision, we need God's advice on all that concerns us. John Bunyan would have us remember that "He that is ever humble,/Has God to be his guide."

How blessed we are to know that all whom He guides, He protects from all enemies, preserves amid trials, and provides in any time of need! Having redeemed us by the precious blood of His Son, God has made us His charge and care. He is willing to supervise all that concerns us until we reach the celestial city above. How encouraged we are to have faith and to know that God's reputation as a perfect guide has never been questioned or tarnished! He never takes a wrong turning or loses His way. With faith and confidence we sing with William Williams:

> Guide me, O thou great Jehovah,
> Pilgrim through this barren land;
> I am weak, but thou art mighty;
> Hold me with thy powerful hand.

The living hope the psalmist gives us is that when we reach the end of our earthly pilgrimage, our loving Guide directs us to heaven to behold His glory. As we await our translation, we must surrender to Him to be guided how and where He pleases, and we must trust Him to direct our steps correctly through the encircling gloom. We must take no step without His order and aid, if we would experience the full joy of being received by Him the moment we find ourselves in His immediate presence.

October 3

"Unless you are converted and become as little children, you will by no means enter the kingdom of heaven." MATTHEW 18:3

What a definite and drastic declaration of the Savior! The conversion Jesus spoke of was not that of turning to Himself as Savior and Lord, for those He addressed were His disciples already. The conversion they had to experience was that of turning from pride, self-exaltation, and ambition to the simplicity and innocency of childhood. Small children are weak and frail, have little strength or wisdom of their own, and are dependent upon others. Many grownups are too self-sufficient to enter the kingdom. But the childlikeness Jesus spoke of as being essential for the assurance of eternal life can be acquired anew into undying life. St. Theresa of Lisieux called the above verse "The Little Way," or the way of the little child. A saint of a few centuries ago prayed: "Each day and every day I surrender myself utterly and in all things to Divine Providence . . . like a little child in the bosom of its good and tender-hearted mother, to want everything and yet to want nothing—everything that God wills, nothing that He does not will."

What are some of the characteristic features of a child we must emulate if we would enter the kingdom of heaven? In the happy face of a child are no lines of self-pride, no blatant self-assertions, only the look of helplessness and dependence upon others. God's best is only ours as we realize that without Him we have nothing, are nothing, and can do nothing. Just as a child trusts its parents for everything, so personal trust in God alone is our passport to heavenly life. Another aspect of childhood is that of love and affection. How pleasant it is to watch how a child clings to and caresses its mother! Such childlike devotion is the shrine of love, unbounded and real. What a love-look the eyes of a child manifest! Is this childlike quality ours? Unless we have experienced the transforming power of God's love and love Him whom we have not seen, what hope have we of entering His kingdom?

May we be as teachable children, resting a trusting hand in the loving hand of our heavenly Father, and be at peace!

October 4

I was left alone
when I saw this great vision. DANIEL 10:8

Although the word *solitude* is not found in the Bible, all it represents and produces is clearly evident in the spiritual experiences of its saints. When he was alone, Daniel received a great vision from God. Only when we are alone with Him do we receive the deepest truths.

Wordsworth described how he felt as a poet alone, when thoughts would flash upon "That inward eye/Which is the bliss of solitude." The poet also declared: "How gracious, how benign, is Solitude." Cowper's request was this: "But grant me still a friend in my retreat/Whom I may whisper—solitude is sweet." Solitude is always sweet when we are alone in the presence of the Friend who sticks closer than a brother. This tranquil solitude is precious when we are alone with Him, with whom we are never lonely.

The apostle Paul knew all about the solitude of captivity. How did he react to life in a prison? He could look over the top of his prison wall and over his enemies and write of himself not as a prisoner of Caesar but as the "prisoner of the Lord." His solitude was a sanctuary and his prison, a palace. Since the apostle's time, a long line of imprisoned saints has followed in his path. We think of John Bunyan, silent in his prison, but his solitude gave birth to the greatest book in the world next to the Bible—*Pilgrim's Progress*, of which he said: "I was at home in prison and I sat me down and wrote, and wrote, for joy did make me write." Eternity alone will reveal all the treasures solitude produced. Alone with God, we are never lonely, for one with Him is a majority.

Alone with thee amid the mystic shadows,
  The solemn hush of nature newly born;
Alone with thee in breathless adoration,
  In the calm dew and freshness of the morn.

October 5

All things work together for good. ROMANS 8:28

Among believers, Paul's great declaration is one of the most often quoted passages of the Bible. Before considering, however, the glorious truth of the six simple words above, we must remember that such providential goodness of God does not extend to all. The apostle makes it clear not all persons can have the assurance that God is overruling in their lives, protecting, preserving, and providing for them unless they love God and have been called according to His will. Only Christians can view everything as having a place in God's plan for their lives.

All things. All circumstances, events, and experiences, whether pleasing or painful, are directed by God for His purposes. Omnipotence has servants everywhere, and whether they come dressed in happy colors or garments of distress, the child of God is assured that He is able to bring good out of evil.

Work together. Work suggests a careful planning and activity. Day by day God labors at His task of preserving all that is worthy in His dispensations. Because of His perfect wisdom, harmony prevails in the ordering of our lives. There is never any conflict, for in His marvelous way He is able to fit all pieces into a complete and perfect pattern. Those who love God are assured that nothing can occur that ought not to arise and that nothing is ever out of joint. Because of all God is in Himself, He cannot make mistakes. For this reason, the believer in the spirit of true resignation can pray: "What You send is best."

For good. How heartening is this assertion, affirming as it does the harmonious overruling of our gains and losses, joys and sorrows, successes and failures, resulting as our present and eternal good! How appropriate are the lines of J. J. Lynch who wrote:

> Say not my soul, "From whence can God relieve my care?"
> Remember that Omnipotence has servants everywhere.
> His method is sublime, His heart profoundly kind,
> God never is before His time, and never is behind.

October 6

The day of the LORD so comes as a thief in the night. 1 THESSALONIANS 5:2

Robbers or bandits are frequently mentioned in the Gospels, but the word Paul uses here as *thief* means "one who breaks through and steals secretly under the cover of darkness." This describes the unexpected coming of our Lord. This same word is applied to Judas, who as a thief secretly raided the money box. In reference to the particular day Paul mentions on which the Lord will suddenly appear, we must note the distinction between "the day of Christ" and "the day of the Lord." The former is associated with the Rapture and reward of the saints when Christ returns; the latter is related to final judgments. In "the day of the Lord" He will come as a thief in the world's last night. Suddenly and unexpectedly, the Lord will swoop down upon the godless, and anguish will overtake them as a woman in travail. None will escape.

"The day of Christ" is different. A thief does not send us advance word that he will attack the home he has chosen to plunder. But Christ has given us previous signs that will herald His coming for His true church, such as "distress of nations, with perplexity, . . . men's hearts failing them from fear." Then came His exhortation, "Now when these things begin to happen, look up and lift up your heads, because your redemption draws near" (Luke 21:25, 26, 28). We are witnessing the beginning of our Lord's prediction, for international and national events are heavy with prophetic significance. The phase of redemption will be experienced when we see Him in the redemption of the body, in the possession of a glorified body—our "building from God, a house not made with hands, eternal in the heavens" (2 Cor. 5:1).

A thief comes equipped to carry out his purpose. He has a key to unlock doors, a bar to force his way through any barrier, and weapons to destroy any who hinder him. Our responsibility is to warn the godless. After Christ's return for His own, He will make a desolation in the earth.

October 7

"He who is bathed needs only to wash his feet, but is completely clean; and you are clean, but not all of you." JOHN 13:10

The Master became a slave when He girded Himself and washed the feet of His disciples. Usually feet-washing was the task of a slave in a household. Many lessons can be gathered from Jesus' lowly act, which was more than a sign of His love for His friends. It was more than a manifestation of humble service. In light of the conversation between Jesus and Peter, the feet-washing was an acted parable with a twofold application.

In the first place, Jesus was facing His betrayal, and He knew that Judas, whose heart had resisted Him, would sell Him to His enemies. The rest of the disciples, however, loved Jesus. They were all clean. But Judas was not, and he died tragically in his uncleanness. Jesus knew who would betray Him and said, "You are not all clean." He knows all of those who have been washed in His blood.

A second application is that every saint requires a daily cleansing from the travel stains of the day. Coming home from the dusty lanes, the traveler does not need to wash all over. He needs only to wash his feet. The soul made clean by the blood cannot be reborn a second time, yet many require a daily renewal of cleansing by which travel stains are washed away. How comforting and assuring is the truth, "you are clean"! From an unknown source we learn:

> Once definitely and irrevocably we have been bathed in the crimson tide that flows from Calvary, but we need a daily cleansing. Our feet become soiled with the dust of life's highway; our hands grimy, as our linen beneath the rain of filth in a great city; our lips as the white doorstep of the house are fouled by the incessant wrong of idle, unseemly, and fretful words; our hearts cannot keep unsoiled the stainless robes with which we pass from the closet at morning prime.

What a blessing it is to know that when we get soiled and stained from the day's travel, we can find relief. We can pray!

Before we retire at night we need cleansing from the contagion of the world's slow stain, and we need to pray: "Wash me, and I shall be whiter than snow" (Ps. 51:7).

October 8

By reason of breakings they purify themselves. JOB 41:25 KJV

The most remarkable conversation in history is that between Jehovah and Job, which pointed to the contrast between the mighty power of God and the littleness or inferiority of Job. During this long conversation, reference was made to a creature whose heart was as hard as stone but whose hardness was subject to breakings, resulting in purification.

The Bible is replete with illustrations of how God uses for His glory those people and things that were broken. He could say, "This is My body which is broken for you" (1 Cor. 11:24). He loves broken things, even the sacrifices of broken and contrite hearts. Breakings in health and wealth, in self-will and self-ambitions, in worldly reputation and associations, are used by God for His glory: "The lame take the prey" (Is. 33:23).

The breaking of Jacob's natural strength occurred at Peniel, where God met him. As the result of his broken body, spiritual power came. Moses had to break the rock at Horeb so that the thirsty could have water to drink. Under the warrior-leader, Gideon, three hundred soldiers had to break their vessels, symbols of their brokenness of spirit, that light blinding their adversaries could be manifest. As for the poor widow, God multiplied her oil, enabling her to pay her debts, once she broke her small oilpot. Only as we are prepared to be broken up as a grain of corn with self-burial can we bring forth fruit to the praise and glory of God.

With Thomas T. Bunch let us pray:

O break my heart; but break it as a field
  Is by the plough up-broken for the corn;
O break it as the buds, by green leaf sealed,
  Are to unloose the golden blossom, torn.
Love would I offer unto love's great Master,
  Set free the odor, break the alabaster.

October 9

Christ is all and in all. COLOSSIANS 3:11

The writings of the apostle Paul convey his consuming passion to magnify and exalt the Lord Jesus, to whom he owed so much. His epistle to the Colossians is an illustration of his Christ-glorifying ministry. Summarizing the various ways in which he had described Christ, he affirmed that Christ "is all and in all."

Before all things at creation, Christ was the beginning of the creation of God. He made all things: "All things were made through Him, and without Him nothing was made that was made" (John 1:3). As the original of all things, He upholds all things by the Word of His power. "He is before all things, and in Him all things consist" (Col. 1:17). Christ "is all and in all," for He was the author of our redemption. "There was no one to uphold/Therefore My own arm brought salvation" (Is. 63:5). "Nor is there salvation" for the lost apart from Christ (Acts 4:12).

In His graces and gifts, He "is all and in all." All grace is stored in Him, and "of His fullness we have all received, and grace for grace" (John 1:16). Christ is the author, developer, and finisher of all graces. He gives us faith to receive Him and sheds abroad in our hearts the love of God. Paul also declared that Christ "is all and in all," when it comes to the ministry of the Word. He ordains the called to "preach Christ crucified" (1 Cor. 1:23).

The question is: Do we recognize Christ as having the right to be "all and in all" in respect to every phase of our lives? To have Christ in this way means that we own Him, love Him, believe in Him, obey Him, worship and adore Him, and live and labor in the light of His promised return. Can we say of Him that He is Lord over all? If He is not Lord *of all,* then He is not Lord *at all.* May grace be ours to crown Him Lord of all we are and have!

October 10

I have been anointed with fresh oil. PSALM 92:10

The symbol of oil illustrating the personality and ministry of the Holy Spirit indicates that in all His activities, He is ever fresh, never stale or faded. His anointing is always active and powerful. As an article of value, oil was used for many purposes, all of which point to the various activities of the Spirit whose anointing we have received.

Oil has a healing, softening, and mollifying nature, which is what the man who fell among thieves needed. It is thus that the Spirit opens the heart and searches it. If it is hard and unyielding, He softens it in a gracious way, making it willing and pliable to God's will.

Oil is effective if the body is attacked by venom or poison. The Holy Spirit is with us to counteract all that is of Satan, the old serpent. "The flesh lusts against the Spirit, and the Spirit against the flesh; and these are contrary to one another" (Gal. 5:17). "Walk in the Spirit, and you shall not fulfill the lust of the flesh" (Gal. 5:16).

Oil can warm and refresh us when applied while bathing. As the Spirit of life, He comforts and invigorates us. How able He is to quicken the mortal body! Jesus promised the Spirit as a comforter. May we ever be delivered from quenching such a source of spiritual life!

Oil also is an efficient lubricant, preserving from friction and enabling easy movement. We read of "the unity of the Spirit." How able He is to preserve the redeemed from irritations and frictions that disturb their oneness in Christ.

Oil was considered by ancients to have a nourishing quality as food. As a fat it was deemed beneficial to the body. Oil is used in cooking much of the food we eat today. Is it not through the Word that the Spirit feeds our souls?

Oil has an illuminating property when used in lamps. The Holy Spirit is the spiritual oil enabling us to give light. May we shine as lights amid the darkness of the world!

October 11

*Having risen a long while before daylight,
He went out and departed to a solitary place;
and there He prayed.* MARK 1:35

How the morning watch prepares us for trials, difficulties, and obligations the day may hold for us! Some of us are able to give more extended hours than others to seasons of prayer. But the majority of saints have laborious, demanding days that seem to leave little time for relaxation or spiritual worship; they need to begin each day with God. That way they may prepare themselves for difficult tasks ahead and receive poise and balance to live and labor through the working of each day. Thus the custom of Jesus, whose days were crowded with preaching, teaching, and miracle working, was to rise early in the morning and pray.

We may not be able to retire to a deserted hideaway and prayerfully prepare ourselves for the day ahead; yet we have a quiet spot within our home where we can begin the day with God. If we are not able to provide space for silence and solitude in our daily lives, we can find opportunities even on crowded buses or in busy classrooms. We need times consecrated to much prayer. It is essential to allot as much time as possible to the early morning traffic with heaven. If our day starts out prayerless, we cannot expect to be kept in perfect peace amid the problems, decisions, and tasks awaiting us.

A thirteenth-century German saint, Mechthid of Magdeburg, left us this tribute to prayer, so appropriate as we begin our daily tasks:

> Prayer makes a sour heart sweet, a sad heart merry, a poor heart rich, a foolish heart wise, a timid heart courageous, a sick heart well, a blind heart full of vision, a cold heart ardent. For it draws down the great God into the little heart; it drives the hungry soul up to the plenitude of God; it brings together those two lovers, God and the soul.

"Early will I seek You" (Ps. 63:1). Let us seek to meet the Lover of our soul early in the morning and journey with Him through the rest of the day!

October 12

Be anxious for nothing. PHILIPPIANS 4:6

These four words, taken by themselves, seem impossible to achieve in our complex, troubled world. The word Paul used for *anxious* means "a distracting care to be troubled about," "drawn in opposite directions," "a fretting, worrying frame of mind." When Paul expressed his desire to see the Corinthians "without care," he did not mean that they need not be careful about life and living but that they should live above the fretting, mistrusting attitude of mind. William S. Gilbert, poet of the nineteenth century, gave us this questionable advice:

When you're lying awake with a dismal headache,
And repose is taboo'd by anxiety,
I conceive you may use any language you choose
To indulge in, without impropriety.

But for the child of God, the secret of a tranquil heart lies in Paul's advice. By prayer and supplication, with thanksgiving, we need to make our requests known to God.

In *Much Ado About Nothing*, Shakespeare informs us: "What though care killed a cat, thou hast mettle enough in thee to kill care." But we do not have mettle of our own to kill worry and disquietness within. Our victory is in the promise: "You will keep him in perfect peace,/Whose mind is stayed on You" (Is. 26:3).

Nothing can be gained by troubled care, resulting in a downcast countenance and a joyless spirit. Why sink by the struggles we have, when by faith we can be more than conquerors over all that is alien to the calm and restful heart of Him who is our peace?

Grant us Thy peace throughout our earthly life,
Our balm in sorrow, and our stay in strife;
Then when Thy voice shall bid our conflict cease,
Call us, O Lord, to Thine eternal peace.

October 13

"The Angel of the LORD appeared to him in a flame of fire from the midst of a bush." EXODUS 3:2

It was a truly dramatic episode in the life of Moses when God revealed Himself in a burning bush and gave His chosen servant his commission for service. The presence of God in such a way on holy ground was one of His miraculous acts. The bush burned fiercely but was not consumed. As the "consuming fire," God burns up all impurities, without self-destruction. Moses could not forget that bush. When he came to bless the twelve tribes just before he died, he referred to the "favor of Him/who dwelt in the bush" (Deut. 33:16). Both Mark and Luke mentioned the memorable bush (see Mark 12:26; Luke 20:37).

Throughout history, teachers of the Word have seen in the burning bush a fitting symbol of the church of Jesus Christ, which has suffered great affliction and severe trials. Yet it remains a witness to God's preserving care. The incident can also be applied to Israel's severe afflictions in Egypt.

Why should the church be compared to a burning bush when it is described by other symbols laden with excellent qualities? Although there may have been magnificent, stately, highly valued trees around from which God should choose, He condescended to use a common bush by the roadside as the medium of revelation. The church of God has been thought contemptible in the eyes of the world. Paul, the great leader of the church in his day, wrote of the world treating him as "the offscouring of all things" (1 Cor. 4:13). The true church may not be clad with outward beauty, but she is all glorious within. Further, a bush is of small value and fit only to be cut down and burned. As those who are members of the church, Christ's body, we have no worthiness of our own. Yet He takes the weak things to confound the mighty. Of ourselves we may be like a common thornbush, but if we are aflame with the presence of God, we are the media of revelation to those around us.

The best of us are but thorny briars, but by the power of Him who dwelt in the bush, we are safe. God is a wall of fire about us and our defense and glory.

October 14

"Have you entered the springs of the sea?/Or have you walked in search of the depths?" JOB 38:16

These personal and pertinent questions were put to Job by God as he witnessed the display of God's omnipotence. As nature has its secrets, so has its God. Until He reveals them to us, we can but trust His wisdom and His love. In one of his great sermons, C. H. Spurgeon said,

> Let me not strive to understand the infinite, but spend my strength in love. What I cannot gain by intellect I can possess by affection, and I let that suffice me. I cannot penetrate the heart of the sea, but I can enjoy the healthful breezes which sweep over its bosom, and I can sail on its blue waves with propitious winds.

John Howe wrote, "There is a key to let us out of earth and a key to let us into the unseen; and both keys dangle at the Savior's girdle, and are there for us to appropriate and use." We are indeed wise when we confess that human knowledge, no matter how extensive it may be, has its limits beyond which it cannot pass. With all our searching, we cannot find God out. We are no more able to fathom deep and dark truths, to discover the motive of God's actions, than we can comprehend the depth from which the ancient ocean draws her watery stores. Said St. Teresa of Avila: "It is only in this life that we have the chance of walking by faith and not by sight." When in our glorified beings we are with God, we will have the privilege of walking in the recesses of the deep truths of His being as we cannot presently do with our finite minds.

Now God is past finding out, but in heaven wonderful revelations of the mystery of His ways will be granted us. Now we see through a glass darkly, but then face to face. Let us remember that love to God and obedience to His will are more profitable than trying to walk in the recesses of the deep.

May our prayer be: "My Lord, I leave the infinite to You and pray You to put far from me such a love for the tree of knowledge as might keep me from the tree of life."

October 15

"Abraham Your friend forever." 2 CHRONICLES 20:7

In assuring Israel of God's help, Isaiah gave as the guarantee of such assistance the precious friendship existing between God and Abraham. God called him, "Abraham My friend" (Is. 41:8). What are the qualifications of true friendship? True friendship requires an intimate knowledge, which God had with Abraham; He knew him through and through as no other. True union is another mark of deep friendship. God's heart was knit to Abraham's heart as Jonathan's heart was knit to David's heart. Intimacy and frequent access to each other characterize true friendship. God and Abraham remained friends forever, for there was never any friction between them to disturb their close relationship. Their hearts were one. Without mutual love and affection, no foundation exists for a highly prized friendship. This is why God said: "Shall I hide from Abraham what I am doing?" (Gen. 18:17). John Keats's tribute to divine friendship appears in his poem "Endymion":

> Wherein lies happiness? In that which beckons
> Our ready minds to fellowship divine,
> A fellowship with essence,
> The crown of these
> Is made of love and friendship, and sits high
> Upon the forehead of humanity.

More than any person, Abraham seems to have had such "fellowship with essence" in abundance in order for God to call him: "My friend forever." We have been brought into a fellowship of heart and mind with a sharing of the thoughts and purposes of the Lord Jesus. As He prepared to leave His disciples, His precious word was, "No longer do I call you servants, for a servant does not know what his master is doing; but I have called you friends, for all things that I heard from My Father I have made known to you" (John 15:15).

> Jesus is all the world to me,
> I want no better friend;
> I trust him now, I'll trust him when
> Life's fleeting days shall end.

October 16

Where many were gathered together praying. ACTS 12:12

Crises in the lives of God's people call for constant, unceasing intercession, and He is always near as the "Savior in time of trouble" (Jer. 14:8). The book of Acts is certainly a book of crises in the days of the early church, as the imprisonment of Peter proves. United intercession was made on his behalf, for prayer is the link connecting us with God in whom all things are possible. Alas, too often we forget that prayer is the bridge that spans every abyss and carries us over every chasm of danger or of need. The early church was the church militant, because she lived on her knees. Her witness was dynamic, for behind it was that persistent, prevailing prayer, conquering even the proud legions of Rome.

In my volume, *All the Prayers of the Bible,* the following quotation appears under the portion in Acts 12:5, 12–17:

> Early in its existence the Church knew what it was to have fellowship with Christ in His death. James had been killed by the sword and Peter was sentenced. The Church went to her knees, yet the praying disciples would not believe it when the answer to their prayer was at the door. God is greater than our prayers. The prayer-watchers prayed without ceasing unto God for the release of Peter, and their prayer meeting was interrupted by a knock at the door. When told it was Peter they could not believe it and told Rhoda she was mad. "Too good to be true"—"impossible"—"it cannot be" were the feelings of those who were praying for Peter's release, but who failed to pray believingly. It is not sufficient to pray for great things from God. We need to have faith to *expect* great things from Him. Peter's miraculous release while the saints were praying for it is a striking illustration of God hearing our cry before we cry (Is. 65:24). As the hymnist says:
>
> Father, hear the prayer we offer;
> Not for ease that prayer shall be,
> But for strength, that we may ever
> Live our lives courageously.

October 17

Who, contrary to hope, in hope believed. ROMANS 4:18

The Weymouth translation has this verse: "Under hopeless circumstances he hopefully believed." Chapter 4 as a whole is taken up with the wonderful faith of Abraham, who was called by the Holy Spirit "the father of us all" (Rom. 4:16). Persons who tread in the steps of Abraham resemble him in his faith. In respect to Abraham's outward circumstances, he had no cause to expect the fulfillment of the divine promise. Yet he believed what God had said and anticipated the time when his seed would be as the stars of heaven.

George Mueller, that great man of faith, never asked for a cent for the support of the hundreds of orphans in his homes. He relied absolutely upon God for all that was necessary. Mueller once wrote, "Remember it is the very time for faith to work when sight ceases. The greater the difficulties, the easier for faith; as long as there remains certain natural prospects, faith does not get on even as easily as where natural prospects fail."

Abraham had only a single promise to rely on, but he held tenaciously to it. In the goodness of God we have a quantity of exceedingly great and precious promises before us. These promises should intensify our confidence in the Word of God. Although, with Abraham, we sometimes feel that God delays in the fulfillment of a promise, He has the wondrous manner of stepping forth to help us at a time when there is the least appearance of it. We are apt to trust upon what we see or feel and not upon the Word itself that never fails.

Emphasizing the truth that the just live by faith and that God, who cannot lie, will fulfill His every promise in His own time and way, the prophet Habakkuk gives us this exhortation: "Though it tarries, wait for it;/Because it will surely come" (Hab. 2:3).

Jesus, my strength, my hope,
   On thee I cast my care,
With humble confidence look up,
   And know thou hearest my prayer.

October 18

"The truth shall make you free." JOHN 8:32

In this context, our Lord exalts the emancipating power of the Word of God. The poet William Cowper has the phrase: "He is the freeman whom the truth sets free." And all whom the truth sets free are slaves—slaves of Him who is their deliverer. Cowper, also in his "Table Talk," expresses it thus: "Freedom has a thousand charms to show,/That slaves, howe'er contented, never know."

The liberating truths Jesus taught have indeed "a thousand charms" and proclaim a glorious liberty of which contented slaves of sin are grossly ignorant. The double curse of sin is that it both blinds and binds. That it blinds is evident from the assertion of the Jews who, having listened to Jesus as He preached freedom, said, "We have never been in bondage to anyone" (John 8:33). Somehow they had forgotten the long and bitter slavery of Egypt. The eyes of their understanding were "darkened" (Eph. 4:18). Prejudice had blinded them.

Our Lord's two phrases, "the Son makes you free" and "the truth shall make you free," are not contradictory but complementary, for He had said, "I am the Truth." Freedom, then, from the tyranny of sin must come from without; it is ours through Him who mastered Satan and sin. He provides a glorious liberty for all who receive Him as Savior and crown Him as Lord of their life. Sin binds and enslaves those who think they can take up sin and lay it down at their will.

The double curse has a double cure, for Christ has provided salvation from the power of sin as well as its penalty. What we must not forget is that our spiritual freedom does not mean we may continue to do as we like. Emancipation from sin does not imply license. In the Lord's service, we have perfect freedom to do only what pleases the Savior.

October 19

Christ as a Son over His own house,
whose house we are. HEBREWS 3:6

Paul used the same figure of the house in dealing with the mystery of godliness—"the house of God, which is the church of the living God, the pillar and ground of the truth" (1 Tim. 3:15). The word *house* is applied to the temple of old as well as the church. Christ spoke of His disciples as His household. Peter wrote of the church as a "spiritual house" (1 Pet. 2:5).

The comforting illustration of the church as a house, or home, can be used in several ways. A house is a habitation, which a builder erects on a solid foundation; the church's one foundation is Jesus Christ her Lord. In the construction of a house, many different materials are used. Is this not true in the formation of the church? No two members are exactly alike, yet all are saved by grace and are "living stones . . . built up a spiritual house, a holy priesthood" (1 Pet. 2:5). The stones are prepared by the Spirit and the Word. The principal parts of a house are its beams, rafters, and pillars, all different in their shape, form, and use. The disciples are spoken of as pillars. The promise of Christ is, "He who overcomes, I will make him a pillar in the temple of My God" (Rev. 3:12). All the varied parts of a house are fitted together in one perfect whole; the church's members, with various gifts, are placed so that there should be "no schism in the body" (1 Cor. 12:25). Above all, the house is the abode of love and fellowship; it is a resting place. The same is true of the church in which there is spiritual repose: "My people will dwell in a peaceful habitation,/In secure dwellings,/and in quite resting places" (Is. 32:18). The church awaits her glorious consummation of peace forevermore:

Till, with the vision glorious,
Her longing eyes are blest,
And the great Church victorious
Shall be the Church at rest.

October 20

"He comes forth like a flower/ and fades away." JOB 14:2

Among the ways by which man is portrayed in the Bible, the symbol of a flower is a most pleasing and instructive one. "As for man," said David, "his days are like . . . /a flower of the field, so he flourishes" (Ps. 103:15). Poets also find flowers to be a favorite topic. Tennyson could write of "the white flower of a blameless life." John Milton, thinking of a baby who died of a cough, composed the lines: "O fairest flower, no sooner blown but blasted,/Soft silken promise fading timelessly." Musing on early springs, Wordsworth affirmed: "'Tis my faith that every flower/Enjoys the air it breathes."

As a flower, the believer not only enjoys but benefits by the air of heaven he or she constantly breathes. One of the old ballads pictures life as a flower in that it fades and dies: "The finest flower that ere was seen/Is wither'd to a stalk." All of us are grateful when winter passes and flowers appear on the earth. When Scripture speaks about persons being in "the flower of their age," it means they have reached full manhood or womanhood. Just as a flower springs from a root to grow and flourish, so men have one common root from which they sprang, namely, the first Adam. Some flowers are more beautiful, rare, and valuable than others. In God's garden there are human flowers more worthy and excellent than others. They may not appear as beautiful to those with carnal eyes, but some have a more sweet and fragrant disposition. Scripture describes flowers, even the most beautiful of them, fading away and returning to the dust from which they sprang. Man, like a flower, may wither and fade, but the Word of the Lord endures forever.

October 21

In a race all run,
but one receives the prize. 1 CORINTHIANS 9:24

The saint as a runner in the celestial race is depicted in the epistle to the Hebrews: "Let us lay aside every weight . . . let us run with endurance the race that is set before us" (12:1). Running is variously dealt with in Scripture. The psalms often employ such a symbol: "For by You I can run against a troop . . . I can leap over a wall" (Ps. 18:29); "The sun . . . rejoices like a strong man to run its race" (Ps. 19:4–5). Solomon used the figure of a runner: "When you run,/you will not stumble" (Prov. 4:12). God's promise is, "They shall run and not be weary" (Is. 40:31).

To become acquainted with the course over which he is to run, a runner will make many practice runs. As runners, believers ought to be familiar with the way to run with Christ. They must follow in His steps. Two other requisites of a runner are physical fitness and the absence of garments that would encumber running. All in the spiritual race must be strong in the Lord if theirs is to be a speedy course toward the goal. The garment of holiness and humility is necessary if the prize is to be obtained. Every other weight must be laid aside. Then, all runners know that they must give careful attention to their diet, for being overweight can slow them in the race. Christians must also take heed that they are not hindered in their running by being "weighed down with carousing" (Luke 21:34) and with the cares and pleasures of this world.

Not all runners in a race obtain a prize, only the one who runs the fastest. But in the spiritual race all may obtain the reward if they have run well. Terms like *running, wrestling, fighting, striving,* and *warring* indicate that the race is by no means easy. All the obstacles we meet well should serve to stir up the greatest diligence imaginable. We believe that heaven will make amends for all.

October 22

[God] said, "I will surely treat you well." GENESIS 32:12

As the God whose goodness never fails He can do nothing but good for His own. Although this promise was given to Jacob, it was not his exclusively. It is intended for all his spiritual seed.

What a gracious promise for your heart and mine as we face another day! We have no foreknowledge of what this new day may hold for us, but we do know and believe that God, because of His omniscience, knows the end from the beginning. As the day continues its course, He will superintend events for our good. What we may deem good and best for ourselves may result in loss, but the infinitely wise God cannot err in His provision for us.

As we read the history of David, we note all the troubles that beset him, but his acknowledgment was, "It is good for me that I have been afflicted" (Ps. 119:71). When losses and crosses are ours, we tend to cry: "All these things are against me." However, God is always with us to do us good, even though He gives us medicine as well as pleasant food. He may try, sift, and humble us, but He knows what is best for our soul's welfare. With His omniscient eye, Jehovah has anticipated and made provision for every need that may arise.

Only by His grace can we look at all our trials and say, "This also shall turn to my salvation." Looking back over the past, we should confess that "goodness and mercy followed me all the days of my life." Looking in every direction, we should resolve, "I will trust and not be afraid." As we look to the future, we can rejoice because ours is the assurance that "the Lord will give that which is good." He is the God of beneficence!

> Through days of toil when heart doth fail,
> God will take care of you;
> When dangers fierce your path assail,
> God will take care of you.

October 23

Let us continually offer the sacrifice of praise to God. HEBREWS 13:15

Do we consider praise or gratitude to God as a sacrifice? What does it actually cost us to magnify and adore God for His rich bounty? Such a sacrifice is one with which God is well-pleased. Paul would have us remember that it is "the will of God in Christ Jesus" for us "in everything" to give thanks (1 Thess. 5:18). In the Anglican Order of Service is the following petition that we should make our own: "We beseech Thee to make us truly sensible of Thy mercy, and give us hearts always ready to express our thankfulness, not only by words, but also by our lives, in being more obedient to Thy holy commandments."

Paul did not say, "*For* everything give thanks," but "*In* everything give thanks." Certain trials and calamities overtake us, and it is beyond us to kneel down and express gratitude to God *for* them. But we can give thanks even *in* the depth of our anguish, knowing that our all-wise God never errs. What He permits must be for His glory and our good. Paul did not say for *some* things give thanks but for *everything*. We do not find it difficult to be grateful for the good things of life, but for the bitter things, it is more difficult. Yet the dark threads are as necessary as the threads of gold and silver in God's pattern for your life and mine. Without His supporting grace, it is hard to pray as did an unknown poet: "Through dark and dearth, through fire and frost,/With emptied arms and treasures lost,/I thank Thee while my days go on."

We are urged to offer the sacrifice of praise continually. Unfortunately, we are not constant in our expression of thanks. Whittier has the phrase, "each loving life a psalm of gratitude," and such a psalm is only possible as we take time to meditate upon all the benefits so freely and fully bestowed upon us. Praise Him from whom all blessings flow!

October 24

The LORD will give grace and glory. PSALM 84:11

Scripture has a unique way of uniting relative truths: faith and works, receive and give, life and death, praise and prayer, and so forth. In the verse before us the psalmist presents the twin truths of grace and glory. Of them, C. H. Spurgeon wrote, "The little conjunction *and* in this verse is a diamond rivet binding the present with the future; grace and glory always go together. God has married them, and none can divorce them. The Lord will never deny a soul *glory* to whom He has freely given to live upon His *grace.*"

Grace represents the unmerited favor of God, who is presented as "the God of all grace" (1 Pet. 5:10). If we drop the *g,* we have *race,* and grace has been abundantly given for all within the human race. God so loved the world that all who repent and believe can receive the free gift of grace. Saved by grace, we are given "grace for grace." Grace is ours to fit us for service, support us in trial, and sanctify our hearts through life.

Glory is grace in perfection. Grace is now ours; the glory is to follow. If by His grace we have been saved, then we shall be glorified with Him. God cannot deny glory to those to whom He has given grace. While there are differing original words for the English word *grace,* the aspect is that of the glory land. To quote Spurgeon again: "Glory is nothing more than grace in its Sabbath dress, grace in full bloom, grace like autumn fruit, mellowed and perfected. Glory to the glory, Heaven, to glory of Eternity, the glory of Jesus, the glory of the Father, the Lord will surely give to His own." As we await our entrance into glory, may the God of all grace and glory enable us to live and labor in the light of all awaiting us.

Praise the Lord for His grace and glory.

October 25

To make the author of their salvation perfect through sufferings. HEBREWS 2:10

No child of God can expect preservation from suffering of some sort or another. Believers come to learn that there is a joy that seeks them through pain. The story is told of a gifted artist who discovered a wonderful red which no other artist could imitate, and his secret died with him. After his death, an old wound was found over his heart, which revealed the source of the matchless color in his pictures; he had mixed his blood in his paint. Does this legend not teach us that everything of value in the world costs the heart's blood? The sufferings we encounter cannot injure us if blended with submission to Him who provided the world with salvation from sin through all He willingly suffered on its behalf.

Cortland Myers related a story of a mother who brought into her home a crippled boy who was also a hunchback. He was to be her son's companion. She warned her boy to be very careful with him and not to touch the sensitive part of his life but to play with him as if he were an ordinary boy. She listened to her small son as the two boys were playing, and after a few minutes he said to his playmate, "Do you know what you have got on your back?" The little hunchback was taken by surprise, but the boy said, "It is the box in which your wings are, and some day God is going to cut it open and then you will fly away, and be an angel." How slow we are in learning that our weights can be our wings enabling us to rise nearer God who seeks to bring us to a crown through a cross! When George Matheson, the Scottish preacher and poet, was buried, friends lined his grave with red roses in memory of his life of sacrifice and in appreciation of his words:

O Cross that liftest up my head,
  I dare not ask to fly from thee;
I lay in dust life's glory dead,
And from the ground there blossoms red
  Life that shall endless be.

October 26

The floods lift up their waves./
The LORD *. . . is mightier . . .*
Than the mighty waves of the sea. PSALM 93:3–4

In Scripture floods often refer to the afflictions and troubles of life. All satanic forces are illustrated by raging storms: the storm of adversity rises against us; the storm of despondency obscures the sky; the storm of temptation carries the soul hither and thither by its blast; and the storm of God's holy displeasure goes against sin. Like the little boat of the fishermen on the Galilean sea, my little boat is tossed, and rowing is hard toil.

A flood is the gathering together of many waters and symbolizes attacking enemies that are combined against the righteous. Many are the adversaries and afflictions of the righteous. Pharaoh and the Egyptians belched out their threatenings against Israel. When a flood comes suddenly, overflowing all banks and bounds, how helpless man is to subdue it. At times affliction comes suddenly and violently upon both saint and sinner. God, however, can enable His own dear children to ride upon the storm, even as He did for Noah and his family in the ark. "The LORD," we read, "sat enthroned at the Flood" (Ps. 29:10). He sits there as the restrainer of it. "Surely the wrath of man shall praise You;/With the remainder of wrath You shall gird Yourself" (Ps. 76:10).

How comforting is the truth that the Lord is mightier "than the mighty waves of the sea"! The disciples proved this when the sleeping Christ in their storm-tossed boat arose and commanded the angry waves: "Peace, be still!" And there was a great calm. As the master of ocean, sky, and earth, He can enable us to face all trials with a victorious assurance. And through the hurricane's eye He draws us closer to His heart, confirms our confidence in Him, and gains for us a glorious conquest. With Christ in our boat, we can laugh at any storm.

When the storms of life are raging,
Stand by me.
When the world is tossing me
Like a ship upon the sea,
Thou who rulest wind and water,
Stand by me.

October 27

There remains therefore a rest for the people of God. HEBREWS 4:9

Rest is attributed to both God and man but with a vital distinction. With us, rest is necessary after strenuous physical and mental exercise. Because of our human limitations and frailty, rest is essential. Jesus offered: "Come to Me, all you who labor and are heavy laden, and I will give you rest" (Matt. 11:28).

With God, it is different, for *rest* simply means "completion." After the creation of the world, He rested. He was not tired or exhausted after six days of marvelous creation. As the omnipotent God, He is never weary but is in full strength and vigor after His labors. "He rested" simply implies the completion and perfection of His task.

The term *rest* appears over two hundred times in Scripture. It is not only a gift from heaven but a virtue we must seek and find. "Peace," "quietness," "to be at ease," "to lean or rely upon" are some of the meanings of the original words used for the English word.

In some passages *rest* implies "Sabbath." Wordsworth embodies the thought of rest as a Sabbath:

> Every day should leave some part
> Free for a Sabbath of the heart.
> So shall the Seventh be truly blest,
> From morn to eve with hallowed rest.

Such a rest does not imply cessation from work or freedom from conflict and suffering. As Cowper expressed it: "Absence of occupation is not rest,/A mind quite vacant is a mind distress'd."

The precious thought to remember is that our daily rest is not something but someone, not a possession but a person: "Thou art my Rest." The Lord Himself is the true peace of the heart.

> My Saviour, Thou has offered rest;
> Oh, give it then to me;
> The rest of ceasing from myself,
> To find my all in Thee.

October 28

His soul shall dwell at ease. PSALM 25:13 KJV

The modern world seeks for ease. What tranquility of heart we would have if victory over inner turmoil were ours! It is pleasant to walk on Easy Street. John Bunyan expressed it: "The delicate plain, called *Ease*."

The noun *ease* is understood as signifying "freedom from pain, annoyance, constraint, or anything that disquiets or oppresses." In this verse from the psalmist, the word does not imply laziness or indolence. A woe was pronounced upon those who were at ease in Zion. God never intended His children to live idly. Shakespeare would have the ghost find Hamlet, "duller shouldst thou be than the fat weed/That rots itself in ease." The original root of the word *ease* has several meanings, such as "good," "goodness," "prosperity."

Job's lament was, "I was at ease, but He has shattered me" (Job 16:12). In the darkest, saddest, and loneliest hour, the soul can find a home in the goodness of God. Our hearts can only be free from slavish fears and from soul-distressing anxieties and dwell in a state of contentment and solid peace when the promises of God are claimed. Then our cares are replaced with a realization of His omniscience and omnipresence. We long to please Him in all things, fear to offend Him in anything, and ceaselessly desire His return, when perfect ease will be ours. Do we have the ease that comes because we are at peace with God? Are we lodging in Him who is the source of supply for any need that may arise and the one who alone can silence all our fears? With God as our portion, we have His infallible Word as our security. With Jesus as our constant advocate and heaven as our final home, why should we charge our soul with any care? Although we live in a restless world, grace can be ours to be at home in ease. Let your heart rejoice in the One who gives divine ease.

There is a place of quiet rest,
Near to the heart of God;
A place where sin cannot molest,
Near to the heart of God.

October 29

"I will visit their transgressions with the rod." PSALM 89:32

The word *rod* is from an original root word signifying "a sprig or bough" taken from the stock of a tree and usually seen in the form of a cane. The psalmist, however, speaks of "a rod of iron" (Ps. 2:9) that God uses as an instrument of punishment.

Scepter and *rod* are the same term in the Hebrew language. Scepters usually have the shape of rods. The scepter of a king is the emblem of authority and power. Wordsworth wrote of "a rod/To check the erring, and reprove."

The rod is principally used in Scripture as an instrument of punishment. Thus Job prayed, "Let Him take His rod away from me" (Job 9:34). "He who spares his rod hates his son" (Prov. 13:24). It is comforting to know that the rod of correction is in the hand of our heavenly, loving Father and that He does not use it as often as we deserve its stroke. "He has not dealt with us according to our sins,/Nor punished us according to our iniquities" (Ps. 103:10). Solomon said, "The rod and reproof give wisdom" (Prov. 29:15). The rod of divine punishment and correction is for the godly, and the iron rod of wrath is for the wicked. If only the godless would heed the cry of the prophet: "Hear the rod!" (Mic. 6:9).

Another aspect of the rod Scripture presents is that of a Person. Moses declared that "the scepter [or rod] shall not depart/from Judah," nor a lawgiver in their midst until the arrival of a prophet of Christ who would come as "Shiloh" to minister the judgments of God (Gen. 49:10). Isaiah depicted the coming of "a Rod/from the stem of Jesse" (Is. 11:1). Jesus came as "a root of Jesse." David could find comfort as God employed His rod: "Your rod and Your staff,/they comfort me" (Ps. 23:4). He had learned how to submit to the rod in the hand of God, not to strive or struggle against it. David knew, as we must come to know, that God corrects with the rod as He deems profitable in respect to spiritual discipline, the degree and kind of which He alone knows.

As He is loath to use the rod, may we obey and please Him who is slow to wrath in all things.

October 30

Do not be conformed to this world, but be transformed by the renewing of your mind. ROMANS 12:2

Let us study the important word *conform*. Paul reminded the believers in Rome that they were "predestined to be conformed to the image of His Son" (Rom. 8:29). Peter warns us as "obedient children" not to conform ourselves to "former lusts" (1 Pet. 1:14). This implies the shaping of one thing after another or like another. We are not to mimic or ape the world in any way. Emerson, poet and essayist of the nineteenth century, would have us know that "Whoso would be a man must be a nonconformist." In Great Britain, a nonconformist is one who does not adhere to the established Church of England, while a conformist is one who acts in harmony with all the edicts of that church.

Those of us who are members of *the* church, which is the Lord's body, are all nonconformists. Why? We have no agreement with or likeness to a godless world. Every believer should have a nonconformist's conscience when it comes to separation from the ways of the world. We are urged to come out from among unbelievers and not touch the unclean thing; we need to be transformed by the renewing of the mind. As confessing Christians, we must be marked and distinct disciples. The miracle of Pentecost was the placing of the church in the world. The masterpiece of Satan is the placing of the world in the church, which results in spiritual barrenness. The follower of Christ Jesus should not live in a godless society, subject to its worldly maxims and modes of life.

The Gospels reveal the Lord Jesus as an unflinching, unashamed nonconformist. Think of His positive assertion: "I am not of this world"! How separate He was from the practices and pleasures of the world! Follow the example of Jesus; hate sin but love the sinner.

The only way to be transformed, rather than conformed to the world, is by the renewing of your mind with the power of the Holy Spirit. Notice Jesus' commendation of His own for being in harmony with His nonconformity: "They are not of the world, just as I am not of the world" (John 17:16).

May we ever be found among God's nonconformists!

October 31

*"Unless I see in His hands
the print of the nails . . .
I will not believe."*

JOHN 20:25

The most heartbreaking use of nails in Scripture was when cruel men hammered them into the hands and feet of our blessed Lord. It was the marks of these nails He showed to the disciples after His resurrection. These scars led Thomas to cry, as he beheld the prints, "My Lord and my God!" (John 20:28). Those marks still remain and are forever adored by the redeemed in glory (see Zech. 13:6). When those nails fastened Him to the cross, they nailed to it the handwriting that was against us (see Col. 2:14).

Byron in "The Prisoner of Chillon" has the warning: "May none those marks efface!/For they appeal from tyranny to God." The marks Jesus eternally bears testify to the tyranny of those who caused God in the dateless past to surrender His beloved Son to be a sacrifice for the sins of the world. They will never be erased, for they represent our eternal salvation and indelible grace. As the soldiers pierced His hands and feet, the first cry the pain wrung from His lips was a prayer for the forgiveness of those who crucified Him.

Staupitz called to Martin Luther: "Look at the wounds of Jesus." There is no other way to be saved. We must look if we would live. We must reject any religion or plan of salvation that is destitute of the print of the nails. Paul prayed for those who heard him preach that they might bear in their body the marks of Jesus. The blood from those gaping wounds became the blood of redemption.

What thou, my Lord, hast suffered
Was all for sinners' gain;
Mine, mine was the transgression,
But thine the deadly pain.

Can we ever praise enough the willing Savior who let His hands and feet be punctured by cruel nails for our salvation?

November 1

"Behold the Man!" JOHN 19:5

What a gruesome sight Jesus must have been as He stood there in the court, whipped and flogged by Pilate's soldiers, His bare back all torn and bleeding. His heart was breaking. His face was marred through the blows received and blood-covered as the thorny crown was pressed upon His brow. To add to the insult, the soldiers gave Him a mock coronation as king when they dressed Him up in the purple robe of royalty. Smiting Him, they cried: "Hail, King of the Jews!" How far removed was such a pitiable object from the One who came as "the brightness of His glory and the express image of His person" (Heb. 1:3)! Yet Jesus was never more sublime than in His sufferings. As the man of sorrows, He revealed the depth of His love for us, and by His stripes we are healed. Then, standing before Pilate, so despised and rejected in His broken, bleeding body, He teaches us patience, meekness, and resignation under insult and disgrace.

That grim spectacle also presents the Roman governor Pilate as one guilty of inconsistency because, pointing to the holy Sufferer, he said, "I find no fault in Him" (John 19:4). If in the trial, Pilate came to the decision that Christ was innocent, he should have released Him. But by flogging Him, he intimated that He was guilty. Even in His anguish and shame, in Him dwelled the fullness of the Godhead. By all that He endured, He became the only foundation of the church's hopes and the only source of eternal salvation. So, behold and love! Behold and adore!

What language shall I borrow
  To thank Thee, dearest friend,
For this Thy dying sorrow,
  Thy pity without end?
O make me Thine forever;
  And, should I fainting be,
Lord, let me never, never
  Outlive my love for Thee!

November 2

As a sheep before its shearers is silent,/ So He opened not His mouth. ISAIAH 53:7

Solomon affirms that there is a time to be silent. Our blessed Lord manifested such a time when He was oppressed and afflicted, refusing to defend Himself before Caiaphas, Herod, and Pilate. With us, if a person is wrongly accused, slandered, or defamed, he takes his accuser to court and protests and proves his innocence before a judge. The judge, affirming defamation of character, awards damages to the accused for slander. But in Pilate's court, Jesus was the silent sufferer: "Being accused . . . He answered nothing. . . . He answered him not one word, so that the governor marveled greatly" (Matt. 27:12, 14). Peter, writing to the pilgrims of the dispersion, encouraged them as they suffered for doing good. By their conduct and character, they could refute those who defamed them as evildoers.

Another aspect of the Master's silence is found in the way He responded to the cry of the woman of Canaan for the relief of her demon-possessed daughter: "He answered her not a word" (Matt. 15:23). His delay was not a denial, for ultimately He commended the woman for her great faith and healed her daughter.

Often the Lord tarries in response to our prayers in order to try our faith, patience, and perseverance. Then, when He breaks His silence, He proves His faithfulness, pity, and love. Therefore, we should not be discouraged though His ear appears to be deaf to our entreaties. We must plead with persistence, await His time, be willing to receive what we seek in His own way, and be concerned that He might be glorified in the way He answers our petitions. Being Christ's, we rest in Him and wait for Him, knowing that His silences are as eloquent as His speech.

> I know not what the future hath
> Of marvel or surprise,
> Assured alone that life and death
> God's mercy underlies.

Let us learn from our loving Master that in many cases silence is still golden.

November 3

The LORD takes pleasure/ in those who fear Him. PSALM 147:11

This verse reveals what does not please the Lord and what gives Him joy. He assures us that He takes pleasure in His people, beautifying them with salvation. Christ finds a deep and satisfying joy in those who have been redeemed by His blood and are living in obedience to His will. God could say to Him, "This is My beloved Son, in whom I am well pleased" (Matt. 3:17). As the children of God through grace, we have the privilege of giving God pleasure. It is on record that Job was well-pleasing to God. It seems as if God almost boasted about His servant Job when He asked, "Have you considered My servant Job, that there is none like him on the earth?" (Job 1:8).

Can God find the same pleasure or bliss in you and me? Is He delighted in us because we love Him, share His thoughts, obey His will, and serve the cause so dear to His heart? How saddened He is when He cannot find in us the fellowship He desires! May we strive to live in unison with His will so He can rejoice over us with singing!

> But saints are lovely in His sight,
> He views His children with delight;
> He sees their hope, He knows their fear,
> And looks, and loves His image there.

This same thought of divine delight is expressed by the seventeenth-century poet Thomas Traherne: "O my soul, ours is far more bliss/Than His is ours; at least it so doth seem/Both in His own and our esteem."

Our gracious Lord could say, "I always do those things that please Him" (John 8:29), which is one of His examples we should follow. Paul instructs us how "to walk and please God" (see 1 Thess. 4:1–12). The apostle also instructed young Timothy on how to "please him who enlisted him as a soldier" (2 Tim. 2:4).

Will you strive to become a beloved daughter or son in whom God is well-pleased?

November 4

The servant of the man of God arose early. 2 KINGS 6:15

Among the references to the word *early* are those associated with time as well as age, so we have those phrases referring to the morning watch: "Early will I seek You" (Ps. 63:1); "I will awaken the dawn [early, KJV]" (Ps. 108:2); "Those who seek me diligently [early, KJV] will find me" (Prov. 8:17). Our Lord, facing a long day of preaching, teaching, and healing, realized how essential it was to meet God before He faced the world. We read of Him: "Now in the morning, having risen a long while before daylight, He went out and departed to a solitary place; and there He prayed" (Mark 1:35). Horatius Bonar urges us to

> Take thy first walk with God!
>   Let Him go forth with thee;
> By stream, or sea, or mountain path,
>   Seek still His company.

History records that those who accomplished great things for God were early on their knees. Matthew Henry, author of a famous commentary of the Bible, would be in his study at four in the morning and remain there until eight A.M. After breakfast and family prayers, he would return to his work for several hours. Philip Doddridge was another who proved the value of the morning meeting with God. He would rise around five A.M. to work on his renowned expository volumes.

If we face another day with all its work and witness in our own strength alone, we will not be victorious. We must first meet Him who promised to be with us all the days of our life. With His Word open before us, we must seek counsel and direction from Him and then go forth into the day confident that He will be with us, upholding, sustaining, and controlling in all events and endeavors.

> Holy, holy, holy! Lord God Almighty!
>   Early in the morning our song shall rise to thee;
> Holy, holy, holy! merciful and mighty;
>   God in three persons, blessed Trinity!

November 5

*"I will be to them like a lion;/
Like a leopard . . . like a bear."* HOSEA 13:7–8

God, the creator of all animals, condescends to the peculiar traits of several to illustrate His judgments. Through the use of similes, the quotation compares Him to three animals in His condemnation of a rebellious people.

The *lion* is one of the most feared and terrible creatures. When it roars, other animals tremble and lie quiet. Of God, it is said that "the LORD also will roar from Zion" (Joel 3:16). The lion terrifies less powerful animals, and when God expresses the anger of His incensed majesty, the sinful and impenitent tremble. Once a lion takes its prey, none can rescue it from the ravenous beast. Isaiah would have us know "there is no one who can deliver out of [God's] hand" (Is. 43:13).

The *leopard* is a very swift and fierce creature. This beast is peculiar in that it flies into the face of a person and seeks the eyes. Man may fight against God, but all in vain, because He is a swift witness against the wickedness of man and leaves him in darkness: "Speedily I will return your retaliation upon your own head" (Joel 3:4). A leopard, when it spots its prey, leaps upon it suddenly. God may appear to tarry before punishing the wicked, but when He does, He comes upon them "as a thief," unexpectedly and suddenly.

The *bear* does not willingly fight with a man. Renowned for love of its young, it is furious when robbed of them. God loves His own with a love exceeding that of a woman for her young ones. God declares that He will deal with the wicked for destroying His own, as "a bear deprived of her cubs" (Hos. 13:8). "Shall God not avenge His own elect who cry out day and night to Him, though He bears long with them? . . . He will avenge them speedily" (Luke 18:7–8).

May the joy that springs from resting in all God *is,* be ours!

November 6

Let us who are of the day be sober,
putting on . . . as a helmet
the hope of salvation. 1 THESSALONIANS 5:8

Consider the importance of the helmet to the soldier of Christ. Paul wrote, "Take the helmet of salvation" (Eph. 6:17). In ancient times, the helmet was a part of a soldier's armor. Saul put on David's heart a "helmet of brass," a protection against the sword of an enemy. In a future time of judgment, God will be found with "a helmet of salvation on His head" (Is. 59:17). In the Christian's armor, the helmet is "salvation" and "the hope of salvation." The believer is thus fortified against wicked spirits in the world.

What are we to understand by Paul's assertion that the helmet is our hope? We do not hope for salvation from the guilt and penalty of sin, for this aspect became ours when we received Christ as our personal Savior. But we still have our old sinful and sinning nature with which we were born. Hence, the constant conflict; when we would do good, evil is present. We must deal with this.

The phase of salvation for which we hope is the complete deliverance from our old nature, which will be ours when we are finally with Christ, transformed into His likeness and image. Then we shall be saved to sin no more. What a glorious hope—a divine and supernatural grace or fruit of the Holy Spirit! May we shun false hope, described as a spider's web, and foster the blessed hope, enabling us to be victorious in the spiritual warfare with the enemies of our soul! This is the hope of salvation that does not fail or disappoint us.

Unless we are clad with the whole armor of God, we are not able to withstand satanic assaults. A soldier knew that his helmet could not be removed until the battle was over. It is so in the spiritual combat, as the Word, our weapon in warfare, declares: "We desire that each one of you show the same diligence to the full assurance of hope until the end." Such a hope is "an anchor of the soul" (Heb. 6:11, 19).

Let us go into daily battle against satanic forces wearing the helmet of the hope of salvation.

November 7

Jacob went on his way,
and the angels of God met him. . . .
He said, "This is God's camp." GENESIS 32:1–2

The Revised Standard Version translates this last phrase as "God's army." This same angelic army heralded the birth of Jesus. The term *angel* signifies a "messenger" and is used of such as a mystic representation of the divine presence. Angels are referred to as God's host or army not because He needs them to protect Himself or to suppress His enemies, since He is stronger than all armies, but as the evidence that He condescends to employ His creatures to fulfill His purposes.

An army, with its various companies, must have a general to lead and command them. The Lord's hosts have Him as their commander, or leader, who is described as the head of principalities and powers. That such an army is vast in numbers appears in the phrase, "an innumerable company of angels" (Heb. 12:22). Christ Himself declared "twelve legions of angels" were ready to do His bidding (Matt. 26:53). As for David, he believed that "the chariots of God are twenty thousand,/Even thousands of thousands [angels]" (Ps. 68:17).

The Romans counted their armies by legions. The number of a legion was approximately 6,000; therefore, "twelve legions" numbered close to 72,000—a magnificent army, indeed, composed of degrees or orders such as archangels, cherubim, seraphim, principalities, and powers. What a comfort to know that such a magnificent, undefeated heavenly army is our protection (see Rev. 12:7)! As the prophet has assured us: "Do not fear, for those who are with us are more than those who are with them" (2 Kin. 6:16). What is the power of any earthly monarch compared to God's heavenly army? How gratified we should be to be surrounded by such legions, because they are constantly encamped "all around those who fear Him" (Ps. 34:7). "Angels to beckon me/Nearer, my God, to thee;/Nearer to thee!"

November 8

My times are in Your hand;/Deliver me from the hand of my enemies. PSALM 31:15

How grateful we are to David for his consoling affirmation of God's omniscience! Is it not wonderful to know that every event in your life and mine is under His control? He leaves nothing to chance. As Shakespeare expresses it: "There's a divinity that shapes our ends,/Rough-hew them how we will."

The hand of the Lord is in all that occurs, overruling and sanctifying to our good. What peace of mind should be ours! He measures out our days; therefore, our hours should obey His loving will. Not by chance are we living in times like these, and we must be careful not to drift carelessly through such times of divine opportunity.

Because of international and national crises, we face difficult days when people's hearts are failing them through fear. But all events are under God's control. Whether our own personal times are glad or sad, He daily orders all each day brings forth.

Twice over in "Rabbi Ben Ezra" Robert Browning agrees with David:

Our times are in his hand.
Who saith, "A whole I planned,"
My times be in Thy hand!
Perfect the cup as planned.

David assures us that by being in God's hands, we are delivered from the hand of our enemies. May grace be ours, then, to rest in the revelation that hour by hour our varied experiences are molded by God into His program for our lives. He will never cause any child of His a needless tear.

God of our life, through all the circling years,
  We trust in Thee;
In all the past, through all our hopes and fears,
  Thy hand we see.
With each new day, when morning lifts the veil,
  We own Thy mercies, Lord, which never fail.

November 9

He will receive the crown of life which the Lord has promised to those who love Him. JAMES 1:12

Crowns, which may signify royalty and victory, are used symbolically in many ways in Scripture. "An excellent wife is the crown of her husband" (Prov. 12:4). Paul spoke of those he led to Christ as his "joy and crown" (Phil. 4:1).

In the New Testament, the crown is more a symbol of victory than of royalty. It is applied to Christ and to the twenty-four elders in heaven who cast their crowns before the throne. Paul mentioned the contrast between a perishable crown and an imperishable crown (see 1 Cor. 9:25). He referred to the perishable crowns worn by victors in ancient contests and to the imperishable crowns of Christians, such as "the crown of righteousness," "the crown of life," and "the crown of glory." These are different aspects of the same crown, of which we are exhorted to beware that no man take from us.

One of the Greek words for crown is *diadem,* the word used for the royal crown of ancient Eastern kings and applied in Scripture to the Lord Jesus upon whose head were many diadems. The most conspicuous crown is the one made up of very sharp thorns placed in derision on the head of Jesus, thereby mocking Him as both a king and a victor.

The crown of life, which saints are to receive after death, may refer to those who laid down their lives for Christ on earth in exchange for a more glorious life in heaven—a short life for an everlasting one, a life of sorrow for one of joy, a life of bondage in sin for one of perfect freedom. As heirs of such a never-failing crown, we should be joyful in the prospect of its eternity.

All hail the power of Jesus' name!
Let angels prostrate fall;
Bring forth the royal diadem,
And crown him Lord of all.

November 10

"I must journey today, tomorrow, and the day following." LUKE 13:33

By His specific statement, our Lord seems to indicate that man is immortal, or imperishable, until his work on earth is completed. It was so in His own experience while here below. At the outset of His ministry He affirmed: "My food is to do the will of Him who sent Me, and to finish His work" (John 4:34). In spite of satanic and human efforts to kill Jesus before the accomplishment of the divine plan, He was preserved until Calvary, where as He died He cried, "It is finished!" (John 19:30).

His pronouncement formed part of His answer to the Pharisees and to Herod who sought to take His life before His God-appointed time. The time periods *today* and *tomorrow* represent the days of His continuing gracious ministry. The *day following,* or "the third day," was to be the day when He would be perfected, the day of His death, not by those of earth but by the prearranged counsel of God. Jesus came as the Lamb slain before the foundation of the world.

Thomas Fuller in his *Church History of Britain* has the sentence: "God's children are immortal while their Father has anything for them to do on earth." Whether our days are long or short makes little difference. In the purpose of God, it is not the length of life that counts but its quality. Our blessed Lord was only thirty-three years old when His task was finished, but what marvelous things He accomplished in the three years of His ministry. As we seek to be in true fellowship with Him, we have the assurance that until our life's work is ended, no hostile power is able to prevent us from finishing our course with joy. Matthew Henry's comment on today's verse reads: "It is a comfort to us, in reference to the power and malice of our enemies, that they can have no power to take us off as long as God has any work for us to do." We may lament when a child of God is suddenly cut off because of unfinished tasks left behind. But from the divine point of view, that person's task was completed.

Let the truth grip your heart, that you too are immortal until your work is done.

November 11

The LORD's mercies . . . His compassions . . . are new every morning. LAMENTATIONS 3:22–23

As we greet the early hour as we rise each morning, our salutation should be: "This is the day which the LORD has made;/We will rejoice and be glad in it" (Ps. 118:24). We may not know what awaits as we journey from the morning hour, but we have Jeremiah's assurance that the mercies of the Lord will crown the day ahead. Because God's mercies and compassions are new every morning, our lives manifest perpetual originality. Our mornings may differ in nature, some clear, some dark, yet God's finger touches each one. His love has planned what the succeeding hours may hold for us. If He sends the messenger of joy or the messenger of sadness, His mercy goes with both. For this we praise Him.

New every morning! What a herald of hope with which to begin a day! No anxieties and worries can appear from which God is not well able to deliver us. No inward doubts and griefs can emerge that He is not ready to dissipate. As Alexander Smellie stated:

> God's goodness is always in the present tense. It runs on without cessation. The blood of Jesus *cleanseth*—the Father *worketh*—the Holy Spirit *teacheth.* Are there any sins so dark and strongly entrenched that Heaven will not forgive and overcome them? No, there is not one. Patiently Jesus of Nazareth passeth by. Today God is He that blotteth out my transgressions for His own sake. Surely I should dismiss any auguries of fear, and should keep a gladsome mind, and should abound in hope.

Great in faithfulness, God will prevent any day from becoming insipid, dull, and fruitless if only we begin the day with the promise given to Asher: "As your days, so shall your strength be" (Deut. 33:25).

How gentle God's commands!
  How kind His precepts are!
Come, cast your burdens on the Lord,
  And trust His constant care.

November 12

"Behold! My Servant whom I uphold." ISAIAH 2:1

The original words for *servant* convey the idea of a bondman or slave. In biblical times some servants were bought with money, others were taken in war. Paul, James, Peter, and Jude all wrote of themselves as bondmen of the Lord. Words of encouragement were addressed to Christian bondservants addressed as the Lord's freemen. Jesus could say of Himself: "I am among you as the One who serves" (Luke 22:27). Now in heaven, He serves as our intercessor advocate. He also spoke of a future time when He will gird Himself and cause His servants to "sit down to eat, and will come and serve them," as a minister to servants (Luke 12:37). Jesus illustrated His servitude when He laid aside His outer garment, girded Himself, and washed the feet of His disciples—a slave's task.

A master choosing a servant looks for one who is qualified to serve in a particular way. God could say of His beloved Son: "My Servant whom I have chosen" (Is. 43:10). Appreciation is also found in Psalm 89:19: "I have given help to one who is mighty;/I have exalted one chosen from the people." In every way, Jesus was well qualified for the glorious task assigned Him. The sphere of a servant implies subordination and subjection, and Jesus in His humiliation became subject to His Father's will. He thus made Himself of no reputation. Yet it pleased the Father that in His Servant-Son all fullness should dwell and in Him all the treasures of wisdom and knowledge were hidden. Another comparison we can make is that a true servant will not seek his own glory or the furtherance of his personal ambitions. As God's servant, Jesus sought not His own glory but His Father's glory. "I honor My Father" was His confession (John 8:49). He always sought the glory of His Father.

Ye servants of God,
Your Master proclaim,
And publish abroad
His wonderful name.

November 13

"Call upon Me in the day of trouble;/ I will deliver you." PSALM 50:15

Because no person is without trouble of some kind, this precious promise is for all troubled hearts. Job reminds us that "man is born to trouble,/As the sparks fly upward" (Job 5:7). But the psalmist declares that the Lord knows all about our troubles; we need not worry whether He will understand. If we need His help, He demands that we call upon Him. Days of troubles are often permitted so that we might prove His ear is always open to our cry. A friend in need is a friend indeed, and the Lord is such a friend, even as one "who sticks closer than a brother" (Prov. 18:24). The Apocrypha asserts that "a faithful friend is the medicine of life." How true this is of Him who condescends to offer Himself as our friend! He is always within call and has boundless resources to help those He calls His friends. He assures us that His hand is not too short to save us nor His ear so heavy that it cannot hear us.

When trials overtake us, we must not look to others to undertake for us until God has proved that He cannot or will not lift our burden—*and that will never be.* Because of all He is in Himself and all that He has promised, He must respond as we call upon Him. God's heart is too kind and His word too faithful for Him to turn a deaf ear to our request.

Are you facing a particular trouble? Then, without hesitation, pay God a visit, lay your whole case before Him, and expect His sympathy, aid, and blessing. He will deliver you, and you will glorify Him. As you trust Him as your friend, you honor Him. As you expect Him to undertake for you in the hour of your need, you have the assurance that He will not fail you, for He is always to be found by those who seek Him in all sincerity. Ask and you will receive!

I've found a Friend,
Oh, such a Friend!
He loved me ere I knew Him;
He drew me with the cords of love,
And thus He bound me to Him.

November 14

Blessed be the LORD,/
Who daily loads us with benefits,/
The God of our salvation! PSALM 68:19

The words above are sometimes translated: "Blessed be the Lord, who daily bears our burden,/The God who is our salvation." *Benefits—burden,* often in life a burden turns out to be a benefit. The reverse is also true because a benefit can become a burden. "Daily loads us with benefits"—"Daily bears our burden." Both aspects suggest that God not only daily bestows benefits, but also bears our burdens.

We are encouraged to know that we have God as our daily burden-bearer upon whom we can cast our care. Trials, frailties, weaknesses will be ours as long as life lasts, but the heart of God is willing to carry them all. He is more compassionate than a woman and more lordly than a man. There are, of course, self-imposed burdens that should not be borne, alien to the mind of God. Graciously, He promised to break the yoke of such burdens and to destroy them with the anointing oil—a symbol of the Holy Spirit who is with us to deliver us from unlawful yokes. How blessed we are to realize that God is not too high, too involved with the control of the universe, to stoop and lift a weight off our hearts! Lord Tennyson said to "Cast all your cares on God; that anchor holds."

That our heavenly Burden-bearer is tireless in His ministry is proven by the truth that He daily undertakes for burdened ones: "He who keeps Israel/Shall neither slumber nor sleep" (Ps. 121:4). No matter what any day may bring forth, His arm is never too short to save us.

Cast thy burden upon the Lord,
  and He shall sustain thee;
He never will suffer the righteous to fall:
  He is at thy right hand.

November 15

She ate and was satisfied,
and kept some back. RUTH 2:14

The story of Ruth the Moabitess is one of the most exquisite in Scripture. Within the world's literature, both sacred and secular, no love story is as absorbing as that of Ruth, who became the ancestress of the Lord Jesus Christ (see Matt. 1:5).

Finding herself in Bethlehem faced with the practical problem of poverty and searching for work, "she happened to come to the part of the field belonging to Boaz" (2:3). The term *happened* does not imply that the meeting with Boaz was accidental. It means "that which she met with"—an issue revealing a divine overruling. There are no accidents in the life of the believer. It was during a break in Ruth's hard toil that Boaz was attracted by the lovely maiden who had come to glean. He offered her some of his own gathered grain. How grateful we are to our heavenly Boaz whose liberality we magnify! As our wonderful host, our Lord daily spreads a bountiful repast. No guest ever goes away unsatisfied from His table.

All desires and needs are met when we know Him and are found in Him. Satisfied, Ruth left, but love bloomed. The end of her story is that she became the wife of the man who shared his meal with her. Surely, this was a rich bounty to follow! Truly, there is always more to follow! Here on earth, we are daily and hourly dependent upon our heavenly Boaz, for without Him we have nothing, can do nothing, and are nothing. He is our all in all. The truth of Scripture is that He who is our Bread of Life will also be the bridegroom. "Blessed are those who are called to the marriage supper of the Lamb!" (Rev. 19:9).

So while we gaze with thoughtful eye
  On all the gifts Thy love has given,
Help us in Thee to live and die,
  By Thee to rise from earth to heaven.

Ask God to care for you in the unforeseen circumstances of life.

November 16

The name of the LORD/is a strong tower;/
The righteous run to it and are safe. PROVERBS 18:10

The tower is often mentioned in Scripture as a place of security. It was also a place of defense on which watchmen were placed. These well-fortified towers were built on the walls of Jerusalem. Towers are also used symbolically, as today's verse indicates. David could say of God: "He is the tower of salvation" (2 Sam. 22:51). As such, He offers firm and substantial protection from the assaults of the enemy of our souls.

Sometimes towers denote proud tyrants, as in the words of Isaiah: "When the towers fall" (Is. 30:25). Shakespeare wrote of King Richard III: "The king's name is a tower of strength." The varied names and titles of the King of kings reveal Him as the mighty tower of His people.

Let us examine the proverb, part by part.

The name of the LORD. "As his name is, so is he" (1 Sam. 25:25). The name above every name is our guarantee of safety and protection. What a shield is the name of Jesus, so sweet in a believer's ear!

Is a strong tower. The strongest towers of men have fallen to enemies or have decayed through lack of use. Although the world around us is rocking on its foundations, God is our refuge that cannot be moved. As tumult rages, we have in God a strong citadel of calm—a shelter in the time of storm.

The righteous run to it. The righteous are those redeemed by the blood of Jesus. For the godless, or unsaved, there is no hiding place from eternal wrath if they die in their sin.

And are safe. What a blessed assurance these three words impart! As believers we are not only saved by grace but are also safe forever. Shelter and security come to all who find in His name a love that never fails, a sympathy always perfect, a sweet omnipotence of grace, and provision equal to every need. Is it any wonder that we run to such a tower?

November 17

*My soul melts from heaviness;/
Strengthen me.* PSALM 119:28

Ours is an age of depression. Disasters, terrorism, unemployment, and sickness all contribute to distress of mind. Although the word *depression* is not in the Bible, all that it depicts is scattered throughout the sacred pages. The idea emerges in phrases such as: "Out of the depths I have cried to You" (Ps. 130:1); "Why are you cast down, O my soul?" (Ps. 42:5); "When my spirit was overwhelmed/within me/Then You knew my path" (Ps. 142:3). David was often despondent. John Trapp said of the psalmist's sighs: "David chideth David out of the dumps." Our Lord warned against the cares of this life weighing us down.

All of us have days when a weight seems to lie on the spirit and the soul melts for heaviness. A mist hangs over our world, work becomes a weariness, and depression seizes us. Physical weakness or mental stress can produce moments of spiritual darkness and the drying up of our spiritual lives. When such heaviness of spirit overtakes us, a cure for our depressed state is to put on the garment of praise. Hope in God!

Often brighter days dawn as we leave our brooding over our own troubles and seek to help others who are downcast. John Keble's wise word is apt: "When you find yourself overpowered as if it were by melancholy, the best way out is to go out and do something kind to somebody or other." New hope and strength are ours when we seek to carry cheerfully another's load.

The consoling thought is that even in the gloom, Jesus, who promised never to leave us, is with us. He promised to undertake for us "all our days"—days of despondency and cheerlessness as well as days of joyous sunshine. He is always at hand to strengthen us. Only such a faith can save us from despair and bring to us treasures out of darkness.

November 18

My people will dwell in a peaceful habitation. ISAIAH 32:18

The metaphor of a habitation, house, or dwelling place often depicts the Lord's residence. "LORD, You have been our dwelling place/in all generations" (Ps. 90:1). The following four descriptions of our habitation differ greatly from each other, but they are alike in that they are shrines and sanctuaries of peace.

"Our earthly house, this tent" (2 Cor. 5:1). Paul called the body the soul's brief and fragile house. It is earthy in that it is perishable and earthly in that it will rise again at the Savior's touch. Although it is only a tabernacle, or tent, and has not eternal permanency, He has redeemed it and made it His present peaceable home.

"You have made the LORD, . . . the Most High, your habitation" (Ps. 91:9). Our habitation, then, is not only a place but also a person. No matter how beautiful a material dwelling place may be, it is transitory. God is our abiding home both now and through eternity.

"If I wait for the grave as my house" (Job 17:13). Although we hope that the Rapture is at hand and that the sky and not the grave will be our goal, the grave may be the body's lone, gloomy, but temporary house. But even the grave is an inn for the traveler on his way to his eternal home in heavenly attire.

"In My Father's house are many mansions" (John 14:2). What a glorious revelation and assurance our Lord's heartening Word gives of our perpetual and blessed home! What a precious word to chase our fears and tears away! Surely, the things of earth should grow strangely dim in the light of such a blessed dwelling place that no plague can approach. Perhaps soon it will be our joy, by the mercy of the King of the mansions, to dwell with Him forever. There is no place like our heavenly home.

November 19

Tell me . . . where you feed your flock. SONG OF SOLOMON 1:7

The illustration of God's people as a flock of sheep occurs frequently in Scripture. The people of Israel were like sheep gathered by God their shepherd, and they were called Jehovah's flock. Our Lord united Jews and Gentiles into one flock with Himself as their shepherd. Zechariah prophesied that the leaders of Israel would be judged for not caring for the remnant, the poor of the flock. Jesus spoke of His own as a little flock, bidding them not to fear, because their Father's good pleasure was to give them the kingdom. Paul, in his sermon to the Ephesian elders, exhorted them to take heed in all the flock, since wolves never spare sheep. Peter urged the elders to "shepherd the flock of God which is among you" (1 Pet. 5:2). All shepherds have the blessed hope that when the Chief Shepherd appears, the unfading crown of glory will be theirs. How comforting, then, is our Lord's word, "Do not fear, little flock" (Luke 12:32)!

A characteristic of a flock of sheep is that they love to be together, feed together, and lie down together. It is no easy task to divide and scatter them. If separated by wolves, foxes, or dogs, they quickly seek to get together again. When one of the flock strays away or dies, its presence is missed by the rest of the sheep. As God's sheep, we are one in Christ Jesus and form a fellowship like that above. We believers love to assemble together: "Those who feared the LORD/spoke to one another" (Mal. 3:16). Although modern criticism of the infallibility and authority of Scripture and even of the deity of our Lord has brought lamentable division into Christian ranks, the fact remains that true saints love to assemble together. It is hard to divide the Shepherd's choice sheep, for their hearts are knit together as Jonathan's heart was to David's. Although satanic forces sought to scatter the early church through persecution, the believers soon got together again. "Blest be the tie that binds/Our hearts in Christian love."

November 20

But grow in the grace and knowledge of our Lord and Savior Jesus Christ. 2 PETER 3:18

The two areas in which believers must develop are grace and knowledge. The more we come to know Christ in all His fullness, the deeper is our appreciation of His matchless grace. The aspect Peter emphasizes is that of a personal spiritual growth. As those professing to be the Lord's, we must never rest with present attainments. We can never be static in the Christian life. If we have no continuous spiritual advance, then we have spiritual decay. A tree planted in good soil grows in both root and branches, and the believer rooted in the love of God grows up in conformity to His will and purpose. Such growth results in the discovery of our own inherent sinful nature with its weakness and misery, but we also become aware of the preciousness of the perfect provision Christ has made for us. Divine grace always leads us out of self to Him who is our all-sufficiency.

What we must bear in mind is the truth that we cannot grow *into* grace but only *in* it. Saving grace is the gift of God; in contrast to the law and to works, it represents the favor and graciousness of God to guilty sinners. The grace that we are to grow in is the daily grace God grants to the saints all along the way. Such continuous grace is combined not only with knowledge but also with mercy. It has been said that grace refers more to the source and character of the sentiment. Mercy refers to the state of the person who is its object. Grace may give me glory; mercy contemplates some need in me. Mercy is great in the greatness of the need; grace is the thought of the person exercising it. May we constantly receive grace, for God loves to bestow it. Grow in grace, for God commands it.

Marvelous grace of our loving Lord,
  Grace that exceeds our sin and our guilt,
Yonder on Calvary's mount outpoured.
  There where the blood of the Lamb was spilt.

November 21

"Yes, He loves the people;/All His saints are in Your hand." DEUTERONOMY 33:3

While it is perfectly true that God loves the world composed of saints and sinners alike, Moses was referring to God's love for the people. These include the saints who are in His hand, who sit at His feet, and who love Him because He first loved them. His love is shed abroad in their hearts, indwelled by the Holy Spirit. Such love passes knowledge; it is eternal and matchless, the bottomless abyss in which our sins are swallowed up. Who were the people God said He loved and of whom He said: "You will not be forgotten/by Me!" (Is. 44:21)? He spoke of Israel—a rebellious, hard-hearted, stiff-necked, and unworthy people. How tender, merciful, and loving God was not to forget His erring people!

In his final blessing upon the people of Israel, Moses implied that because God loves and pities us, He distinguishes us from others around us who are in the orbit of His grace. He did not spare His beloved Son but delivered up this Son for the salvation of all the world. Only those who have received Him as Savior have Him as their substitute and representative at the right hand of God. As God loves His Son, so He loves those saved by the precious blood Jesus shed on their behalf. The rays of God's love for His people center in Jesus.

How glorious is the mystery of God's infinite and eternal love! It is the love that will not let us go, the love into which Jesus alone can direct our hearts. May this love become the center and the circumference of all things in our life! So, fellow believer, as we go forth into another day with all that it may hold for us, may we remember that we are encircled forever by the love of God.

O Love that wilt not let me go,
  I rest my weary soul in thee;
I give thee back the life I owe,
That in thine ocean depths its flow
  May richer, fuller be.

November 22

"How much more will your Father who is in heaven give good things to those who ask Him!" MATTHEW 7:11

Jesus would have us know that there is no limit to the generosity of His Father. God does not stop at a given boundary; He always journeys beyond it. In Scripture His numerous "much more's" speak of His beneficence. *Superfluous* can mean "overflowing," "more than is necessary," "an excess of that which is sufficient." Voltaire, the renowned atheist, coined the phrase: "The superfluous is necessary."

The "much more" Jesus mentioned reveals that His Father is not proscribed or limited in His provision but is superabundant. Jesus Himself illustrated such divine excess when, after He had fed a hungry crowd of thousands, there was the overflowing in the twelve baskets full of fragments gathered up. He is able to provide above all we ask for or need.

In the narrative containing today's verse, Jesus interprets the bountiful heart of God. If an earthly father gives his child what he asks for, our heavenly Father wants to give His children greater and more numerous good things. So let us hide these three words—*how much more*—in our hearts. Human love is a symbol of the divine love, but the symbol often fails. Jesus said, "If you then . . . know how to give good gifts" (Matt. 7:11). But fathers do not always know and in ignorance sometimes bestow gifts that prove detrimental. Our heavenly Father, however, always knows what is best for His children and in His loving wisdom gives only good gifts—His dear Son, the Holy Spirit, the Holy Scriptures, grace, and glory. Are we receiving and rejoicing in such a divine sea without a shore? Here and now, the abundance of God is at our disposal, but how much more is in the hand that bled to make it ours in the superabundance of heaven.

Thank the Father for His generosity.

The King of love my Shepherd is,
  Whose goodness faileth never;
I nothing lack if I am His,
  And He is mine forever.

November 23

"Who then is that faithful and wise steward?" LUKE 12:42

Let me direct your attention to the important position of steward. Since every saint is a steward of God, all must function as His "good stewards" (1 Pet. 4:10). The scriptural significance of a steward is one who acts as a house manager, one who has authority over the servants of a family in assigning their tasks, and one who generally manages all affairs and accounts. Such persons were generally slaves but could be free men, as seen in the history of Eliezer (see Gen. 15:2) and Joseph (see Gen. 39:4). They also had charge of the monetary affairs of sons in a family; thus, they differed from tutors.

Christians are stewards, having both spiritual and temporal goods, described as "talents," committed to them for service on the part of others. They must expect to be called to account for their service: "Give an account of your stewardship" (Luke 16:2). This is to be the purpose of the judgment seat of Christ at which "each of us shall give account of himself to God" (Rom. 14:12). If we have grabbed much of the Master's property, using it for ourselves, then no reward will be ours. There will be nothing to our account. Ours will be a saved soul but a lost life.

Gospel pastors and preachers are spiritual stewards of God. A steward is a servant of the rich and noble, and the believer is a privileged servant of the Prince of Glory, King of heaven and earth. At all times stewards must be faithful in all things, not seeking their own personal advantage or pleasure, but only the honor of serving their master. Believers, as stewards, must be faithful to their heavenly Master in all things, seeking at all times His interests and honor. How sad it is that too many of us are among those who "seek their own, not the things that are of Christ Jesus" (Phil. 2:21). The unfaithful steward was in the mind of our Lord when He said, "Give an account of your stewardship, for you can no longer be steward" (Luke 16:2). May we so live and serve as to merit His commendation at the end of the day: "Well done, good and faithful servant."

November 24

"Yes, gray hairs are here and there on him,/ Yet he does not know it." HOSEA 7:9

The Bible says that hair is given by God as a protection and ornament for the head. Specific instructions were given as to the care of hair in the books of Leviticus and Deuteronomy. Premature baldness was considered a token of judgment (see Is. 15:2).

The prophet Hosea depicts Ephraim, God's people, as having gray hairs they did not know they had—a symbol of unconscious spiritual decay. While persons may become gray long before old age overtakes them, usually gray hairs are the sign that the strongest days are past and that youth has departed. For Ephraim, however, the gray hairs were not so much a sign of old age as of a nation old in wickedness. Such hairs are symptoms of the loss of youthful vitality, and the appearance of an old and withered look, all of which the people did not realize. So, such hairs represented the whoredom of Ephraim who permitted "strangers to devour his strength." Pride was another gray hair: "The pride of Israel testifies to his face" (Hos. 5:5). The prophet goes on to say that goodness, "like a morning cloud,/And like the early dew . . . goes away" (Hos. 6:4). Added to such a gray hair was another, symbolized by the description, "Ephraim is a cake unturned" (Hos. 7:8), baked on one side, raw on the other. The people were not thoroughly the Lord's; they had halted between two opinions. Another national gray hair appears in their being an empty vine, bringing forth fruit to itself and thus barren toward God. Ephraim "feeds on the wind,/And pursues the east wind" (Hos. 12:1), indicating that they pursued vanity and fed upon the empty things of the world.

May we search for gray hairs we do not know about and, discovering symptoms of spiritual decay, then allow and trust God to bring us into full harmony with His will and purpose.

November 25

The LORD God planted a garden. GENESIS 2:8

As soon as God created man, He fashioned a garden for the promotion of his enjoyment of the Creator and called it "the garden of the LORD" (Gen. 13:10). The Garden of Eden was well-watered and therefore a fruitful place. Symbol of great blessing, the restoration of Israel will resemble "a well-watered garden" (Jer. 31:12). Essayist Francis Bacon, who was an ardent lover of gardens, wrote, "God Almighty first planted a garden; and it is the Purest of human pleasures." A garden rests the soul and cheers the heart. Thus we should pray that in our heart and life God may find a garden of His own planting where He can talk with us in the cool of the day.

Although the first home of Adam and Eve was a pleasant garden, the Bible records sad tales in the history of its gardens. On a Welsh churchyard tombstone, this epitaph is found:

In a garden the first of our race was deceived;
In a garden the promise of grace was received;
In a garden was Jesus betrayed to His doom;
In a garden His body was laid in a tomb.

A garden may be looked upon as a place of delight, as it is often figuratively used in the Song of Solomon. A garden is also depicted as being the secluded place of sin and judgment (see Is. 65:3; 66:17). In *Othello,* Shakespeare wrote, "Our bodies are our gardens, to the which our wills are gardeners." If we consider our bodies to be the temple of the Holy Spirit, then, like watered gardens, they will be of rare fragrance. Rudyard Kipling's poem, "The Glory of the Garden," says:

Oh, Adam was a gardener, and God who made him sees
That half a proper gardener's work is done upon his knees.
So when your work is finished, you can wash your hand and pray
For the glory of the garden, that it may not pass away.

Only once in Scripture is the term *gardener* found, and then it was associated with Jesus, who alone can make your heart and mine as a fragrant, fruitful garden (see John 20:15).

November 26

Our heart is enlarged. . . .
be ye also enlarged. 2 CORINTHIANS 6:11, 13 KJV

To enlarge means "to extend, broaden, elaborate, or magnify." In photographs, an enlargement is a print larger than the negative. Paul wrote of the Corinthians whose faith increased and of the way by which they enlarged his ministry. Samuel Johnson was somewhat cynical when he wrote, "Enlarge my life with multitude of days," for he went on to say, "Life protracted is protracted woe."

How we need to be enlarged in our knowledge, love, hope, faith, and generosity! God, who always seeks to enlarge our hearts, disapproves of any contraction in the lives of believers. All of His great and precious promises guarantee enlarged experiences. God would have us open our hearts as wide as possible to receive all He is willing to bestow. Because He waits to gratify enlarged spiritual desires, we should exhibit a constant development in prayer, benevolence, pity, and compassion in all our efforts for His glory.

We must guard ourselves against narrow views, or efforts, because the heart of God is large. The love of Christ is beyond measure. The gospel commission is wide. The provision of mercy and the mansions of God are expansive. We need to pray for our narrow hearts to expand to contain all that God waits to bestow: "O Lord, broaden my contracted heart, that I may abound in hope, by the promise and aid of the Holy Spirit!"

Philip P. Bliss would have us sing:

Have you on the Lord believed?
 Still there's more to follow;
Of His grace have you received?
 Still there's more to follow.
Oh, the grace the Father shows,
 Still there's more to follow.
Freely He His grace bestows,
 Still there's more to follow.

November 27

"I will also command the clouds/
That they rain no rain on it." ISAIAH 5:6

As we read the Bible, we realize that clouds appear as the celestial veil of God's presence, His chariot, and the hiding place of His power. He manifested Himself to Israel in a cloud. It was by "the pillar of cloud" that He guided the children of Israel through the wilderness. This visible symbol of God's glory is often called the *shekinah.*

Clouds have many metaphorical notations in Scripture:

1. They may represent calamities or great afflictions. "The LORD has covered the daughter of Zion/With a cloud in His anger!" (Lam. 2:1).

2. An innumerable company of witnesses is compared to a multitude of clouds (see Heb. 12:1).

3. God's army is vast in appearance, even as a large cloud covering the earth (see Ezek. 38:9). Dwelling in light unapproachable, His presence is shrouded by clouds.

4. False teachers with their vanity and emptiness are described as clouds without rain (see 2 Cor. 11:13, 26). Godly teachers are filled with refreshing rain.

5. Those present at the transfiguration of Christ were overshadowed by a cloud, out of which they heard the divine voice (see Luke 9:34–35). At His ascension, a cloud became His chariot, taking Him to heaven (see Acts 1:9).

6. At the Rapture, the saints are to be caught up to meet the Lord in the air (see 1 Thess. 4:17). His return to earth will be in the clouds (see Luke 21:7).

The clouds obey the voice of their Creator and will act as He commands. Thus they represent His severe judgments upon those who fail to obey Him. Let us never cease to pray that the church may always have spiritual clouds full of divine rain and a divine light shining brightly for God's glory.

November 28

As a wise master builder
I have laid the foundation. 1 CORINTHIANS 3:10

Builders and their tasks loom large in Scripture. In the cradle of human society, Cain built a city and gave it his son's name, Enoch (see Gen. 4:17). Abraham, so often without a permanent home, looked for a city whose builder was God. The concept of building is used symbolically of raising up a spiritual edifice to God (see Eph. 2:20–21). Paul called himself a wise architect and builder, building on the foundation that is Christ. All builders are warned as to the materials they use in the building of God's house. The use of wrong materials means loss of goods and reward. Christ is referred to as the chief cornerstone, refused by the Jewish nation as such but highly exalted of God.

A Hebrew word for *builder* means "to build or rear a house or city." God is presented as the chief builder: "He who built all things is God" (Heb. 3:4). Christ is the great builder, and He declared of His work: "On this rock I will build My church" (Matt. 16:18). A wise builder is most careful about having a stable foundation upon which his structure is to be built. The apostles, as instruments in God's hand, were most careful as to the presentation of the foundation of faith and salvation in their effort to add to the church of the living God. "No other foundation can anyone lay than that which is laid, which is Jesus Christ" (1 Cor. 3:11).

An efficient builder also takes great care to prepare all necessary materials before he raises his house or building. Solomon emphasized this necessity in his injunction: "Prepare your outside work,/Make it fit for yourself in the field;/And afterward build your house" (Prov. 24:27). All who witness for the Lord are hewers, and their ax is the Word of God. By their teaching, they make disciples and, thereby, function as co-builders with Christ in His effort to complete the church, which is His body (see Matt. 28:19–20).

Volunteer your help in Christ's great task of building His church.

November 29

"What do you want Me to do for you?" MARK 10:36

How gratifying it is when a friend, who knows all about us, says: "Now, whatever you do, let me know if I can help you at any time. Don't fail to call upon me, if any need turns up. I'll be only too willing to do all I can to relieve you."

What blessed assurance is ours when the Friend closer than a brother meets us with the question: "Ask! What shall I give you?" (1 Kin. 3:5)! As we begin each new day, the Lord is before us, saying, "Now, let Me know what I can do for you. Whatever you ask, in prayer, believing, you will receive." To the blind man Jesus met near Jericho, He posed the same question: "What do you want Me to do for you?" (Luke 18:41). Without hesitation, Jesus sweetly answered the blind beggar's request for sight and said, "Receive your sight." Our Lord is gracious to place Himself at our disposal and to assure us: "Remember, when any trouble appears, let Me know about it, and I'll release you." The Lord is always near us and is aware of our question before we present it. He is ready to deliver us out of all our troubles.

As we begin each day, may we hear Him ask us what He can do for us throughout the unknown hours ahead. May our petition be ready to present, since His ear is always open to our appeal. As He asks, "What shall I give you?", we should readily answer, "O Lord, grant me victory over inward corruption. Purify my heart. Make me a vessel of honor fit for Your service. Impart holiness. Write Your Word upon my heart, enabling me to be a living epistle with Your precepts written large over my life. Fashion me into Your likeness and enable me to live for the honor and glory of Your free and sovereign grace!"

Remember that Jesus is always at His pardon office, sitting on a throne of grace, and always in a gracious and loving attitude to give us what we ask of Him.

November 30

The sacrifices of God are a broken spirit,/ A broken and a contrite heart. PSALM 51:17

Several years ago, the novelist Harold Begbie produced his *Broken Earthenware,* which described the stories of men and women broken and crushed by sin but all of whom had been transformed by God through the ministry of The Salvation Army. We still live in a world full of broken earthenware—so many brokenhearted people who, through one cause or another, are crushed in spirit and mind.

The Bible, a faithful mirror of human life, has much to say about broken hearts and about the causes of such crushing grief. Jeremiah, the weeping prophet, reflected the sorrow of God when he cried: "My heart within me is broken/Because of the prophets. . . . For the land is full of adulterers" (Jer. 23:9–10). Do the apostasy and adultery of our times move our hearts as deeply? Do rivers of tears run down our faces because of a powerless religion and a corrupt society? "Reproach has broken my heart" (Ps. 69:20) is said of Jesus, and He literally died of a broken heart, as evidenced by the blood and water from His pierced side. Because of such a death He is able to heal the brokenhearted.

How poignant is Paul's lament over the efforts of friends to deter him from his glorious task: "What do you mean by weeping and breaking my heart?" (Acts 21:13)! Solomon reminds us: "By sorrow of the heart/the spirit is broken" (Prov. 15:13). Is yours a broken spirit? Are you, either through your own mistakes or the action of others, broken and crushed? Then claim the promise that the Lord is near to the brokenhearted and ready to deliver those crushed in spirit. He alone has the secret of mending broken hearts and lives. In "The Ballad of Reading Gaol" Oscar Wilde has the couplet: "How else but through a broken heart/May Lord Christ enter in?"

December 1

"Blessed are those who have not seen and yet have believed." JOHN 20:29

The apostle John himself was not one of those he describes. For some three years, he was a close companion to Jesus, the disciple Jesus loved. John's benediction, then, is for those who have never seen the face of Jesus yet love Him and believe in Him as a living, bright reality. We have the axiom: "Seeing is believing." But the reverse is true, "Believing is seeing," as Peter confirmed when he wrote, "Though now you do not see Him, yet believing, you rejoice with joy inexpressible and full of glory" (1 Pet. 1:8). In our Christian life here below as "we walk by faith, not by sight" (2 Cor. 5:7), we are among those who have dared to make the venture of faith.

The snare of things that are seen can be strong; therefore, it is necessary to live in an unseen world. If a bird seeks to keep near the ground, it will not fly well. It must keep away from visible things and trust its buoyant wings to fly upward. Sometimes we find it hard to believe what God teaches us when He says not to look for things seen and temporal. We need to trust Him where we cannot trace Him, thus making His Word real in fact as well as in faith. "No one has seen God at any time" (1 John 4:12), but by the Holy Spirit we can see all that He is in His invisible self—His love, His compassion, His glory, His power, and His works. How appropriate are the lines of E. M. Winter:

I do not ask that He must prove
   His Word is true to me,
And that before I can believe
   He first must let me see.

It is enough for me to know
   'Tis true because He says 'tis so;
On His unchanging Word I'll stand
   And trust till I can understand!

While we sojourn in our earthly tabernacle, our eyes will not behold His radiant form. But once the veil of sense is removed, the glorious vision will be ours, and we will see His face (see Rev. 22:4).

December 2

James, Cephas, and John, who seemed to be pillars. GALATIANS 2:9

Several Hebrew words are translated *pillar.* One of these means "to set," "to place" and implies anything that is set up. It is the word used twice by Jacob in different circumstances (see Gen. 28:18; 35:14). Pillars were also associated with idolatry. Another Hebrew word refers to the pillars of the tabernacle and the temple, and to the pillar of cloud and the pillar of fire. The same word is used symbolically of the pillars of the heavens and the pillars of earth.

The New Testament word means "any firm support." In this sense the three apostles were like columns in the church at Jerusalem. All church matters were referred to them. Paul functioned in a similar manner. The true church of God is described as "the pillar and ground of the truth" (1 Tim. 3:15), that is, the witness maintaining the truth on earth. As a pillar is designed to support a building, so believers support the house of God on earth.

Many pillars serve for beauty. Those of Solomon's temple were beautifully adorned with lily work and other attractive additions. The church possesses many adorned by the Holy Spirit with gifts and graces, enabling them to witness well for the Master. Peter wrote of "the incorruptible ornament of a gentle and quiet spirit, which is very precious in the sight of God" (1 Pet. 3:4). To believers, Peter said, "Be you all of one mind," reflecting the mind of Christ. It is incumbent upon us to uphold and support, in every way, the section of the church of God of which we are members, in both local and missionary activities.

Jesus shall reign where'er the sun
  Does his successive journeys run;
His Kingdom stretch from shore to shore,
  Till moons shall wax and wane no more.

December 3

Having nothing,
and yet possessing all things. 2 CORINTHIANS 6:10

What a seeming contradiction this appears to be! How can one be both poor and rich at the same time? It has been said that man is a bundle of contradictions. All Bible students know that the Word possesses many paradoxes and is a bundle of apparent contradictions. The majority of the Lord's people are not materially rich but have just enough to get along. More affluent persons may look at them and feel they have nothing to make them content and happy. But how wrong they are in their assessment! Even the poorest are heirs of God, having Him as their portion and inheritance. While they do not have much of this world's wealth, theirs is gold tried in the fire, making them spiritually rich.

James Smith, who gave us *Daily Remembrancer,* wrote:

> His eternity is the date of our happiness; His unchangeableness, the rock of our rest; His omnipotence, our constant guard; His faithfulness, our daily security; His mercies, our overflowing store; His omniscience, our careful overseer; His wisdom, our judicious Counsellor; His justice, our stern avenger; His omnipresence, our sweet company; His holiness, the fountain from which we receive sanctifying grace; His all-sufficiency, the lot of our inheritance; His infinity, the extent of our glorious portion.

Although we may have little of this world's goods, we have a marvelous fortune at our disposal in God. He waits to give us all He has, richly to enjoy. Ours is the privilege of living as heirs of heaven, poor yet rich, unknown by the world as heirs of eternal wealth and as those fully known by Him who is the owner of all. Though poor, we can make many rich, said Paul, who owned little more than the clothes he wore and the books and parchments he loved.

May we pray: Give us from Thy heavenly store, and we shall be rich, indeed.

December 4

"Ephraim is a cake unturned." HOSEA 7:8

In biblical times cakes were usually mingled with oil. The unleavened cakes typify the Lord Jesus in His perfect humanity begotten by the Holy Spirit. Ephraim, or Israel, is compared to a cake not turned, indicating it was not palatable, "neither cold nor hot" (Rev. 3:16). In her quest for alliances, Israel was brought into a situation in which she was neither truly Israelite nor truly foreign; she was half-baked, like a pancake cooked on only one side. The nation was kind and good to neighbors but not obedient and good toward God.

Unturned implies not "thorough," or not through and through. Ephraim was not wholly the Lord's. Grace was hers, but such grace had not gone to the very center of her being so as to be felt in all thoughts, words, and actions. A cake not turned is soon burned on the side nearest the fire, a symbol of one who is "saint in public, but a devil in practice. The assumed appearance of superior sanctity frequently accompanies a total absence of all vital godliness," said C. H. Spurgeon, who added the prayer:

> If I am cake burned on one side, and dough on the other, O Lord, turn me! Turn my unsanctified nature to the fire of Thy love and let it feel the sacred glow, and let my burnt side cool a little while as I learn my own weakness and want of heat when I am removed from Thy heavenly Flame. Let me not be found a double-minded man, but one entirely under the powerful influence of reigning grace; for well I know if I am left like a cake unturned, and am not on both sides the subject of Thy grace, I must be consumed forever amid everlasting burnings.

We need to pray a similar prayer as followers of Him who was holy all through.

I am Thine, O Lord, I have heard Thy voice,
  And it told Thy love to me;
But I long to rise in the arms of faith,
  And be closer drawn to Thee.

December 5

"I must be about My Father's business." LUKE 2:49

Among the various original words translated *business*, one refers to one's own business or affairs: "Mind your own business" (1 Thess. 4:11). Another term implies the business or duties of another, which is the implication in today's verse. At the outset of His ministry, Jesus affirmed that He was in the world to finish the work of His Father. Here He declares He is active in such a task.

Shakespeare wrote, "To business that we love we rise betime,/And go to 't with delight." The Son delighted to do the will of His Father and would often rise early to converse with His Father about the business entrusted to Him. The words of this verse were His first recorded words, uttered when He was only twelve years of age. The words indicated that even at an early age He knew what His purpose was in a world of need. This saying is also significant because it gives us the key to the whole of His life and mission. As Dr. G. Campbell Morgan stated, "The compelling force, the *must* behind all His doing and teaching, was ever the same: the things of His Father. He lived and wrought only to do the will of God."

How happy are parents when their children relate their lives to God by the *must* of complete surrender to do His will! Are we doing the King's business not only with haste but also with delight? Are we being borne along by the Master's compelling force to finish the task the Father has allotted us? Unfortunately, the majority around us have no idea why they are in the world. Having never discovered the divine plan for their lives, they drift with the tide. If we are the Lord's, then no matter what our legitimate business may be, the Father's business must always have top priority. His affairs must be our chief concern. As Dr. S. D. Gordon signed in my autograph book: "The greatest passion that can burn in the human heart, is to know the will of God, and get it done."

Let us put the Father's business first.

December 6

They were forbidden by the Holy Spirit
to preach the word in Asia.
. . . they tried to go into Bithynia,
but the Spirit did not permit them. ACTS 16:6–7

Paul always sought to be guided by the Holy Spirit and declared that all led of the Spirit are the sons of God. The apostle went through the cities of Derbe and Lystra, and he strengthened the existing churches in their faith and established further churches. Yet when he crossed into Asia, he was forbidden by the Holy Spirit to preach the Word there and also was restricted by the Spirit when he tried to go into Bithynia. If the divine commission was to go into *all* the world and preach the gospel to every creature, why were these prohibitions issued, since Asia was part of the world? Why was the door shut by Christ's own Spirit? Why did He hinder Paul from preaching the gospel there? By some undesignated reasons the Spirit indicated that the apostolic witness was inadvisable.

The omniscient Spirit, however, knew the exact moment for precise action. There is a specific time for a specific task, and He knew that the precise moment for Asia had not yet come. Later on, Paul went to Ephesus, the chief city of Asia, and experienced a mighty movement of the Spirit.

As servants of the Lord, we must be guided by the Spirit and move each moment at His will. When Paul reached Bithynia, the Spirit would not permit him to witness there. The next day Paul and his companions came to Troas, a leading seaport, where Paul had a vision of the man of Macedonia. As a result of these events, the gospel reached Europe.

A lesson we gather from these apparent interruptions in service is that the Spirit has not only a service of work, but a service of waiting. If doors of usefulness seem to be closed against us, the Spirit has a blessed way of finding in them a new ministry into God's service. How appropriate are lines from "Streams in the Desert":

> When I cannot understand my Father's leading,
> And it seems to be but hard and cruel fate,
> Still I hear that gentle whisper ever pleading,
> God is working, God is faithful, ONLY WAIT.

December 7

"I do not know how." . . .
the LORD *knows how.* 1 KINGS 3:7; 2 PETER 2:9

I will take the liberty of weaving these two phrases, separated by time of utterance, to illustrate the difference between our ignorance and God's perfect wisdom. In one of his renowned essays, Francis Bacon wrote, "If you dissemble sometimes your knowledge of that you are thought to know, you shall be thought, another time, to know what you know not." In spite of all our acquired knowledge, we do not know everything. Solomon humbly said, "I am a little child; I do not know how to go out or come in" (1 Kin. 3:7). The king asked for an understanding heart and discernment of character, and God granted his request.

We do not know the way we should take in many decisions that have to be made, but God knows. When He has tried us, we come forth as gold. Job's great triumph of faith can be ours if we have learned to sing: "In every hour, in perfect peace, I'll sing, He knows! He knows!" We may not know how to face the burdens of tomorrow, but do we need to know? Is not today's burden enough, and has not God said, "As your days, so shall your strength be" (Deut. 33:25)? Why, then, add tomorrow's load to today's? If you feel tomorrow's burden may crush you, let it happen tomorrow, not today. The Lord knows how and when to deliver the godly out of the trials awaiting them. We do not know how we are to meet each problem, situation, choice, and sorrow but the Lord knows how. As we rest in Him, He makes our pathway plain.

Perhaps you have recently been bereaved and are saying to your heart: "I do not know how I can face the coming days without the loved one who was so much a part of my life." But God knows how you will survive, for He has made every provision for the vacant place in your heart and home. Why not leave tomorrow in His hands?

O magnify the Lord with me,
With me exalt his name;
When in distress to him I called,
He to my rescue came.

Trust His perfect knowledge to lead you.

December 8

He will guide you. . . .
led by the Spirit of God. JOHN 16:13; ROMANS 8:14

The unredeemed person does not have it in himself to direct his steps aright. He is not the master of his fate or the captain of his soul. He has no inner light to lead him amid encircling gloom; he needs a guide. The believer turns to Him who has promised to be our guide, even to death. God is indeed the noblest, wisest, and strongest of all guides. He is the only guide in whom we should place our confidence and the One ready to guide us with His unerring counsel.

Among the various original words for *guide,* one means "a leader," "one who goes on before and leads the way." Another word indicates "one who guides a stranger toward a given object," which is the way the Holy Spirit functions. He guides us into all truth and leads us as strangers and pilgrims toward Jesus whom He glorifies and toward the celestial city.

An earthly guide, because he is human, is liable to err in respect to time, distance, and location. The gracious Holy Spirit, who is perfect in every way, is incapable of making a mistake. His guidance, therefore, bears the imprint of His perfection. As the One who searches for all things, He alone can guide us in the Word and ways of God. He guides us continually with His eye (see Ps. 32:8), the eye indicating His omniscience. "His eyes behold" everyone in every place and are always open "on the righteous" (Ps. 11:4; 34:15). Hagar named the Lord who spoke to her, You-Are-the-God-Who-Sees, for she said, "Have I also here seen Him who sees me?" (Gen. 16:13). We should praise God for such an all-seeing, perfect guide and teacher as the Holy Spirit. The Spirit is always with us to lead us with faith.

Guide me, O thou great Jehovah,
  Pilgrim through this barren land;
I am weak, but thou art mighty;
  Hold me with thy powerful hand;
    Bread of heaven,
Feed me till I want no more.

Let us put out our hands and trust the Holy Spirit to be our guide.

December 9

Deliver yourself like a gazelle from the hand of the hunter, / And like a bird from the hand of the fowler. PROVERBS 6:5

Hunter and fowler are used symbolically of Satan, from whose traps God delivers His children. When judgment fell upon Israel, her prophets became as the traps of the fowler (see Hos. 9:8). Many parallels between the hunter and Satan, who is the hunter and destroyer of men's souls, can be traced. For instance, a hunter is one who follows his prey with all kinds of enticement. He is tireless in his pursuit, and he greatly delights in his search for game. How like Satan, who uses many wiles to entrap men's souls. He is never weary but always has delight in his hunt.

Another comparison is evident in the objective of the hunter, who consumes the animals or birds he has caught. The ultimate design of Satan in the capture of souls is that he might destroy them. David could say of his enemy: "You hunt my life to take it" (1 Sam. 24:11). Peter would have us know about the satanic fowler "seeking whom he may devour" (1 Pet. 5:8). A hunter also resorts to many devices and schemes to trap innocent game. Craftily, he spreads nets for birds. Paul could say, "We are not ignorant of his devices" (2 Cor. 2:11). But God has provided us invincible armor enabling us to resist all the tricks of Satan: "He shall deliver you from the snare of the fowler" (Ps. 91:3).

Avid hunters do little else but hunt. Nimrod is described as a mighty hunter. Such was his life! We do not realize sufficiently that Satan is an untiring hunter, with nothing else in mind except the captivity of souls. Think of the millions he has caught and destroyed already! "But thanks be to God, who gives us the victory through our Lord Jesus Christ" (1 Cor. 15:57).

The powers of death have done their worst,
  But Christ their legions hath dispersed;
Let shouts of holy joy outburst.
  Alleluia!

December 10

These are wells without water.
. . . clouds without water. 2 PETER 2:17; JUDE 12

Under the inspiration of the Holy Spirit, writers of holy Scripture were enabled to express, in picturesque and symbolic language, aspects of divine truth. For instance, these waterless wells and clouds signify false teachers who are destitute of the only true source of life. Jesus spoke of the fountain of life, which was symbolic of the Holy Spirit that Christ bestowed upon His church. The Spirit is the power of life springing up within the soul toward its heavenly source.

Wells are receptacles for water. If a person comes to draw water but finds the well empty, he is deceived and disappointed. Clouds without water imply the same deception of being full, yet rainless. Ministers of the Word should be filled with grace and gifts of the Spirit, enabling them to impart spiritual instruction. But false teachers, in spite of their appearance as faithful preachers of the Word, are barren of the truth as it is in Christ Jesus. They are empty wells and clouds, carried about with the wind of delusion and untrue doctrine.

When Solomon referred to drinking "running water from your own well" (Prov. 5:15), he referred to the privileges and blessings within one's own house. The direct application is associated with a man enjoying all his heart's desires in the wife of his youth, instead of seeking joy and satisfaction elsewhere. Solomon also recorded that "the mouth of the righteous is a well of life" (Prov. 10:11), which implies that the life of a Christian should emanate the virtues of love, sympathy, and kindness, all enriching the lives of others. Isaiah 12:3 speaks of the value of a water-filled well: "With joy you will draw water/From the wells of salvation."

The unlimited treasures of which the Lord makes us the recipients are called wells because they convey untold blessings to the hearts of those within God's family. The manifold fruit of the Spirit can represent the wells from which we are to drink deeply with confidence and gladness.

December 11

He turns the shadow of death into morning,
And makes the day dark as night. AMOS 5:8

The various biblical uses of the word *shadow* mean different things: the shelter of a home (see Gen. 19:8); a representation or sample which gives an idea of the real thing (see Col. 2:17); a symbol of sorrow and death (see Ps. 23:4); of heavenly protection (see Ps. 91:1); of the hidden energy of God (see 2 Chr. 5:8); and of adversaries (see Is. 16:3).

The opposite actions in connection with morning and night indicated by the prophet Amos are emphatic as being the prerogative of God the creator. Poets have given us many descriptions of death as somber as the event itself. We have phrases such as "death's dark night," "the terrors of death," "the icy hand of death." But the declaration of Amos is that God turns shadow into substance, night into morning, and day into night.

Faith in God enables us to count death as the signal of retreat from the dark shadows of this world into the glorious abode above. Death is the passageway from the mortal into the immortal. During World War II, an unknown Christian soldier was instantly killed in battle, but some time before his death he had set forth his conception of leaving death's shadow for a glorious morning above:

> Best loved of all I leave behind, I see
> O Heaven, pity those who cannot see!
> Glory on glory—glory on that face
> So near, so dear; gold glory on the wave,
> Purple and gold and darting tongues of flame;
> Calm glory on the cloud-filled dome of heaven;
> Glory of fire on earth's great face.
> So slips my soul, scarce heeding of the change,
> From glory unto glory! Heaven breaks
> Eternal glory, on the face of God.

The death and resurrection of our gracious Lord give us the assurance that in Him alone the shadow of death will be transformed into glory and joy unspeakable.

December 12

You who set Your glory above the heavens!/
Out of the mouth of babes and infants/
You have ordained strength. PSALM 8:1–2

Here David is emphasizing two of God's witnesses, namely, a star-bespangled sky and a newborn human soul—the latter being more convincing than the former. The plural, *heavens,* refers to the firmament or wide expanse of the sky in which the sun, moon, and stars are set. The scriptural record sets forth several meaningful phrases in reference to the heavens: the dwelling place of God; Satan has no entrance into it; the third heaven Paul was caught up into; the heaven of heavens; the final abode of saints; the new heavens and earth. While the aerial heavens glorify God, His ultimate glory is above them, even in heaven, His eternal abode.

The heavens are voiceless, but children can speak. As Alexander Smellie stated it:

> Through the immensities of the firmament, and from its abysses, no articulate message comes to my spirit. It is a silent book, which I must interpret and rouse into life; for, without me to ponder and explain them, "the thick inlaid patinas of bright gold" would have nothing to say. But the child of three or four summers may learn the Gospel, and tell it out in simple accents of his own; and then he outruns Arcturus and the Pleiades. He can hold a blessedness in his bosom, and sing a winsome psalm with his lips, to which no fabled music of the spheres may ever be compared.

Stars testify to the greatness of God, but children testify to His grace. Many years ago in a London school for girls, the renowned theologian Adolph Monod heard the girls sing: "All hail the power of Jesus' name!" Overwhelmed, Monod said, "My weak heart gave way, and I could not but weep instead of singing. The whole of sacred criticism is not worth my little girl of six years old, opening her mouth and saying to angels, Jews, Gentiles, and Christians—*Crown Him Lord of All*"!

O that with yonder sacred throng
We at His feet may fall!
Join in the everlasting song,
And crown Him Lord of all!

December 13

"When He has tested me,/ I shall come forth as gold." JOB 23:10

Gold typifies the pure doctrine of the gospel and the grace and benefits of Christ received through the Word. Gold is most precious and one of the rarest things on earth. The saints are choice in God's sight: "The precious sons of Zion,/Valuable as fine gold" (Lam. 4:2). In the chapter before us, in the midst of Job's bitter complaint and sighing after God, he flashes forth a most remarkable evidence of the tenacity of his faith. He was confident that God was behind his trials. God was seeking the vindication of the true gold in His servant.

In the furnace of affliction, the Divine Goldsmith was transmuting Job's life into a most precious vessel. Malachi assures us that God sits as the refiner and purifier of silver (see Mal. 3:3). Often the best that God has to give us comes out of the furnace of affliction. The potter never sees the clay take on rich shades of silver or red or cream or brown until after the burning in the furnace. Is this not universal in the law of life? When did the most godly persons we have known or read about receive their beautiful character? As with the clay, their beauty and glory came after the darkness and burning of the furnace. The trials and testings produce the fine gold. It was in the thick darkness where God was that Moses talked with God and received from Him laws for the people.

Perhaps you are presently being sorely tried and somewhat mystified by what God has permitted to overtake you. Remember that He dwells in darkness as well as in light. God is with you in your furnace, trying you, sifting out the impurities, and transmuting your life into a golden vessel more fit for His use.

O Joy that seekest me through pain,
I cannot close my heart to thee;
I trace the rainbow through the rain,
And feel the promise is not vain
That morn shall tearless be.

December 14

"God resists the proud,/
But gives grace to the humble." JAMES 4:6

The contrast between pride and humility, in word and in deed, is prominent throughout Scripture. Jesus was emphatic in His teaching regarding these opposite qualities. To Him, the only way up was down. Childlike humility is the way to high honor in heaven, and only "he who humbles himself will be exalted" (Matt. 23:12). When in His Sermon on the Mount He spoke of the humble as being "poor in spirit," He did not imply poor-spiritedness. What He taught was that honor would come to those who place their own righteousness in proper relationship to the thrice-holy God. Their own fleshly wisdom was but folly to Him. Only those who do not shun the valley of humiliation find it to be a place of blessing and hope. Only as we learn of our own poverty and ignorance are we ready to learn of God and to trust Him. Warning against "false humility," Paul urged the saints to don as a garment, "humbleness of mind" (Col. 2:18; 3:12).

Contrary to worldly policy, humility is the root of all progress in knowledge. Some of the greatest persons in knowledge or personality were extremely humble. All who are Christ's, who was Himself meek and lowly in heart, should always seek to adorn the garment of true humility. The consistent teaching of Jesus was that the gates of the kingdom of God are always open to the lowly hearted and to those who know there is nothing between them and gross darkness beyond but the love, pity, and provision of God. Thomas à Kempis would have us pray: "Surely my heart cannot rest, nor be entirely contented, unless it rest in Thee, and rise above all gifts and all creatures whatsoever." Only as we realize that we are nothing, have nothing, and can do nothing apart from God can we be graced with the humility that James declared comes as God's gift.

And thus my hope is in the Lord,
And not in my own merit;
I rest upon his faithful word
To them of contrite spirit.
That he is merciful and just,
Here is my comfort and my trust;
His help I wait with patience.

December 15

"He has stripped me of my glory,/ And taken the crown from my head." JOB 19:9

James exalted the patience and perseverance of Job (5:11). Job was "blameless"; he "feared God and shunned evil" (Job 1:1). The stripping process by God must have meant the exercise of much patience by the patriarch. In a most poignant way, Job relates how God had denuded him of his glory, his crown, his honor, his loved ones, his familiar friends, his possessions and position, leaving him as a barren tree. As I glance out of my study window and gaze for a moment at several trees that during the summer had abundant and beautiful foliage, I see they are now gaunt, bare, leafless, and stripped of all their summer glory. This must have been the way Job felt in his wretched, lonely condition.

Does your life seem desolate and bare, a leafless tree? Perhaps you have been stripped of all that made life worth living, a dear one so precious to your heart and upon whom you were so dependent was taken from you. In that one's death your own heart seems to have died. Now you stand on the bleak summit of your deep grief, no longer sheltered by the loved one but stripped like a tree of all its summer dress and beauty. May the good Lord, who always seeks your highest and best, save you from yielding to despair and inspire you to live in hope that, as a tree planted by the Lord in His garden, you will blossom again and no longer appear as a naked tree. Job lost everything in his trials but lived to see the day when God gave him back twice as much as he had lost. His latter end was more richly blessed than his beginning. Above all, think of Jesus who was stripped of all and died naked on a leafless tree but is now clothed and crowned with honor and glory.

O Light that followest all my way,
  I yield my flickering torch to thee;
My heart restores its borrowed ray,
  That in thy sunshine's blaze its day
May brighter, fairer be.

December 16

Who makes grass to grow on the mountains. PSALM 147:8

Grass often represents human frailty: "Surely the people are grass/The grass withers, the flower fades" (Is. 40:7–8). Jesus used the figure of grass not only as divine clothing for the earth but also as an illustration of man's frailty, growing one day, the next day a fuel for the oven. Walt Whitman in his *Leaves of Grass* gave us this beautiful aspect of grass:

> A child said *What is the grass?*
> fetching it to me with full hands.
> Oh I guess it is the handkerchief of the Lord.
> A scented gift and remembrance designedly dropt,
> Bearing the owner's name someway in the corners,
> That we may see and remark and say, *whose*?

As children are clothed with attractive and beneficial garments, so God clothes the fields with various lovely grasses. "He causes the grass to grow for the cattle" (Ps. 104:14). How could cattle or we humans exist without it? Where would our milk, butter, cheese, and wool come from if it were not for the grass? Grass is not only for our provision but also for our pleasure. One of the most pleasing sights is the lovely green, covering the hills like a carpet.

If God so clothes the earth with grass, surely He will not fail to care for His children, as Jesus clearly taught in His reference to the grass. The psalmist's affirmation that God grows grass upon mountains implies that He can make it grow in the least likely and most difficult places. The word *makes* reminds us that the power of God is under the root of the grass, causing it to grow even in a shallow place that is not nurtured. If life for us is not in some sheltered valley but exposed in a most difficult sphere, is it not encouraging to know that God can enable us to grow in grace and in knowledge of Him in the least likely place? Having charmed us with the color of grass, He is able to make us pleasing in His sight—and in the sight of others.

Praise your marvelous Creator for all His abundant blessings.

December 17

Examine me, O LORD, and prove me;/
Try my mind and my heart. PSALM 26:2

This triad of requests expresses David's desire for every phase of his life to be in harmony with God's will. The psalmist sought heaven's vindication of his character and so used three forcible words in addressing God, namely, *examine, prove, try.* Another translation puts it: "Examine me, O Lord, and try me;/Test my heart and my mind."

Examine. Desiring no wicked way to remain within his heart, David asked God, a thorough examiner, to search his life for any hidden sin or weakness. He wanted everything known to God to be made known to himself. Examinations as a rule are not pleasant experiences. Young people dread them at school. Yet failures in such examinations often create a determination never to fail again and are therefore profitable. Searchings of our persons and possessions for security reasons at airports are inconvenient but not to be feared if we have nothing to hide. For medical reasons, examinations are beneficial. We are to work with the Lord in the necessary examination of the heart: "Let a man examine himself" (1 Cor. 11:28). We are to examine ourselves whether we be in the faith. It is possible to work *for* the faith yet not *in* it.

Prove. Such an action is necessary, showing something to be true by argument. God proves His people and desires His people to prove Him.

Try. This kindred term means "to sift out," "to test or make trial of." "Many shall be purified" (Dan. 12:10). "Faith . . . tested by fire" (1 Pet. 1:7). Fire, a symbol of the Holy Spirit, consumes all that is contrary to the holy will of God.

Mere self-introspection can result in despair. It is far better to pray with David: "Search me, O Lord." He alone knows how to throw light into the darkened cells where passion reigns supreme. Blessed be His name! What His search reveals, His blood can cleanse.

Search me, O Lord, and from the dross of sin,
  Refine as gold, and keep me pure within.
Search Thou my thoughts whose springs Thine eyes can see;
  From secret faults, O Savior, cleanse Thou me.

December 18

Old and patched sandals on their feet. JOSHUA 9:5

The first mention of sandals in Scripture was when Moses was told to put off his shoes, for the ground on which he stood was holy because God was there. The same was said of Joshua. With bare feet the priests ministered in the temple. It was an ancient custom when transferring a possession to deliver a sandal (see Ruth 4:7–8). Shoes of biblical times were mostly sandals, or soles fastened to the feet by strings or thongs.

In *Idylls of the King,* Tennyson describes a "race of miserable men," who "Do forge a lifelong trouble for ourselves,/By taking true for false, or false for true." Joshua had to face a good deal of trouble as the result of taking the false for the true in his encounter with the deceiving Gibeonites. They came with the intent of misleading the wise leader of Israel and cleverly succeeded. Joshua was beguiled by the wily Gibeonites with their tattered clothes, worn-out shoes, and moldy bread because he "did not ask counsel of the LORD" (Josh. 9:14). Joshua was famous for his stratagem as leader of Israel's forces. But because he acted on his own as he listened to the fabricated story of the Gibeonites, he was found wanting in keen discernment. The deceivers likely had large wardrobes, wealth, fine homes, and plenty of good food, but they acted as if they were very poor, not only to gain sympathy but also to save themselves from death. What a dramatic scene!

The lesson we learn from such duplicity is never to act what we are not or to be deceitful in righteousness. A sign of the times is the way multitudes will believe a lie, even as Joshua did. Satan is the archdeceiver who beguiled Eve through his subtlety and who, although the fiend of darkness, can transform himself into an angel of light. Our protection against satanic wiles is the constant effort to seek the Lord, praying that spiritual intuition may be ours to detect immediately that which is not of the Lord.

Ask the heavenly Father for His wisdom today.

December 19

The wind was contrary. . . .
the wind ceased. MATTHEW 14:24, 32

Wind, which is air in motion with varying degrees of velocity, is used figuratively in Scripture to describe how God works out His purposes with people. Because it comes unseen and goes we know not where, it is a fitting symbol of the activities of the Holy Spirit, whose power is felt and whose results abide. Wind also illustrates the unseen influence of Satan who carries out his evil designs by it. Wind may denote things that are vain and empty. In our Lord's miracle when He walked on the sea, a contrary wind probably came as a gentle breeze and then became a violent force. Often in human experiences there are contrary winds, but there is a glory of the Master seen only when the wind is contrary and our little ship is tossed about with waves. Jesus is perfect security in storms. He has never promised an easy passage, only a safe landing.

No person has ever seen the wind, for its movements surpass human perception. It is thus with the invisible Holy Spirit, whose operations can be seen and felt. That His ways and workings are of a hidden nature is emphasized by Paul in his teaching of the Spirit's activities: "The natural man does not receive the things of the Spirit of God" (1 Cor. 2:14). As God holds the wind in His fist, so the operations of the Spirit are from God, who causes and commands spiritual winds to operate in our lives.

The wind blows freely, and we cannot command its movements. Scripture reveals the Holy Spirit as a free agent, to act as He pleases. He works "distributing to each one individually as He wills" (1 Cor. 12:11). Our personal responsibility is to be ready for any movement from Him who is the Spirit of love.

Spirit of our God, descending,
  Fill our hearts with heavenly joy,
Love with every passion blending,
  Pleasure that can never cloy;
Thus provided, pardoned, guided,
  Nothing can our peace destroy.

Ready, ever ready, we stand, O Spirit, waiting for Your Movement.

December 20

He who talked with me had
a gold reed to measure the city. REVELATION 21:15

It is quite proper that a gold reed is to measure the city of pure gold. Ancient experts looked for a philosopher's stone to transmute the baser elements into that which was precious and peerless. Yet no one but God can create "the source of sapphires,/And it contains gold dust" (Job 28:6). Such a miracle is His prerogative. The measuring aspect, however, interests us, for one wonders how we could exist without measure in many phases of life. The houses in which we live represent precise measuring, as do the clothes we wear and the food we eat. Light and gas come through a *meter,* a word meaning "that which measures."

The Lord has the measuring rod to test your life and mine to see whether they conform to His standard measurement. The Bible is God's law from heaven for our sojourn on earth, and it presents Jesus as our infallible standard. Paul prayed for grace to measure up to the stature of the perfect man in Christ Jesus. As cities and towns are subjected to endless measurements in their creation, so the Holy City indicates perfect planning. Precise measuring is found in details in the city that lies foursquare.

A lesson we learn from all this is that God wills us to order our lives systematically, conforming to His standards. Long ago people measured with their thumbs, an inch represented by the distance between the knuckle and first joint. This became known as "the rule of the thumb," but it was not very exact. God, who measures our days, would not have us plan life in such a haphazard way, but by His certain and perfect standard. To bring our lives up to the divine measurement, we have the guidance and power of the Holy Spirit, who is given to us without measure.

Holy Ghost, dispel our sadness;
  Pierce the clouds of nature's night;
Come, thou source of joy and gladness,
  Breathe thy life, and spread thy light.
From the height which knows no measure,
  As a gracious shower descend,
Bringing down the richest treasure
  Man can wish, or God can send.

December 21

"Why have you been standing here idle all day?" MATTHEW 20:6

Jesus, in His parable of workers in the vineyard, had every right to ask such a pointed question. In the days of His flesh, He labored unceasingly for the glory of His Father and for the good of all people. What particular day was Jesus referring to? Many different days are mentioned in Scripture, and it is necessary to distinguish their differences. The day in our Lord's question is the day of grace He instituted, the day of the building of His church, of the calling out of people for His name. This is "man's day," his "day of salvation," and as he hears the divine voice "today," he is warned against hardening his heart toward God. "Standing here idle" means to be living without labor, doing nothing, being lazy. Paul quoted a saying about Cretans as "lazy gluttons" (Titus 1:12). Peter also warned us against barrenness and unfruitfulness (see 2 Pet. 1:8).

To us a day is a period of twenty-four hours, but Scripture's today is an unknown period. It is said of Jerusalem: "If you had known, even you, especially in this your day, the things that make for your peace!" (Luke 19:42). Because the day is the time of our labor, we should not be idle. When the day is ended and night overtakes outdoor laborers, they can no longer work. As laborers for God, we can only witness and work for Him as He continues the day of grace, for the night comes when no person can work. May we be found laboring for the Master from dawn to setting sun! Amos pronounced a woe upon those "at ease in Zion" (Amos 6:1). How can we who are children of the day remain indolent and slothful as we think of the millions in heathen darkness awaiting the coming of missionaries to lead them into the light of the gospel? May He, who died for the sin of a lost world, create within our hearts a deep passion for souls!

We hear the throb of surging life,
  The clank of chains, the curse of greed,
The moan of pain, the futile cries
  Of superstition's cruel creed;
The peoples hunger for thee, Lord;
  The world is waiting for thy Word.

December 22

I know a man in Christ. . . .
I know such a man. 2 CORINTHIANS 12:2–3

In his defense against false teachers and their false visions, Paul, referring to his conversion fourteen years earlier, defends his authentic visions and revelations as a regenerated man in Christ Jesus. Such a precious and personal indwelling is emphasized by the apostle in other similar phrases: "in Christ," "in Him," "in whom." The mutual indwelling of which Christ spoke, "Abide in Me, and I in you," was dear to the heart of the apostle, who fully realized all the spiritual benefits he had by being in Christ.

In Christ, he died and was buried. Before his regeneration, Paul was bent on slaying all the saints believing in a crucified Savior. However, on the Damascus road the miracle happened, and he came to know what it was to be crucified with Christ and to become dead to sin.

In Christ, he had the assurance that he stood before God, freely and fully justified because of the Savior's death and merit. Paul considered himself to be the chiefest sinner, but a sinner made whiter than snow and transformed into a child of the King.

In Christ, he found the center and the circumference of the true life. Paul came to write, "Christ in you, the hope of glory" (Col. 1:27). On earth he believed that he was inhabited by Christ, the monarch of his life. In Christ, he put on Christ. Retaining his own impressive individuality, Paul is shown with the Light, daily reflecting the image of his meek and majestic Lord.

In Christ, he had the undying hope that ultimately he would depart from this life to live with the glorified in Christ's immediate presence, which would be far better than life below. Paul, knowing that the Lamb is all the glory in Immanuel's land, was happy when he could say, "The time of my departure is at hand. . . . There is laid up for me the crown of righteousness" (2 Tim. 4:6–8).

Let cares like a wild deluge come
And storms of sorrow fall!
May I but safely reach my home,
My God, my heaven, my all.

December 23

"Make them sit down in groups of fifty." LUKE 9:14

Such a command reveals how Jesus could organize a crowd. If added to the five thousand men were women and children (see Matt. 14:21), then the multitude may have been as large as ten thousand. Believing that order is heaven's first law, Jesus seated the people in groups of fifty, knowing that this would prevent confusion and make serving easier. Had the large crowd rushed upon Him, crowding around Him in a confused, feverish fashion, He would not have been able to dispense the good things He had provided to satisfy their hunger. What a sight that must have been, with thousands looking up into the face of the One who was the object of their hope, who alone knew how to command a well-nigh unmanageable crowd!

Philip Brooks once preached a powerful sermon on the phrase, "Make the men sit down," in which he indicated that at that moment all the confusion subsided. Instead of the people pushing toward and surging around Jesus, they were made to sit down, ready to receive what He was to give. Such order, Brooks went on to show, illustrates two stages in Christian experience. First, when people rush hurriedly after good things, their religious life is full of tension and even worry. Second, when they sit down, their restlessness and confusion give way to calm patience and watchful waiting. This is an essential part of spiritual experience.

Our perfect Lord was ever the master of assemblies, knowing how to act in an emergency. He never lost command. Thus, as His followers, we should never lose our composure in the presence of tumultuous trials and cares. Like Mary, we should always be found sitting at His feet, ready to be fed by Him. When we fulfill the Master's commands, we discover that there is always more than enough to satisfy our hunger for the bread He alone can give.

December 24

"Forgive us our debts,/
As we forgive our debtors." MATTHEW 6:12

A *debt* is "something we owe another," whether it be to God or man, an obligation or indebtedness we should earnestly endeavor to pay or discharge. In His model prayer, Jesus was teaching His disciples who were in debt to God. The *Wycliffe Commentary* calls debts, "sins viewed as moral or spiritual debts to God's righteousness. These are not the sins of the unregenerate—only disciples are taught this prayer—but of believers who need to confess them." As believers, then, we are all debtors, or debt-owers, who must expiate our guilt.

Often people find themselves encumbered by heavy financial debts without sufficient money to meet their needs. This was the case in our Lord's parable of the unforgiving servant, who owed his master ten thousand talents. Moved by compassion, the master forgave him his debt. In turn, however, the forgiven servant acted wickedly when he demanded of a fellow servant who owed him money: "Pay me what you owe!" (Matt. 18:28). Being very poor, the debtor was not able to pay and, in spite of his cry for patience, was cast into prison. Forgiven by his king, the wicked servant failed to forgive.

In the prayer Jesus taught His disciples to pray, He assured them that God would forgive their debts in the same way they forgave their debtors. According to the *Wycliffe Commentary,* "The case of a believer confessing his sin and asking God's forgiveness while withholding forgiveness for someone else is not only incongruous but hypocritical. A forgiving spirit is made easier for Christians when they consider how much God has already forgiven (Eph. 4:32). An unforgiving spirit is sin, and should itself be confessed." An attribute of our God of forgivenesses (note the plural) is that when He forgives, He forgets: "Their sin I will remember no more" (Jer. 31:34). Too often we grudgingly forgive other persons. Although we profess to forgive them, we will not forget the debt they owed. The glory of grace is that Jesus cleared the handwriting of debt that was against us, nailing it to His cross.

Let us follow our Savior's example of willingness to forgive.

December 25

"There is born to you this day . . . a Savior." LUKE 2:11

Today is celebrated as the day of Christ's birth almost two millennia ago. This is the day when the Lord of glory clothed Himself with the garment of our humanity in order to die as the Savior of the world. Why should we limit our recognition of this greatest event in world history to only once a year? All saved by His matchless grace should have a Christmas every day as their unceasing, grateful remembrance for all Jesus accomplished by becoming the Holy Child. Paul clearly understood the inner significance of Christmas when, in writing to young Timothy, his son in the faith, he declared: "This is a faithful saying and worthy of all acceptance, that Christ Jesus came into the world to save sinners, of whom I am chief" (1 Tim. 1:15). If the chief sinner has been saved, then there is hope for all other sinners!

How hopeless we would have been if Jesus had not turned aside from the ivory palaces and entered a world of woe! But glory to His name, He came, as predicted, the Son of a virgin. He bore the name of "Immanuel"—*God with us* (Is. 7:14). The prophet Isaiah also foretold that Jesus in His birth would combine deity with humanity and appear as the God-man: "For unto us a Child is born,/Unto us a Son is given" (Is. 9:6). As a child He was born of a virgin, but as a Son He is a giver: "God so loved the world that He gave His only begotten Son" (John 3:16). Throughout His earthly ministry, a union of our Lord's two natures is evident. As a man He slept in the storm-tossed boat, and as God He calmed the angry deep with His divine command: "Peace, be still!" As the Man, He knows all about our human needs, and as God He can meet every one of them. Such, then, is the significance of Christmas.

Gentle Mary laid her Child
  Lowly in a manger:
There He lay, the Undefiled,
  To the world a stranger.
Such a Babe in such a place,
  Can He be the Savior?
Ask the saved of all the race
  Who have found His favor.

December 26

"Bring Me a denarius that I may see it." MARK 12:15

A denarius, sometimes translated "penny," was a common Roman coin. With a value of about eighteen cents, it purchased a great deal more than the same sum would today. In Christ's time it was a laborer's wage for a day. Is there not an evidence of His assumed poverty when He said, "Bring Me a denarius," implying that He did not have one of His own to use? What a sermon that penny preached! When we want to emphasize the influence money wields, we say, "money talks." The small coin in Jesus' hand certainly did talk, although its witness was silent until Jesus gave it a voice in His question. Pointing to Caesar's profile on the coin, He asked, "Whose image and inscription is this?" It bore the name and likeness of the emperor, which indicated that he had claim upon it. Distributed among his subjects, such money represented his imperial power and the right to rule.

When the people replied, "Caesar's," He said, "Render to Caesar the things that are Caesar's, and to God the things that are God's" (Mark 12:17). No wonder the people marveled at His sermon on obligations, heavenward and earthward, that He made that coin preach. The emperor's image was stamped upon silver that had been purified and made ready for use. The question each heart must ask is: Am I purified as silver, fit for the Master's use and therefore qualified to bear His stamp upon my heart and life?

All who are redeemed by the blood of Jesus are His coinage, and He seeks to use them as His current coin in the world wherever they go. Bearing His image, they are recognized as His property. By their spirit, conduct, actions, and speech, they glorify God as their owner and fulfill in the world what is legally expected of them, no matter who their governing Caesar may be.

December 27

"There stands One among you whom you do not know." JOHN 1:26

Confronted by the priests and Levites as to whether he was one of the prophets or the promised Messiah Himself, John the Baptist confessed: "I am not the Christ." When asked who he was, the Baptist replied he was only a voice crying in the wilderness, preparing the way for the Christ but unidentified by the Jewish hierarchy. Ovid, the Latin philosopher, affirmed of himself: "Nor, if you were suddenly to see me, could you recognize me?" Jesus appeared suddenly, but many failed to identify Him as the Messiah. When asked, "Are You the Christ?", He readily answered, "I am."

One of the mysteries of the ages is the stupidity of human beings, who, although surrounded by natural objects, took thousands of years to discover what God had put by their side for use. Sorrowfully, the Savior of the world lamented: "There stands One among you"—the supreme fact of life—"whom you do not know"—the supreme folly, for to know Him is eternal life. John, the man of vision who heralded the advent of Jesus, had no hesitation in proclaiming who He was and the purpose of His mission to earth.

How privileged we are to have God's beloved Son standing among us! His presence is an inspiration, and His grace is sufficient for every need. The tragedy, however, is that so many people do not know that He is standing at the door waiting for recognition and admission to their hearts as the Redeemer. Many persons fail to see in Jesus the brightness of God's glory and the express image of His person, and they neglect the great salvation He secured for them by His supreme sacrifice at Calvary. How blessed we are, if with Paul we can confidently say: "I know whom I have believed" (2 Tim. 1:12). We then have the assurance of life everlasting as ours through knowing, loving, obeying, and serving Him who came as "the image of the invisible God" (Col. 1:15). The day is coming when "the earth shall be full of the knowledge of the LORD" (Is. 11:9).

December 28

"He found him . . . He encircled him, He instructed him,/He kept him as the apple of His eye." DEUTERONOMY 32:10

Describing most accurately God's care for His people, Moses reminded them that the eye of God was fixed upon Israel in a fourfold way: He found him; He encircled him; He instructed him; He kept him. What a blessed foursome of God's operations! James Edmeston, the nineteenth-century hymnist, in one of his sacred lyrics has the couplet: "Guard us, guide us, keep us, feed us,/For we have no help but Thee."

He found him. The Lord who came to seek and save the lost found Israel homeless and helpless in the desert. Can we not see a foreshadowing of ourselves in the plight of Israel? Was it not in the desert-land of sin, the waste-howling wilderness, where there was no refuge for our soul? "I was lost, but Jesus found me,/Found the sheep that was lost."

He encircled him. He encircled him, even as the mountains are round about Jerusalem. Once found, and at home in the Lord, we have His guidance and protection.

He instructed him. When Christ gathered twelve disciples around Him, He began by teaching them the truths of His kingdom. In school with Him, He teaches all about our weakness and His all-sufficiency; our frailty and His constancy; our lack of fidelity and His unwavering faithfulness.

He kept him. This aspect speaks of God's guardianship of His saints, His unceasing vigilance of even His most obscure child.

Wherever the expression, "the apple of His eye," is used, it means that which must be tenderly cherished as a most choice treasure. God preserved Israel as the apple of His eye—the part of the eye especially to be guarded. The apple is the pupil of the eye, in which, as in a mirror, a person sees his own image reflected in miniature.

May we be found resting in the joy of all the Lord is in Himself!

December 29

The path of the just is like the shining sun,/That shines ever brighter unto the perfect day. PROVERBS 4:18

Solomon stressed the contrast between the lighted "path of the just" and the darkened "way of the wicked" (Prov. 4:18–19). Sin always flourishes in the dark. But the believer walks in increasing light. Light is essentially the sun because it is the fountain of light. God is called Light, indicating His majesty, holiness, perfection, and pleasantness. Paul affirmed that God dwells in "unapproachable light" (1 Tim. 6:16). His is a glory, a felicity, no creature can comprehend.

George Meredith wrote of "the rapture of the forward view." Was this not the rapture flooding the soul of Paul when he urged the saints to go forward and upward, to "press toward the goal for the prize of the upward call of God in Christ Jesus" (Phil. 3:14)? As pilgrims, we must make progress and never pause in our heavenly journey. We cannot be static, for we are either advancing forward or going backward. Not until we reach "the perfect day"—the day of Christ's glorious appearing—will we be able to pause and say, "Here will I rest." As those in Christ, our path is a shining light, in spite of any obscurity or gloom that may cloud our path. God's marvelous light enables us to see ahead and make progress. Jesus is always with us as the light to brighten our darkness.

The light Solomon wrote about is progressive, shining more and more. As the dawn of morning creeps gradually to midday splendor, so we journey on from the first dawn of spiritual light to the warmer rays produced by the Sun of Righteousness, who ever shines upon us. The first dawn is the undeviating precursor of the perfect day of glory. How often Scripture exhorts us to advance at all times, never to be weary in well-doing and in holy living, knowing that if we faint not, we shall reap.

I need thy presence every passing hour;
  What but thy grace can foil the tempter's power?
Who, like thyself, my guide and stay can be?
  Through cloud and sunshine, Lord, abide with me.